THE DREAM

THE
DREAM

MARTIN LUTHER KING, JR., AND THE SPEECH THAT INSPIRED A NATION

Drew D. Hansen

An *Imprint of* HarperCollins*Publishers*

Designed by Fearn Cutler de Vicq

Library of Congress Cataloging-in-Publication Data
Hansen, Drew D.
The dream : Martin Luther King, Jr., and the Speech that Inspired a Nation /
Drew D. Hansen.—1st ed.
p.   cm.
Includes index.
ISBN 0-06-008476-6
1. King, Martin Luther, Jr., 1929–1968. 2. King, Martin Luther, Jr., 1929–1968—
Oratory. 3. March on Washington for Jobs and Freedom, Washington, D.C., 1963.
4. Speeches, addresses, etc., American—Washington (D.C.) 5. African-Americans—
Biography. 6. African-American civil rights workers—Biography. 7. Baptists—United
States—Clergy—Biography. 8. African-Americans—Civil rights—History—20th
century. 9. Civil rights movements—United States—History—20th century. I. Title.

E185.97.K5 H273 2003
323'.092—dc21
[B]   2002192739
ISBN 0-06-008477-4(pbk.)

05   06   07   08   09   ❖/ RRD   10   9   8   7   6   5   4   3   2   1

Contents

THE DREAM

Prologue

In 1963, the year that Martin Luther King, Jr., delivered one of the most famous speeches in American history, blacks in America lived under a racial caste system. Twelve million of the nation's nineteen million black citizens lived in the South, where Jim Crow segregation pervaded nearly every aspect of life. Southern towns maintained separate hotels, beaches, bathrooms, restaurants, and drinking fountains for whites and blacks. Nearly a decade after the Supreme Court's decision in *Brown v. Board of Education*, school desegregation was at a standstill. Fewer than one-half of 1 percent of black children in the South attended public schools with white children. Many Southern states operated completely segregated school systems, in open defiance of *Brown*. Not a single black child in South Carolina, Alabama, or Mississippi attended an integrated public school during the 1962–63 school year.

Many counties in the South barred blacks from voting. A 1963 survey by the United States Commission on Civil Rights found that, in one hundred of the South's counties with the highest proportions of black residents, only 8.3 percent of blacks were registered to vote. White voter registrars applied a racial double standard to applications, rejecting black applicants because of minor errors in their applications, while indiscriminately registering white applicants, including one who, in response to a question about a section of the Louisiana Constitution, wrote, "FRDUM FOOF SPETGH." Registrars would sometimes shut down the registration offices when black applicants arrived. In Madison Parish, Louisiana, where blacks of voting age outnumbered whites of voting age by nearly two to one, the electoral rolls held ten times as many white voters as black voters. In Wilcox County, Alabama, none of the 6,085 blacks of voting age were registered to vote. Chief Judge Elbert Tuttle of the Fifth Circuit Court of Appeals began an opinion about voting rights in Panola County, Mississippi, with:

> When this suit was filed by the United States on October 16, 1961, Panola County, Mississippi, had 7,639 white persons, and 7,250 Negroes of voting age. At least 5,343 white persons were then registered to vote. The only Negro registered to vote in Panola County was R.H. Hightower, 92 years old, who had registered in 1892. This does not tell the whole story, because another Negro, E.H. Holloway, was registered on January 5, 1952, but he is now deceased.

Many Southern blacks could not serve on juries. The Supreme Court had struck down statutes that barred blacks from jury service in *Strauder v. West Virginia,* a case decided in 1879, but some Southern counties maintained all-white juries through the early 1960s. White officials responsible for composing jury lists picked jurors based on personal acquaintance, guaranteeing that no blacks would be selected. In Mitchell County, Georgia, jury lists were drawn from color-coded tax returns (yellow for blacks, white for whites), and, as of 1963, none of the county's 9,000 blacks had ever served on a jury.

White Southerners maintained segregation not just by enforcing the Jim Crow laws, but by committing retaliatory acts of violence against blacks who challenged the region's racial caste system. In the summer of 1955, Emmett Till, a fourteen-year-old boy from Chicago, was murdered by two white men after he had allegedly whistled at a white woman in a Mississippi store. His body was found in the Tallahatchie River, with an iron gin-mill fan tied with wire around his neck and a bullet in his head. The Emmett Till murder attracted nationwide media attention, but thousands of similar crimes went unnoticed outside the South. According to the Tuskegee Institute, 3,444 blacks were lynched between 1882 and 1963. Even this figure understates the violence against black Americans under Jim Crow, because it only counts public summary executions by white mobs. Whites frequently perpetrated less public beatings and murders against blacks who tried to exercise constitutionally protected rights. Three months before Emmett Till arrived in Mississippi, the Reverend George Lee, the first black man to register to vote in Belzoni, Mississippi, was shot. One week before Emmett Till arrived in Mississippi, Lamar Smith, a black farmer who had been warned to "quit trying to get Negroes to vote," was shot in the middle of the day in front of a courthouse. No arrests were made in either case.

In the North, there were no "Whites Only" signs, but segregation was no less a reality than in the South. Almost every Northern city was sharply segregated into white and black neighborhoods. The Supreme Court had invalidated racially restrictive covenants in its 1948 decision in *Shelley v. Kraemer,* but blacks were effectively kept out of white neighborhoods by a variety of less obvious devices. White realtors entered into voluntary agreements with one another not to sell to black clients. White bankers practiced "redlining," refusing to lend money to homeowners in black areas. Governments demolished black neighborhoods they deemed slums and displaced residents into public housing projects. Black families who tried to move to all-white neighborhoods in Northern cities were often harassed or attacked by white mobs.

Black Americans were almost totally absent from many sectors of the nation's economy. Blacks owned 2.6 percent of all retail outlets and less than 0.2 percent of all banks or financing institutions. The median income of black men was half that of white men. The median income of black women was two-thirds that of white women. White men had a higher median income in 1948 than black men did in 1963. Black unemployment was twice the white rate; black arrests were five times the white rate.

Black actors were rarely seen in movies, except in roles that Sidney Poitier characterized as "other-cheek-turners." Jackie Robinson had started the integration of baseball, but there were few blacks in golf, tennis, or basketball. There were no blacks in the president's cabinet, no blacks on the Federal Reserve Board, no black members of the New York Stock Exchange, and no black mayors in any city of the United

States. Some white academics scorned black culture and history: In 1963, Nathan Glazer and Daniel Moynihan wrote: "[T]he Negro is only an American, and nothing else. He has no values and culture to guard and protect."

By 1963, thousands of black Americans had participated in the protests against Jim Crow that would come to be known as the civil rights movement. The modern civil rights movement is conventionally thought to have started on December, 5, 1955, the first day of a boycott of the segregated city buses in Montgomery, Alabama. The black women of Montgomery had called the boycott after the arrest of Rosa Parks, an active member of the local chapter of the National Association for the Advancement of Colored People (NAACP), for refusing to stand over a row of empty seats so that a white man could sit in the same row. On the afternoon of the boycott's first day, the black ministers of Montgomery met to set up an organization to support the women's protest. Montgomery is known as the birthplace of the modern civil rights movement because of a decision made at that meeting. When it was time to choose officers, the ministers nominated the Reverend Martin Luther King, Jr., the twenty-six-year-old pastor of the Dexter Avenue Baptist Church, to be president of the new organization.

King was not an obvious choice to lead the Montgomery bus boycott. He had lived in Montgomery for just over a year. His strongest credentials were academic: He had attended college at Morehouse, seminary at Crozer in Pennsylvania, and received a Ph.D. from Boston University. He had not been known as a civil rights activist in college or graduate school. One of the few foreshadowings of his later career was what one of his professors recalled as his "vivid memories" of

King's interest in the prophets of the Hebrew Bible. In an essay on the prophet Jeremiah, King wrote:

> Jeremiah is a shining example of the truth that religion should never sanction the status quo. This more than anything else should be inculcated into the minds of modern religionists, for the worst disservice that we as individuals or churches can do to Christianity is to become sponsors and supporters of the status quo.

Even in seminary, King saw the prophetic vocation as a possible model for his own life. In an essay in which he criticized a book that argued that religion was merely an expression of society's values, King wrote:

> Now I want to be religious, but I have some values that I would like to see conserved which are not socially recognized. Would I be excluded? What shall we call the experience in which a prophet, dissenting from socially recognized values, makes appeal to what he regards as a higher standard?

Since his arrival in Montgomery, King had been active in the NAACP and a local civil rights group called the Alabama Council on Human Relations. He had insisted that his parishioners create a "social and political action" committee at Dexter. But he was scaling back his activism at the time of the boycott. Three weeks before the protest began, King had refused the presidency of the local NAACP chapter. He decided with his wife, Coretta Scott King, that he should not take on any serious community responsibilities, because he had recently finished his dissertation and needed to concentrate more on his parish duties. King wasn't sure why he had been chosen to lead the Montgomery boycott, but he accepted the nomination, saying, "Well, if you think I can render some service, I will."

King's first task as head of the boycott would be to deliver the main address at a mass meeting to be held that evening at the Holt Street Baptist Church. He returned home after his election with about twenty minutes in which to prepare a speech. After telling his wife about his new position, he went to his study, closed the door, and panicked. He had never been asked to do anything like this before. He had given hundreds of sermons, but usually with plenty of time to prepare. He typically spent around fifteen hours each week working on his Sunday sermon. That night, he would have to speak to the entire black citizenry of Montgomery, with members of the media in attendance, in a meeting convened to decide whether a major civil rights protest would continue. After five minutes of anxiety, he prayed and asked God to be with him. He then started to prepare in the remaining fifteen minutes, but he was only able to compose a mental outline before it was time to leave for the church.

As King neared the Holt Street Baptist Church with his friend Ralph Abernathy, he noticed cars parked on both sides of the street and on the driveways and lawns of houses. King and Abernathy both had the same reaction: Surely someone important at the church—perhaps the head deacon, or even the preacher—had died. When they reached the churchyard, they saw a crowd of several thousand gathering under the oaks outside the building. Inside, the sanctuary was packed with at least a thousand people. The meeting opened with two hymns, "Onward Christian Soldiers" and "What A Fellowship, What A Joy Divine." After a prayer, there was a reading from the Psalms, and then it was King's turn to speak.

He began by recounting the indignities suffered on the buses and the story of Rosa Parks's arrest. Then, King said:

> And you know, my friends, there comes a time when people get tired of being trampled over by the iron feet of oppression.

The congregation erupted in applause so loud and so long that King was forced to wait and then shout his next lines over the din. King spoke for ten more minutes, but he did not again reach the reaction inspired by that line. He had cast his audience as heroes in a Biblical contest between good and evil, using the language of the King James Bible to sum up in one sentence the lifelong experience of black Americans under Jim Crow. At the end of the meeting, the congregation voted unanimously to continue the boycott. King had spoken for nearly twenty minutes, without notes or an outline, in a completely extemporaneous address. He would later write that he realized that evening what older preachers meant when they said "Open your mouth and God will speak for you."

The boycott ended almost thirteen months later, when NAACP attorneys won a decision from the U.S. Supreme Court desegregating Montgomery's buses. At the conclusion of the boycott, King and others established the Southern

Christian Leadership Conference (SCLC) to sponsor civil rights campaigns across the South. At a mass meeting after the Supreme Court's decision was announced, King declared: "The Red Sea has opened for us, we have crossed the banks, we are moving now."

Despite King's hopeful words, there were no major civil rights protests for a full three years after Montgomery. The next significant campaign in the civil rights movement began in the early spring of 1960, when black college students in Greensboro, North Carolina, started a series of "sit-ins" at segregated restaurants, in which black students would sit and wait to be served in the restaurants' white sections. John Lewis, at that time a twenty-year-old seminary student, was thrown in jail in Nashville, Tennessee, for disorderly conduct after participating in a sit-in at a Woolworth's lunch counter. Lewis would later become president of the Student Nonviolent Coordinating Committee (SNCC), the organization formed by the students who had been involved in the sit-in movement. In May 1961, another civil rights group, the Congress of Racial Equality (CORE), organized "freedom rides" in order to publicize the Southern refusal to comply with a Supreme Court decision prohibiting segregation in bus terminals used by interstate passengers. At several stops along the route, the freedom riders were beaten by white mobs. In Montgomery, John Lewis, who had joined the freedom rides, was knocked unconscious when a member of a mob hit him in the head with an empty soda bottle crate. The violence that the freedom riders encountered was so severe that members of Congress openly worried what other nations would think of America. Senator Jacob Javits admonished his colleagues with the words of Edward Murrow, then the head of the United States Information Agency: " 'To some the picture of a burning bus in Alabama may merely represent the speed and competence of a photographer; but to those of us in the U.S. Information Agency it means that picture will be front-page tomorrow all the way from Manila to Rabat.' "

But by 1963, despite the successes of the Montgomery bus boycott, the freedom rides, and the sit-ins in drawing the nation's attention to the injustice of segregation, the civil rights movement had also suffered some serious setbacks. SNCC had organized voter registration campaigns in several Southern towns, but its efforts were hindered by the violent resistance of local whites. The SCLC had been unable to provoke a wave of Montgomery-style boycotts across the South, in part because many Southern cities desegregated their buses voluntarily rather than be publicly humiliated by boycotts. The SCLC's most recent campaign, a 1961–62 protest against segregation in Albany, Georgia, had ended in failure. King had accepted an invitation from SNCC staff members in Albany to join a burgeoning local protest movement, but he soon realized that he had entered the city without strategic direction. Albany's police chief, Laurie Pritchett, studied King's tactics after the FBI warned him that King was planning to come to Albany and concluded that he could prevent federal intervention in the city if he avoided violent confrontations with the civil rights protesters. Pritchett boasted afterward that he had "met nonviolence with nonviolence" in Albany. This was false: Marion King, the wife of Slater King, one of Albany's prominent black citizens, had been kicked, knocked to the ground, and beaten by police officers until she lost consciousness. A county sheriff had broken a wooden walking stick over the head of C. B. King, a leading black attorney in Albany, after he had asked to check on the condition of a jailed civil rights worker. But Pritchett successfully kept most of the violence away from the television cameras, thereby avoiding national outrage at the brutality of Albany law enforcement. After a nine-month campaign in which King went to jail three times, the demonstrations in Albany ceased in late August 1962 without any tangible victories for the protesters.

At the beginning of 1963, the civil rights movement seemed to have stalled. The movement's greatest victories— Montgomery, the sit-ins, the freedom rides—were a few years in the past. King knew that the movement needed to rebuild the momentum that had been wrecked by the defeat in Albany. After discussing potential protest locations with his aides, King decided that the SCLC would direct a campaign against segregation at its strongest bastion: Birmingham, Alabama. Birmingham was legendary for its fierce maintenance of Jim Crow under Eugene "Bull" Connor, the city's longtime public safety commissioner. So many black homes and churches had been bombed over the years that many Southern blacks had taken to calling the city "Bombingham." A victory in Birmingham, King thought, would show that segregation could be defeated anywhere in the country.

When the Birmingham protests started in spring 1963, they were so small in scale that it looked as if King was heading for another debacle like Albany. But then in April the Birmingham movement received help from an unexpected source. Bull Connor lost patience with the nonviolent protesters and assaulted them with police dogs and high-pressure fire hoses able to strip the bark off trees at thirty paces. Photographs and television footage of the city's attacks on the protesters were circulated nationwide. National opinion turned instantly against the Birmingham segregationists. President Kennedy saw a picture of a police dog lunging at a black woman and told a group of visitors that it had made him "sick." Under pressure from the Kennedy administration, the city agreed to a settlement providing for the desegregation of many downtown areas. At a triumphant press conference after the settlement was announced, King declared a "great victory" for the movement.

The breakthrough in Birmingham was the catalyzing event that the civil rights movement had been awaiting since Montgomery. The movement's success in Birmingham propelled civil rights to the top of the national agenda. The *New York Times* published more stories about civil rights in two weeks than it had in the previous two years. In the ten weeks after Birmingham, there were 758 racial demonstrations in 186 cities, resulting in 14,733 arrests. House Majority Leader Carl Albert told President Kennedy that civil rights was "overwhelming the whole program." The president agreed. "Civil rights did it," he said. "I mean, this has become everything."

King knew that the movement needed to do something dramatic to keep the nation's attention focused on civil rights. On June 1, in a telephone conversation recorded by the FBI, he conferred with two of his aides to plan the SCLC's next move. One aide recommended that the "Birmingham pattern" be followed in other cities throughout the South. King suggested a grander proposal. "More than ever before is this national determination and feeling that time is running out," he said. "We are on the threshold of a significant breakthrough and the greatest weapon is mass demonstration." King proposed that the next step should be to organize "literally thousands and thousands of people" for a civil rights march on Washington.

At the time of this conversation, preliminary plans for a massive civil rights demonstration in the nation's capital were already being made under the leadership of A. Philip Randolph, the seventy-four-year-old head of the International Brotherhood of Sleeping Car Porters. A march on Washington had been a lifelong project of Randolph's: In 1941, he had used the threat of a march on the nation's capital to pressure President Roosevelt into issuing an executive order to establish a commission that would ensure that federal contractors did not discriminate against blacks. (Roosevelt issued the order only after one of his aides threw it on his desk and screamed at him, "Mr. President, sign it, or the Negroes will march on Washington within the next ten days.") Randolph had been trying since the early spring of 1963 to interest the leaders of the major civil rights groups in an "Emancipation March for Jobs," to be held in Washington, D.C., in October, but he had received only a moderate reception. CORE and SNCC had agreed to join Randolph's march, and King had assented to the use of his name, but he was too preoccupied with the Birmingham campaign to give the project any substantial attention. The leaders of the civil rights groups who had not participated in the mass local protests of the 1950s and 1960s rejected Randolph's initiative. Whitney Young, the executive director of the National Urban League, had declined, citing scheduling conflicts. Roy Wilkins, the executive secretary of the NAACP, was noncommittal. The NAACP had pursued a decades-long strategy of challenging Jim Crow statutes in the courts, and Wilkins thought that demonstrations would not be as effective as continued litigation. This difference in philosophy between the NAACP and the more protest-oriented civil rights groups was captured in an exchange between Wilkins and King during a foundation meeting in 1963. Wilkins leaned over a table toward King and said: "One of these days, Martin, some bright reporter is going to take a good hard look at Montgomery and discover that despite all the hoopla, your boycott didn't desegregate a single city bus. It was the quiet NAACP-type legal action that did it."

"We're fully aware of that, Roy," King replied. "And we in the SCLC believe that it's going to have to be a partnership between nonviolent direct action and legal action if we're going to get the job done."

Wilkins pressed on: "In fact, Martin, if you have desegregated *anything* by your efforts, kindly enlighten me."

"Well," King said, "I guess about the only thing I've desegregated so far is a few human hearts."

Wilkins conceded, nodding, "Yes, I'm sure you have done that, and that's important. So, keep on doing it; I'm sure it will help the cause in the long run."

But when King gave his full attention to Randolph's march, joining SNCC and CORE, the NAACP and the Urban League could not remain uncommitted, at the risk of seeming outside the mainstream of civil rights activism. On June 11, an SCLC representative announced plans for a "massive, militant, and monumental sit-in" demonstration in Washington, to be coupled with "massive acts of civil disobedience all over the nation."

Within hours of the announcement, President Kennedy invited the leaders of the major civil rights groups to meet with him at the White House. In the weeks between the invitation and the meeting, the president sent a sweeping civil rights bill to Congress that included, among other measures, a ban on discrimination in places of public accommodation—a provision that would effectively outlaw Jim Crow. At the meeting, the president tried to dissuade the leaders from carrying out the march on Washington, because he feared it would provoke a congressional backlash against his civil rights bill. He said:

> We want success in Congress, not just a big show at the Capitol. Some of these people are looking for an excuse to be against us. I don't want to give any of them a chance to say, "Yes, I'm for the bill, but I'm damned if I will vote for it at the point of a gun." It seemed to me a great mistake to announce a march on Washington before the bill was even in committee. The only effect is to create an atmosphere of intimidation—and this may give some members of Congress an out.

When the president had finished, A. Philip Randolph gave the march leaders' reply. "The Negroes are already in the streets," he said quietly. "It is very likely impossible to get them off. If they are bound to be in the streets in any case, is it not better that they be led by organizations dedicated to civil rights and disciplined by struggle rather than to leave them to other leaders who care neither about civil rights nor about non-violence? If the civil rights leadership were to call the Negroes off the streets, it is problematic whether they would come." King eventually joined the discussion: "I think it will serve a purpose," he said. "It may seem ill-timed. Frankly, I have never engaged in any direct action movement which did not seem ill-timed. Some people thought Birmingham ill-timed."

"Including the Attorney General," the president noted. "I don't think you should all be totally harsh on Bull Connor," he added wryly. "After all, he has done more for civil rights than almost anybody else." The president ended the meeting shortly thereafter, agreeing not to oppose the demonstration, and urged the leaders to "keep in touch."

In a meeting the next week, on July 2, the leaders of the participating civil rights groups—by then, the Brotherhood of Sleeping Car Porters, the SCLC, SNCC, CORE, the NAACP, and the Urban League—decided to move up the demonstration's scheduled date from October to August, in order to take advantage of the momentum generated by Birmingham and to provide a nonviolent outlet for black protest during the summer. They set the march for August 28, 1963: a Wednesday, so that Jewish leaders keeping the Sabbath and black ministers who needed to return to the pulpit could attend, during a week in which Congress was scheduled to be in session. After the meeting, King announced to reporters that the planned march "will have a two-fold purpose . . . to arouse the conscience of the nation on the economic plight of the Negro one hundred years after the Emancipation Proclamation and to demand strong forthright civil rights legislation."

The change in date left the leaders with just under two months to plan the largest civil rights demonstration in American history. A. Philip Randolph selected Bayard Rustin, a longtime aide who had helped King with administrative duties during the Montgomery bus boycott, to engineer the march's logistics.

Rustin and his staff were headquartered in a four-story Harlem tenement at 130th Street and Seventh Avenue, where Rustin presided over a planning operation at once efficient and chaotic, compared by one visiting reporter to an incipient congressional campaign. In order to avoid the potentially incendiary spectacle of white police officers arresting black marchers, with its echoes of Birmingham and Albany, Rustin established a squad of two thousand black men who would be "marshals" for the March. (The FBI initially seemed somewhat concerned by this all-black security force but was comforted by the D.C. police department's assurance that the marshals were "highly cooperative" with police.) The staff sent out thousands of organizing manuals that orchestrated the details of participation in the march, from where to park a car to what kind of food to pack. Leaflets and flyers were dispatched to civil rights groups, churches, unions, and other sympathetic organizations across the country, calling on all Americans to join in the pilgrimage to Washington, D.C. One of Rustin's aides handled the transportation requests, chartering buses, trains, and airplanes, and assigning a captain to each bus so that the riders would always know where to go. Rustin frequently summoned his team to evening staff meetings for updates on the planning process. By August, the aide in charge of public relations had taken to sleeping on an army cot next to his desk. A banner hung beneath the headquarters' third-story window announced "MARCH ON WASHINGTON FOR JOBS AND FREEDOM—AUGUST 28."

True to its instruction to "keep in touch," the Kennedy administration dispatched a team led by John Douglas, the head of the civil division of the Department of Justice, to coordinate the federal government's response to the event. One team member flew to Chicago and Detroit, scenes of previous civil rights rallies, and queried the local officials on how to ensure a peaceful demonstration. Douglas's team assisted the march planners in thinking through the day's details, down to the adequacy of toilet facilities on the Mall. (The Department of Justice would later secretly pay the bill for the toilets that were rented for the march.) The team also provided the march organizers with an intermediary to the federal and local authorities who would be responsible for security arrangements. There was a brief crisis when the Kennedy team told the D.C. police that they could not use their K-9 unit at the demonstration, because the team thought the sight of police dogs in Washington would remind some marchers of Bull Connor's dogs in Birmingham. The D.C. police balked, and a stalemate ensued until John Douglas took the dispute to Attorney General Robert Kennedy, who got on the phone with the district commissioner and told him, flatly, "No dogs."

In order to get a better idea of how many people would be at the march, and in order to assess potential threats of violence, the Department of Justice team requested assistance from the FBI. In mid-July, and again in August, J. Edgar Hoover's office ordered the FBI's field offices to keep headquarters informed as to who would be participating in the march, including what the director called "Hate or Klan" groups. These requests generated hundreds of pages of reports, usually captioned "URGENT," as agents were deployed to find out which organizations from their areas were planning to attend, how many marchers each organization would supply, and what mode of transportation they would take. By late August, the Bureau had compiled an intelligence file that was probably superior, in some areas, to the information possessed by the march organizers themselves. (The Bureau knew, for example, that marchers from New Britain, Connecticut, could reserve bus tickets through Police Sergeant Clifford Willis at the Willis Barber Shop.) High-ranking FBI officials, ever sensitive to the possibility of criticism, instructed the Bureau's Washington, D.C., divisions to avoid any action on the day of the event that could be embarrassing. Tours of the FBI building were to go on as scheduled. The administration division was encouraged to have plenty of job applications on hand, because the Bureau expected a larger than normal number of applicants on the day of the demonstration.

In the months before the march, civil rights protests exploded across the South. In Jackson, Mississippi, in late May and early June, participants in demonstrations were hauled away in garbage trucks and imprisoned in stockades on the state fairgrounds. Roy Wilkins visited Jackson and told a crowd at a mass meeting, "In Birmingham, the authorities turned the dogs and fire hoses loose on peaceable demonstrators. Jackson has added another touch to this expression of the Nazi spirit with the setting up of hog-wired concentration camps. This is pure Nazism and Hitlerism. The only thing missing is an oven." The next day, Wilkins was arrested during a demonstration. King was pleased by this apparent about-face by the leader who had consistently urged trust in the laws, and he joked to an adviser, "We've baptized brother Wilkins." On May 28, the house of Medgar Evers, the NAACP field secretary in Mississippi, was firebombed. Local police told the family, "It was just some kind of prank . . . It was just some people having some fun, probably." Two weeks later, Evers was assassinated by a sniper in front of his house.

In Danville, Virginia, in June, the city turned fire hoses on sixty-five black protesters, and police beat those who tried to shield themselves behind parked cars. King told a reporter that Danville was "the most critical city in the country at the moment," because "the potential for violence is the worst here." In Americus, Georgia, in early August, police beat and then arrested civil rights marchers. In Mississippi, a sharecropper named Fannie Lou Hamer was returning from a voter registration workshop with several other black Mississippians when they stopped at a bus depot to get some food and to use the washroom. After they entered the "white" side of the terminal, the police arrested them and took them to the county jail. Fannie Lou Hamer later told what happened next:

> I was carried to the county jail, and put in the booking room. They left some of the people in the booking room and began to place us in cells. I was placed in a cell with a young woman called Miss Euvester Simpson. After I was placed in the cell I began to hear sounds of licks and screams. I could hear the sounds of licks and horrible screams, and I could hear somebody say, "Can you say, yes sir, nigger? Can you say yes, sir?" And they would say other horrible names.
>
> She would say, "Yes, I can say yes, sir."

"So say it."

She says, "I don't know you well enough."

They beat her, I don't know how long, and after a while she began to pray, and asked God to have mercy on those people.

And it wasn't too long before three white men came to my cell. One of these men was a State Highway Patrolman. . . . [H]e said, "We are going to make you wish you was dead."

I was carried out of that cell into another cell where they had two Negro prisoners. The State Highway Patrolman ordered the first Negro to take the black-jack. The first Negro prisoner ordered me, by orders from the State Highway Patrolman for me, to lay down on a bunk bed on my face, and I laid on my face. The first Negro began to beat, and I was beat by the first Negro until he was exhausted, and I was holding my hands behind me at that time on my left side because I suffered from polio when I was six years old.

After the first Negro had beat until he was exhausted, the State Highway Patrolman ordered the second Negro to take the blackjack. The second Negro began to beat and I began to work my feet, and the State Highway Patrolman ordered the first Negro who had beat to set on my feet to keep me from working my feet. I began to scream and one white man got up and began to beat me in my head and tell me to hush. One white man—my dress had worked up high, he walked over and pulled my dress down, and he pulled my dress back, back up.

I was in jail when Medgar Evers was murdered.

All of this is on account we want to register, to become first-class citizens . . . [I]s this America, the land of the free and the home of the brave where we have to sleep with our telephones off the hooks because our lives be threatened daily because we want to live as decent human beings, in America?

As the day of the march drew nearer, Rustin and the heads of the sponsoring groups began to draw up a schedule for the day's events. The most contentious issue proved to be the composition of an afternoon program of speeches at the Lincoln Memorial. By August, several important religious and labor organizations had joined the major civil rights groups as cosponsors of the march, bringing the total number of sponsoring organizations up to ten. In order not to slight any of the sponsors, it was decided that one representative from each group would be given an opportunity to speak at the Lincoln Memorial. But in order to ensure that the program would not drag on, the leaders were told that each speech could be no longer than five minutes.

This arrangement annoyed some of King's aides, who felt that King and the more prominent figures on the program should be allowed to make longer speeches. One aide complained to another, in a conversation overheard by the FBI, "This is silly and just doesn't make any sense, when everybody across the nation is coming to hear Phil Randolph and Martin Luther King, and to a second extent Roy Wilkins, but they're certainly coming to hear Martin." King thought the problem could be solved by giving a few people longer speaking slots or by extending the whole program by an hour so that everyone would have enough time to speak. FBI wiretaps picked up a conversation in which King confided to one of his friends that he felt that the leaders of the other groups were trying to throttle him because they were determined not to allow him to make a speech that would arouse a great response from the people.

Five days before the march, the formal program at the Lincoln Memorial was still unsettled. King's aides had contacted the march organizers and made known their displeasure with the five-minute time limit, and Bayard Rustin had called a meeting in New York at which the issue would be discussed. On the morning of the meeting, a reporter from *Newsday* called King to inquire about a "rift" over King's being given only five minutes to speak. King told the reporter that the question would be settled that afternoon and that he should talk to Bayard Rustin about it. Rustin, meanwhile, had asked King not to attend the meeting, and King was happy to demur, as he was not eager to get involved in an unseemly and fractious dispute over the details of the program.

Before the meeting began, A. Philip Randolph asked King's aides not to bring up the topic of time limits. He suggested that the matter be settled surreptitiously: If King's aides made sure that King had the final speaking slot on the program, Randolph would see that he was allowed to take whatever time he needed to make his speech.

At the meeting, the other leaders of the sponsoring groups argued over whether the honor of the day's final speech should go to King or to Roy Wilkins, as the head of the nation's oldest civil rights organization. Bayard Rustin contended that King should speak last, both because of King's prominence in the movement by late summer 1963 and because Rustin thought King was the best orator in the group. The other leaders eventually agreed. Rustin told them, "You are wise because the minute King has finished, he is so popular, everybody is going to head home."

Rustin and King's advisers believed that the other leaders had fallen in line primarily because none of them wanted to speak after King. But a few of King's aides came to believe that there had been an additional reason for the leaders' willingness to let King speak last: Some of the leaders thought that the earlier spots on the program might give them a better chance at being featured on the evening news. King was not scheduled to speak until late in the day. By then, it was thought, the television cameras would already have left to process their film, and none but the assembled marchers would remember the words of the day's final speaker.

chapter one

The March on Washington for Jobs and Freedom

S ome of the marchers left a few days early so that they would be sure to reach Washington by August 28, 1963. A Los Angeles pants presser named David Parker loaded five friends into his Ford and set off across the country because, as he later told a reporter, his people had troubles. In Brooklyn, twelve young members of CORE started walking the 237 miles to the capital. The Local 593 Mine, Mill, and Smelter workers took up a collection at the Anaconda American Brass Company plant in Buffalo and gave it to the NAACP to pay the fares of unemployed workers who wanted to go to Washington. Forty unemployed men from Cleveland, Mississippi, took the bus up North after raising the thirty-three-dollar fare by selling shares in their tickets at a dollar apiece.

In Chicago, the passengers of two chartered trains crowded together at the station to listen to final instructions from their captains. Then the trains took off for the overnight trip to Washington. A three-piece jazz combo set up at the end of one car and played tunes for the riders. Some passengers sang along:

This train don't carry no liars, this train . . .

This train is bound for glory, this train . . .

Six buses left Alabama on Tuesday morning, August 27, with garment bags holding fresh clothes hanging from the overhead handrails. Some passengers started the trip singing, but as the twenty-two-hour journey went on, they began to talk about what it meant for them to go to Washington. Many of the marchers had been beaten by Bull Connor's troops or had spent time in the Birmingham jail. "They ought to know who we are," said one. "After all, we're the ones who started the whole freedom movement."

In the days before August 28, buses, cars, and trains from all over the country set out for Washington. Three buses with more than one hundred demonstrators left from the General Baptist Convention headquarters in Milwaukee. A chartered train left Pittsburgh, and another one left Detroit. A caravan of two hundred cars set out from North Carolina. Buses left Arkansas, Mississippi, and Louisiana.

In Boston, a teacher at the Freedom School in Roxbury abandoned her plans to fly to the march and climbed aboard a bus. A sixty-seven-year-old dressmaker from Memphis said to herself, "I'm going to lay aside my patterns and be a part of it." A cabdriver from New York drove his cab for awhile on Tuesday evening and then said, "That's it. I'm going to Washington because it's a duty that has to be done."

On Tuesday night, a band of SNCC staff members joined teenagers from Albany, Georgia, in a vigil at the Department of Justice. Earlier in August, the Department had indicted several members of the Albany movement for obstruction of justice, in an action arising out of their boycott of a white man's store. Justice attorneys believed the boycott had been called because the store owner had served on a jury that had dismissed a civil suit brought by a black man who had been shot in the neck by a white sheriff. The Albany activists insisted that they were protesting the store's racist hiring practices. They wondered why their relatively insignificant boycott was attracting so much federal attention when the government had not prevented the Albany police from assaulting the city's black citizens. One SNCC member carried a sign that read "WHEN THERE IS NO JUSTICE, WHAT IS THE STATE, BUT A ROBBER BAND ENLARGED?" Another sign proclaimed "EVEN THE FEDERAL GOVERNMENT IS A WHITE MAN."

At one-thirty in the morning on Wednesday, August 28, whole blocks of Harlem had all their lights on as residents gathered at bus depots, community houses, and churches to cheer the departing marchers. "You tell them, tell them for me," yelled people in the crowd as the marchers filed onto the buses that lined 125th street for a block on each side. "They look just like soldiers going off," said an elderly woman. One man shouted, "Tell them I want a job!" A decorated veteran told a reporter, "If I was proud of these medals I wouldn't be on this bus. It makes my blood boil to see Negroes dying for our country and then kids not able to go to school in Little Rock or Virginia." By dawn on Wednesday, according to FBI surveillance figures, 972 chartered buses and 13 special trains, carrying a total of 55,000 people, had left New York for Washington.

The FBI field offices—mindful of the director's insistence

that surveillance of the marchers was the "personal and continuing responsibility" of the special agents in charge—deployed agents across the nation to track the demonstrators' progress. The Knoxville office notified headquarters when an NAACP-chartered bus carrying thirty-five passengers had left Chattanooga. The Phoenix field office provided the names of the four Phoenix residents who were driving to Washington. An agent watched as the Houston delegation boarded a Greyhound bus (license number T-345) and counted the people on it ("fifteen Negro males, and nine Negro females"). One hundred forty field agents were dispatched to Union Station and the D.C. area airports to observe the marchers' arrivals and departures, with instructions to keep a particular watch for "subversives."

As the buses from all over the country rolled through the August night, people who couldn't make the trip gathered on the shoulders of highways to cheer the marchers along the way. At toll booths, passengers noticed that local farmers had brought their children out to watch the caravans. A few buses made an early morning stop at a church, where volunteers had been up all night preparing breakfast for bus after bus that came through. Early on Wednesday morning, the first demonstrators reached Washington. As they drove through the capital's black neighborhoods, well-wishers waved to them from curbs and porches. Finally, after journeys that lasted as long as six days and seven nights, the buses neared the Washington Monument, the scheduled assembly point for the March on Washington for Jobs and Freedom.

Most white politicians in Washington had been nervous

about the march for months. In May, Senator John Stennis of Mississippi apologized to his colleagues for bringing "scare stories or bad news" when he informed them of possible plans for a civil rights demonstration in the nation's capital. The prospect of black Americans coming to Washington to present their grievances terrified most white politicians, who envisioned their black constituents marching down Constitution Avenue throwing stones at them. As the scheduled day for the march drew nearer, the worries of white Washingtonians reached near-hysterical levels. *Life* magazine observed: "Merely contemplating the possibilities for trouble and the logistics of the demonstration has given Washington officialdom its worst case of invasion jitters since the First Battle of Bull Run." A syndicated columnist predicted that the "mob spirit" of the march would erode the foundations of democratic government. Two days before the march, Representative William Jennings Bryan Dorn of South Carolina warned that the demonstration might eventually lead to the overthrow of the republic:

> Mr. Speaker, the Government of the French Congo was overthrown last week by a howling mob in the streets of its capital city. Reports from Saigon, South Vietnam hourly bring incredible tales of mob violence and demonstrations. This friendly government on which we are spending a million dollars a day is in grave danger of being overthrown by mobs.
>
> The march on Washington this week will set a dangerous precedent. It is reminiscent of the Mussolini

Fascist blackshirt march on Rome in 1922. It is reminiscent of the Socialist Hitler's government-sponsored rallies in Nuremberg.

By contrast, President Kennedy's public comments about the march had become almost welcoming. He said at a mid-July press conference that the event would be a "peaceful assembly calling for a redress of grievances" in the "great tradition" of America. A few days before the march, the president privately expressed his fear that the demonstration might fall short. He worried that if fewer than one hundred thousand people showed up, it could cause some members of Congress to conclude that there was not a serious demand for action on civil rights.

Despite its public professions of unconcern, the Kennedy administration took exhaustive security precautions on the day of the march. John Douglas was posted at D.C. police headquarters to coordinate the administration's activities. Justice attorneys assumed observation posts at Union Station, the Baltimore–Washington expressway, and the rooftops of government buildings. The army installed direct phone lines between the Justice stations and the army operations room at the Pentagon. Secret Service agents mingled with the crowd. The National Park Service gave official ribbons to forty FBI agents, who were stationed atop the Lincoln Memorial and the Washington Monument. Two executive orders were prepared for the president's signature, which would effectively have declared martial law in the nation's capital. The first ordered the crowds to disperse, and, if that order was not complied with, the second directed the secretary of defense to use the armed forces to disperse the crowd and "maintain law and order."

The administration was particularly concerned with the security of the public address system during the afternoon program at the Lincoln Memorial. Several Justice attorneys feared that someone—either one of the scheduled speakers or an organized insurgent group able to commandeer the speakers' platform—would use the public address system to incite the crowd to riot. John Reilly, the deputy attorney general in charge of the U.S. attorneys and a member of John Douglas's team, decided to establish a cutoff switch so that he could shut off the speakers if it looked as though a riot was about to begin. The switch was set up on the right side of the Memorial, with a line of sight to the podium. After the cutoff switch was put in place, Reilly realized he did not know what he would do next if he had to cut the sound. He went out and bought a record of Mahalia Jackson singing "He's Got the Whole World in His Hands." If something went horribly amiss, Reilly thought, he would shut off the feed from the microphones and put Mahalia Jackson on the turntable.

On Wednesday, August 28, Washington had barricaded itself against the invaders. The streets downtown were nearly deserted. Many stores were closed and chain-locked. Those few that remained open reported almost no customer traffic during the day. Twenty-two clinics were established around the Mall to handle medical emergencies. The city's General Hospital canceled leave for personnel and was prepared to go on a national disaster plan. At the Justice Department's request, the D.C. commissioners banned alcohol sales in the

District. (Malcolm X, who was in Washington for the event, told some friends on Tuesday night, "No firewater for the Indians tomorrow.") Many whites who worked in Washington had stayed in their homes in Maryland or Virginia. Several members of Congress warned their female aides to stay home because the streets, they said, would not be safe.

The police presence that day turned downtown Washington into one of the most heavily guarded places in America: At dawn, police blockaded one hundred blocks in the center of the city. Thirteen cranes, borrowed from the army, stood ready to tow broken-down buses at the Mall. Police officers and members of the National Guard were posted on every corner. Additional squads of military and civil police provided protection for the congressional buildings. MPs in Jeeps and command cars patrolled downtown. There were so many soldiers on the streets one senator remarked that it looked as though a military coup had happened during the night. The army informed the FBI that it had seventeen thousand combat-ready troops stationed near Washington, and that forty-nine helicopters, some equipped with riot control munitions, had been put on standby at Fort Myer and Bolling Air Force Base, ready to descend on the nation's capital in the event of a riot.

Early on Wednesday morning, while it was still dark, the first busloads of marchers arrived in a city prepared for siege. A bus carrying thirty-eight students from Clarksdale and Greenwood, Mississippi, was the first to arrive. The students got off the bus and started singing. Then a bus from Little Rock, Arkansas, showed up, with thirty-six marchers on board. At Union Station, lines of shuttle buses stood ready at the curb to transport marchers who had traveled by train.

There were probably more police officers than marchers on the Washington Monument grounds. Only about a half-dozen buses had parked around the Ellipse, and few marchers had gathered on the lawn under the Monument. Most of those who had arrived stayed on the buses for an early morning nap after long and uncomfortable journeys. A few teenagers sat on a bench near the parking area, singing freedom songs. Closer to the Washington Monument, three boys napped on the grass, with black derbies over their faces. The march organizers, who had set up base in a green circus tent with a green-and-white striped roof, began to worry that the event would flop. Bayard Rustin was rushed by reporters as he surveyed the Monument grounds. "Mr. Rustin, it is past six o'clock," said one of them. "You promised a march of more than a hundred thousand. Where are all the people?" Rustin looked carefully at a yellow legal pad in his hand. "Gentlemen," he announced, "everything is going exactly according to plan." Standing beside him, one of his deputies noticed that the pad he was looking at was blank.

From his suite at the Willard Hotel, Martin Luther King, Jr., looked down on the mostly empty lawns around the Washington Monument. King had previously confided to Ralph Abernathy that he was worried about a violent incident taking place at the march. "If that happens, Ralph," he had said, "everything we have done in Birmingham will be wiped out in a single day." Now, on the morning of the march, King became anxious that so few people would show up that the event would be labeled a failure. Coretta Scott King awoke to the sound of typewriters and voices in the next room and saw her husband looking out the window at the arriving marchers.

Early television reports said that only a small number of people had assembled. King and his wife departed for the march, subdued by what appeared to be a disappointing turnout. "About twenty-five thousand," the television reporters were saying, as the Kings left the hotel.

At Union Station, the trains were beginning to arrive. The first train to appear was a regular commuter from Baltimore, the second was Southern Railroad's Number 42, the train that, a month earlier, had borne Medgar Evers's body to Washington. Then a "Freedom Special"—a chartered train that had originated in Jacksonville and made stops in Georgia and Virginia—pulled into the station, and nearly eight hundred young people from the South tumbled off, talking and singing. These were the foot soldiers of the freedom movement: Even though most were in their teens or early twenties, they were already veterans of Southern civil rights campaigns. The students sang a massed chorus of "We Shall Overcome," and as the song resounded through Union Station, it seemed to rejuvenate the hundreds of marchers who were wandering around the terminal wondering what to do next. Another train pulled in, and more marchers poured off, also singing:

I woke up this morning with my mind
Set on freedom.
I woke up this morning with my mind
Set on freedom.
I woke up this morning with my mind
Set on freedom.
Hallelu, Hallelu, Hallelujah!

Soon the station was packed with what some authorities later speculated were the largest early morning crowds since the end of World War II. The shuttle buses ferried marchers to the Washington Monument as more trains continued to come in. Between six in the morning and noon, trains arrived in Union Station every ten minutes, disgorged their passengers, and then pulled into sheds and quickly backed out to make room for the next arrivals.

At the Monument, the buses were coming in regularly now. The passengers got off, grabbed pennants commemorating the "MARCH ON WASHINGTON FOR JOBS AND FREEDOM," and walked past the ever-lengthening line of parked buses to the assembly grounds. One group carried a banner that read "NEWMAN MEMORIAL METHODIST CHURCH SCHOOL, BROOKLYN, NEW YORK." Another group wore yellow hats that identified them as members of the Building Services Employees International Union. The crowd at the assembly point was growing fast—by 9:30 A.M. police estimated that 22,800 people were gathered at the Washington Monument. Twenty minutes later, that number had nearly doubled. The marchers soon filled the lawn below the Monument and started to spill over onto Constitution Avenue and the Ellipse. According to the official plan, a program of entertainment was slated to begin at 9:30, on the stage that had been constructed a few hundred yards from the Monument. But many of the entertainers were stuck outside the city, so the program had to be delayed.

This didn't seem to bother the marchers. By midmorning, the Washington Monument grounds had taken on the cheerful anarchy of a gigantic church picnic. Most of the marchers wore their Sunday-best suits or dresses. They sat on the grass with the people they had traveled with, or lined up at the ice cream trucks or the soft drink stands. Several groups started singing, and soon small crowds gathered around to clap hands and join in. Some high school students who had just been released from jail in Danville, Virginia, improvised on a spiritual called "Move On." An onlooker asked them why they wore black bands on their sweatshirt sleeves. "We're mourning injustice in Danville," replied a fifteen-year-old boy who had been arrested three times. "Things haven't changed at all in Danville," said one protester. "They're worse if anything. They have an injunction now that won't let us gather, talk, or even think civil rights." Several young people wearing CORE T-shirts and overalls marched in a circle in front of the headquarters tent. "I'm going to walk the streets of Jackson," sang out one girl. "One of these days," responded the rest. "I'm going to be the chief of police," another sang. "One of these days," the rest answered. Another group sang hymns under signs proclaiming that they had come from Albany and Americus, Georgia. One sign read:

Martin Wilkerson—20 stitches

Emanuel McClendon—3 stitches (age 67)

James Williams—broken leg

"That's where the police beat these people up," explained a fifteen-year-old from Albany.

Finally, enough entertainers arrived for the official program to start. At a little after ten A.M. Joan Baez came over the public address system, singing a spiritual. She was followed by more folksingers, a few celebrities, and still more singers. The people who were pressed against the fence surrounding the stage listened to the program, but the crowd was already too large for the loudspeakers to carry the entertainment to everyone. All around the Washington Monument, the picnic went on. By eleven, many people had started eating the box lunches they had packed for the day. They unpacked camp stools, picnic baskets, and Thermos jugs, and ate their peanut butter and jelly sandwiches (no mayonnaise, the march organizers had warned them—it might spoil in the sun) on the grass while they watched the newcomers arrive. Impromptu reunions took place as friends met around the ice cream trucks or the concessions stands. Groups that had traveled on the buses together posed for pictures in front of the Washington Monument or on the lawn. At twenty minutes before eleven, the loudspeaker broke up the program by announcing the crowd size at ninety thousand. Unknown to the marchers, many more were on the way: Trains kept coming into Union Station, and the Baltimore–Washington expressway was packed bumper-to-bumper with cars and buses.

Earlier in the summer, the FBI's surveillance had turned up evidence of white supremacists who were planning marches of their own on Washington. A leaflet distributed in Los Angeles called for an all-white counter-demonstration: "Make no mistake about it, August 28 the Communist revolution starts in dead earnest—over three hundred thousand red-led blacks are storming your capitol to terrorize and force your Congress to pass the filthy communist public accommodations law—if they terrorize your Congressmen into passing that law, it is the end of private property—it is the end of

America, it is the end of the white race." George Lincoln Rockwell, the head of the American Nazi Party, had asked supporters (he "only wanted radicals," he warned) to join him for an August 28 rally in the nation's capital. Literature distributed by his organization read: "over SIX HUNDRED fighting mad white men from Richmond alone have pledged to stand against the nigger terror with us on August 28th, . . . Be in Washington Monument [sic] at dawn on August 28 with every single white person—man, woman, and child—you can bring . . . MAKE HISTORY—NOT EX-CUSES!" The National Park Service had rejected Rockwell's application for a demonstration permit on the grounds that it could handle only one large event in a day. Undeterred, Rockwell and a small group of about seventy supporters gathered at the Washington Monument early on Wednesday morning. They were immediately surrounded by a double cordon of D.C. police so thick that Rockwell complained that his sympathizers couldn't get through to join him. Rockwell told a reporter that he had been personally warned by "three high government officials" that if he showed up on the Mall, "Bobby Kennedy would have [him] arrested." At a little after eleven, one of Rockwell's deputies began to speak. He said, "We are here to protest by as peaceful means as possible the occupation of Washington by forces deadly to the welfare of our country," and then he was arrested for speaking without a permit. Rockwell's lieutenant would be the only person arrested on the Monument grounds that day.

Peter, Paul, and Mary sang, and then the SNCC Freedom Singers from Albany, Georgia, came on. Miscellaneous dignitaries (an elderly Socialist, the first black flight attendant,

Jackie Robinson) were announced and applauded. At a few minutes before eleven, a voice came over the loudspeaker informing everyone that "we are trying to locate Miss Lena Horne." "Governor Ross Barnett of Mississippi" was also listed among the missing, prompting boos in the crowd that changed to cheers when the announcer added that Barnett was lost beneath the speakers' platform at the Lincoln Memorial.

Just after eleven, the amplifier announced teen idol Bobby Darin. He told the audience that he was "proud, and kind of choked up." And then, without any signal, a few members of the crowd started walking to the Lincoln Memorial. They were quickly followed, and soon thousands of demonstrators were walking down Constitution and Independence Avenues. They didn't form regular lines or keep a set tempo. They just walked, as the *Washington Post* put it, "like people who know where they are going but are not making a show of it."

About twenty minutes after the people had started walking, a voice came over the loudspeakers. "We've lost the leaders' delegation. They are hereby instructed to join the march and go to the Lincoln Memorial. Will the leaders' delegation please sound off?" The original plan was for the heads of the major civil rights groups to emerge from morning meetings with members of Congress and lead the marchers from the Washington Monument to the Lincoln Memorial. But when the first demonstrators started to walk, the leaders were still in their meetings. They came out to find tens of thousands of people walking purposefully ahead of them. "My God, they're *going*," shouted Bayard Rustin, whose carefully planned march had been off schedule from the start. "We're supposed to be *leading* them!" As marshals tried to slow the crowd down, the leaders rushed to get to the front. Eventually a break opened up somewhere in the middle of the throng, and the leaders clasped hands and sang "We Shall Overcome" as they walked in front of a mass of people. But most of the crowd was far ahead of them. From where the leaders walked, they couldn't even see the first marchers.

There wasn't much chanting or singing in the crowd as they walked toward the Lincoln Memorial. A young man from Virginia led some of his fellow marchers in a call and response:

Freedom, freedom, freedom, freedom. Going to take it
  to the President.
Yeah, man.
Going to take it to the Representatives.
Yeah, man.
Going to take it to the press.
Yeah, man.
Going to read it in the paper.
Yeah, man.

Many marchers carried red-white-and-blue placards that had been handed out by the march sponsors. The signs announced: "WE MARCH FOR INTEGRATED SCHOOLS NOW!" or, "WE MARCH FOR MINIMUM WAGE COVERAGE FOR ALL WORKERS NOW!" The marchers had been instructed that only slogans approved by the march organizers would be allowed, but some carried hand-lettered signs, one of which read, "WE DEMAND AN HON-

EST INVESTIGATION OF THE POLICE BRUTALITY IN SOUTHWEST GEORGIA." Aside from the few groups who were singing, most of the crowd walked on in silence. For an hour and a half, nearly the only sounds on Constitution and Independence avenues were the footfalls of the marchers.

As the first marchers neared the Lincoln Memorial, marshals parted the crowd and directed them down both sides of the Reflecting Pool. Before long, the steps of the Memorial were packed with people. The marchers kept filing in and lined the Reflecting Pool for about a third of a mile on each side. Still more people arrived and spread out on either side of the Pool under the oaks and elms. From the Lincoln Memorial, it soon looked as if the crowd stretched for the entire eight-tenths of a mile back to the Washington Monument. The D.C. Police would estimate the crowd size at 210,000 people, but several reporters the next day would place the figure at closer to a quarter million.

The march organizers had scheduled an afternoon program of entertainment before the official speeches, which they began more than an hour early when they saw that the people had already gathered at the Memorial steps. At one in the afternoon, Camilla Williams opened the program with "The Star-Spangled Banner." This began another procession of singers (Joan Baez and Peter, Paul, and Mary made repeat appearances) and speakers. Dick Gregory, newly released from a Chicago jail after a school segregation protest, went up to the microphone and said, "The last time I saw this many of us together, Bull Connor was doing all the talking." Those who had arrived first could hear everything clearly. But there were so many people that the loudspeakers could not carry the program across the entire crowd. Even a third of the way back from the Lincoln Memorial, the speeches were almost inaudible. Many people carried transistor radios, creating an echo effect with the loudspeakers. Spaces in the open with a clear view of the speakers' platform were scarce, and the crowds packed shoulder to shoulder in areas near the loudspeakers or with an unobstructed view. Several children climbed up into the trees for a better look at the Memorial.

Those who could not see or hear, or who didn't want to try to find a better spot, put down their placards under the trees and used them as picnic blankets or sleeping mats. The sun was high in the sky, but a cool breeze kept the temperature just above 80 degrees, making the shaded lawns an ideal place for a picnic. Marchers who had not eaten their lunches at the Washington Monument unpacked them now and munched on sandwiches and fruit. Some found choice spots on the banks of the Reflecting Pool, where they took off their socks and shoes and sat with their feet in the cool water. The marchers snacked and talked with one another, and tried to keep their children from running into the pool.

At some point during the afternoon, the official speeches by the leaders of the groups sponsoring the march began. Most of the speeches were not unusually moving, and even those members of the crowd with the best views started to get restless. Many marchers had been up all night and retreated under the trees for a nap as the speakers droned on. The crowd stirred briefly to lobby for President Kennedy's pending civil rights legislation by chanting "Pass the bill! Pass the bill!" when A. Philip Randolph introduced the members of Congress who had come to the march. Because people were packed so closely together near the front, even the moderate heat became difficult to deal with. Many people stopped paying attention altogether and started to walk back to the buses.

Then Randolph stepped to the microphone and introduced "Brother John Lewis." This caused many in the crowd, especially those from states in the Deep South, to stop fidgeting and pay attention. John Lewis was a twenty-three-year-old leader of SNCC who had spent the last few years working in Southern states on voter registration and desegregation campaigns. The crowd greeted him with sustained cheers as he walked to the podium with his head bowed. He did not even acknowledge Bayard Rustin as Rustin clasped his hand and patted his back. Lewis glanced down at his text and licked his lips a few times. He looked out and saw the crowd and thought to himself, "My." Off to his right, he saw a small group of his friends from SNCC, clapping and yelling to encourage him. "Here it is," he thought, and he began his speech, in a voice thick with the rural accent of the Alabama farm where he had grown up, at a pace that he would think, many years later, might have been too quick:

> We march today for jobs and freedom, but we have nothing to be proud of. For hundreds and thousands of our brothers are not here. They are receiving starvation wages . . . or no wages at all. While we stand here, there are sharecroppers in the Delta of Mississippi who are out in the fields working for less than three dollars a

day, twelve hours a day. While we stand here there are students in jail on trumped-up charges. Our brother, James Farmer, along with many others, is also in jail. We come here today with a great sense of misgiving.

Right away, it was clear to the crowd that John Lewis did not sound like any of the other speakers they had heard.

It is true that we support the Administration's civil rights bill. We support it with great reservation, however. Unless Title Three is put in this bill, there is nothing to protect the young children and old women who must face police dogs and fire hoses in the South while they engage in peaceful demonstrations.

The crowd interrupted him, for the first time, with applause. As he saw the crowd's reaction, Lewis seemed to become more sure of himself, and he spoke more forcefully:

In its present form this bill will not protect the citizens of Danville, Virginia, who must live in constant fear of a police state. It will not protect the hundreds and thousands of people who have been arrested on trumped charges. What about the three young men— SNCC field secretaries—in Americus, Georgia, who face the death penalty for engaging in peaceful protest?

As it stands now the voting section of this bill will not help the thousands of black people who want to vote. It will not help the citizens of Mississippi, of Alabama and Georgia, who are qualified to vote but lack a sixth-grade education. "One man, one vote," is the African cry. It is ours, too. It must be ours.

The crowd clapped and whistled in approval. Many of them knew firsthand of Danville and Americus.

We must have legislation that will protect the Mississippi sharecropper who is put off of his farm because he dares to register to vote. We need a bill that will provide for the homeless and starving people of this nation. We need a bill that will ensure the equality of a maid who earns $5 a week in the home of a family whose total income is $100,000 a year. We must have a good FEPC bill.

My friends, let us not forget that we are involved in a serious social revolution. By and large, American politics is dominated by politicians who build their careers on immoral compromises and ally themselves with open forms of political, economic, and social exploitation.

The crowd shouted its agreement.

There are exceptions, of course. We salute those. But what political leader can stand up and say, "My party is the party of principles?" For the party of Kennedy is

also the party of Eastland. The party of Javits is also the
party of Goldwater.

The audience punctuated the denunciations with cheers.

> Where is our party? Where is the political party that
> will make it unnecessary to march on Washington?
> Where is the political party that will make it unneces-
> sary to march in the streets of Birmingham? Where is
> the political party that will protect the citizens of
> Albany, Georgia? Do you know that in Albany, Georgia,
> nine of our leaders have been indicted not by Dixiecrats
> but by the Federal Government for peaceful protest?
> But what did the Federal Government do when
> Albany's Deputy Sheriff beat Attorney C. B. King and
> left him half dead? What did the Federal Government
> do when local police officials kicked and assaulted the
> pregnant wife of Slater King, and she lost her baby?

The Albany veterans in the crowd joined in to give John Lewis
the greatest applause of his speech so far. Lewis was nearly
shouting now, a defiant jeremiad proclaimed to the hundreds
of thousands at the Memorial and the millions watching on
television.

> To those who have said, be patient and wait, we must
> say that we cannot be patient, we do not want our free-
> dom gradually but we want to be free now! We are
> tired, we are tired of being beaten by policemen. We
> are tired of seeing our people locked up in jail over and

over again, and then you holler "Be patient." How long can we be patient? We want our freedom and we want it now.

And he had to pause, as the crowd screamed its answer.

We do not want to go to jail, but we will go to jail, if this is the price we must pay for love, brotherhood and true peace.

I appeal to all of you to get in this great revolution that is sweeping our nation. Get in and stay in the streets of every city, every village and hamlet of this nation, until true Freedom comes, until the revolution of 1776 is complete. We must get in this revolution and complete the revolution. For in the Delta of Mississippi, in southwest Georgia, in the black belt of Alabama, in Harlem, in Chicago, Detroit, Philadelphia, and all over this nation—the black masses are on the march for jobs and freedom.

You talk about slow down and stop, we will not stop. All of the forces of Eastland, Barnett, Wallace, and Thurmond will not stop this revolution. If we do not get meaningful legislation out of this Congress, the time will come when we will not confine our marching to Washington. We will march through the South— through the streets of Jackson, through the streets of Danville, through the streets of Cambridge, through the streets of Birmingham—

At this point, he had to stop, as the crowd responded to his calling of the roll of the civil rights battlefields from the summer of 1963.

> —but we will march with the spirit of love and with the spirit of dignity that we have shown here today. By the force of our demands, our determination, and our numbers, we shall splinter the segregated South into a thousand pieces and put them together in the image of God and democracy. We must say, "Wake up, America! Wake up!" For we cannot stop, and we will not and cannot be patient.

When he finished, the 250,000 people listening cheered louder than they had for anyone all day. On the speakers' platform, every black speaker rushed up to Lewis to shake his hand and pound him on the back. Every white speaker stayed seated and stared into the distance.

Lewis's speech had been the emotional high point of the day, but the crowd's energy was soon dissipated by the procession of speakers who followed him. Roy Wilkins announced the news of W. E. B. Du Bois's death in Africa. "Remember, this has been a long fight," he said. "Now, regardless of the fact that in his later years, Dr. Du Bois chose another path, it is incontrovertible that at the dawn of the twentieth century, his was the voice that was calling to you to gather here today in this cause." There was a wave of applause that subsided into a reverential silence. "It's like Moses," said a woman. "God had written that he should never enter the promised land."

By the time that Roy Wilkins finished his address, the

crowd was already tired from a long afternoon of speechmaking. More marchers packed up and headed toward the buses. Several people left to go downtown in search of souvenirs. The crowd was dissolving when A. Philip Randolph introduced Mahalia Jackson. At the mention of her name, many in the audience paused. She sang the first two verses of a spiritual, "I Been 'Buked and I Been Scorned," to a silent crowd. Then, she closed her eyes for the third verse:

I'm going to tell my Lord
When I get home
I'm going to tell my Lord
When I get home
Yeah, I'm going to tell my Lord
When I get home.
How you been mistreating me so long.

She drew out the "tell" in the third stanza with a rough blues slide, and the crowd shouted back to her. Martin Luther King, Jr., seated near her at the speakers' platform, was openly enjoying her performance. He clapped his hands on his knees and called out to her, a preacher urging the choir to sing. At the end of the verse, Bayard Rustin came up to the podium, because the song had apparently ended. "Thank you," Rustin said to the crowd, away from the microphone, but Mahalia Jackson was still humming the tune. She went back to the first verse and sang it again. Rustin looked at her, a nervous smile on his face, his pad in hand. But it was too late, and she was already into the second verse. Rustin gave up, and started to sing along with her.

Stand by me, Lord
Stand by me.

She finished, and the marchers cheered for an encore.
Roger Mudd, announcing for the day for CBS News, told the
television audience: "Mahalia Jackson. And all the speeches in
the world couldn't have brought the response that just came
from the hymns she sang. Miss Mahalia Jackson." The crowd
was still applauding behind him as Mudd went on, "They're
demanding an encore, but I'm not sure—yes, she's still there.
She's going to sing again." At his last words, the pipe organ at
the Lincoln Memorial had already set into a rolling bass line,
for an up-tempo spiritual, "How I Got Over." Bayard Rustin
clapped at her side, in time with the crowd. When Mahalia
Jackson finally finished, she left the microphone to a sustained
shouting that sounded like the response of a congregation to a
gospel choir.

After a speech by Rabbi Joachim Prinz, from the
American Jewish Congress, A. Philip Randolph thanked the
organizers of the march, including Bayard Rustin, "a gifted
young man," with a "marvelous capacity for the organization
of men." Then Randolph took off his glasses and said, "At this
time I have the honor to present to you the moral leader of our
nation." Someone in the crowd shouted "Yes, sir!" and the audience applauded. "A great, dedicated, man," said Randolph.
The cheers of the audience almost drowned him out, because
people could see Martin Luther King, Jr., making his way to
the podium. "A philosopher of the nonviolent system of be-
havior in seeking to bring about social change for the ad-

vancement of justice and freedom and human dignity." King was at Randolph's side now. "I have the pleasure to present to you, Dr. Martin Luther King, 'J-R'," Randolph finished, pronouncing each of the last two letters. His voice nearly didn't carry above the cries of the crowd, who cheered loudly in tribute.

King placed his prepared speech on the lectern and looked out over the vast assembly. He wore a dark suit and tie with a white shirt. The "March on Washington for Jobs and Freedom" button was pinned to his lapel. He had a small smile on his face. He nodded a few times and mouthed "thank you" to the crowd. The applause kept going. King adjusted his jacket and looked down at the podium, waiting for the audience to finish. Then he looked up, and it seemed that he would begin to speak, but a "Hip Hip" came from somewhere in the crowd, and a "Hooray!" followed. King looked back down. The two cheers came once more, and the "Hooray!" seemed to surprise him, because he looked up suddenly from his notes. He opened his mouth again, but the "Hip Hip" was already out from the crowd, and King had to wait to listen to the final cheer. This went on a few more times before it merged into a roll of shouts and clapping from the audience. Many people chanted King's name, over and over. Contrary to what some of the civil rights leaders had expected, the television networks had all interrupted their regular programming to broadcast what was happening at the Lincoln Memorial, and millions of Americans witnessed the ovation that King received. King grasped the podium with both hands, waited a moment, and then opened his mouth to speak.

I am happy to join with you today in what will go down in history as the greatest demonstration for freedom in the history of our nation.

The crowd applauded with gracious restraint, as if cheering themselves. When they finished, King began to read from his written text.

Fivescore years ago, a great American, in whose symbolic shadow we stand today, signed the Emancipation Proclamation. This momentous decree came as a great beacon light of hope to millions of Negro slaves who had been seared in the flames of withering injustice. It came as a joyous daybreak to end the long night of their captivity.

But one hundred years later, the Negro still is not free. One hundred years later, the life of the Negro is still sadly crippled by the manacles of segregation and the chains of discrimination. One hundred years later, the Negro lives on a lonely island of poverty in the midst of a vast ocean of material prosperity. One hundred years later—

The crowd had been standing rapt and silent so far, but as they caught the repeated phrase, they responded. King waited for the applause to cease, then went on:

—the Negro is still languished in the corners of American society and finds himself an exile in his own land.

And so we've come here today to dramatize a shameful condition. In a sense we've come to our nation's capital to cash a check. When the architects of our republic wrote the magnificent words of the Constitution and the Declaration of Independence, they were signing a promissory note to which every American was to fall heir. This note was a promise that all men—yes, black men as well as white men—would be guaranteed the unalienable rights of life, liberty, and the pursuit of happiness.

It is obvious today that America has defaulted on this promissory note insofar as her citizens of color are concerned. Instead of honoring this sacred obligation, America has given the Negro people a bad check; a check which has come back marked "insufficient funds."

The crowd applauded this point, and King delivered the one joke of his speech:

But we refuse to believe that the bank of justice is bankrupt.

Many people laughed appreciatively. "Sure enough!" shouted one woman.

We refuse to believe that there are insufficient funds in the great vaults of opportunity of this nation. And so we've come to cash this check—a check that will give us upon demand the riches of freedom and the security of justice.

The crowd responded, and then became still.

We have also come to this hallowed spot to remind America of the fierce urgency of now. This is no time to engage in the luxury of cooling off or to take the tranquilizing drug of gradualism. Now is the time to make real the promises of democracy. Now is the time to rise from the dark and desolate valley of segregation to the sunlit path of racial justice. Now is the time to lift our nation from the quicksands of racial injustice to the solid rock of brotherhood. Now is the time to make justice a reality for all of God's children.

The audience cheered after each "now," and at the end of each line, in a cadence.

It would be fatal for the nation to overlook the urgency of the moment. This sweltering summer of the Negro's legitimate discontent will not pass until there is an invigorating autumn of freedom and equality.

Nineteen sixty-three is not an end, but a beginning. And those who hope that the Negro needed to blow off steam and will now be content will have a rude awakening if the nation returns to business as usual.

At this, the people shouted agreement with the challenge that had been issued earlier by John Lewis.

> There will be neither rest nor tranquility in America until the Negro is granted his citizenship rights. The whirlwinds of revolt will continue to shake the foundations of our nation until the bright day of justice emerges.

> But there is something that I must say to my people who stand on the warm threshold which leads into the palace of justice. In the process of gaining our rightful place we must not be guilty of wrongful deeds.

> Let us not seek to satisfy our thirst for freedom by drinking from the cup of bitterness and hatred.

The crowd clapped in approval.

> We must forever conduct our struggle on the high plane of dignity and discipline. We must not allow our creative protest to degenerate into physical violence. Again and again we must rise to the majestic heights of meeting physical force with soul force.

> The marvelous new militancy which has engulfed the Negro community must not lead us to a distrust of all white people, for many of our white brothers, as evidenced by their presence here today, have come to realize that their destiny is tied up with our destiny—

Here he had to pause, as the applause had slowly welled up in appreciation for those whites who had come to the march.

—and they have come to realize that their freedom is inextricably bound to our freedom. We cannot walk alone.

And as we walk, we must make the pledge that we shall always march ahead. We cannot turn back. There are those who are asking the devotees of civil rights, "When will you be satisfied?" We can never be satisfied as long as the Negro is the victim of the unspeakable horrors of police brutality. We can never be satisfied—

The applause rose gently at this line.

—as long as our bodies, heavy with the fatigue of travel, cannot gain lodging in the motels of the highways and the hotels of the cities.

The crowd shouted back at him, and King repeated the refrain:

We cannot be satisfied as long as the Negro's basic mobility is from a smaller ghetto to a larger one.

We can never be satisfied as long as our children are stripped of their selfhood and robbed of their dignity by signs stating "for whites only."

We cannot be satisfied as long as a Negro in Mississippi cannot vote and a Negro in New York believes he has nothing for which to vote.

The screams of the crowd interrupted him again. He began:

No—

And he surveyed the crowd for a moment, letting the line build, and went on:

—no, we are not satisfied, and we will not be satisfied, until justice rolls down like waters and righteousness like a mighty stream.

A roar broke like thunder from the audience. And seeing the response, King skipped whole paragraphs and headed into his planned conclusion:

I am not unmindful that some of you have come here out of great trials and tribulations. Some of you have come fresh from narrow jail cells. Some of you have come from areas where your quest for freedom left you battered by the storms of persecution and staggered by the winds of police brutality. You have been the veterans of creative suffering. Continue to work with the faith that unearned suffering is redemptive.

Behind him, Mahalia Jackson shouted, "Tell them about the dream, Martin!"

Go back to Mississippi; go back to Alabama; go back to South Carolina; go back to Georgia; go back to Louisiana; go back to the slums and ghettos of our Northern cities, knowing that somehow this situation can and will be changed. Let us not wallow in the valley of despair.

She called to him again, "Tell them about the dream, Martin!" And perhaps because of something in the way the crowd was responding to him that day, Martin Luther King, Jr., left his prepared text and began to preach.

I say to you today, my friends—

The cheers made him stop for a moment.

—so even though we face the difficulties of today and tomorrow, I still have a dream.

It is a dream deeply rooted in the American dream.

I have a dream that one day this nation will rise up and live out the true meaning of its creed: We hold these truths to be self-evident, that all men are created equal.

The crowd shouted, letting themselves be pulled along with him.

I have a dream that one day on the red hills of Georgia, the sons of former slaves and the sons of former slave-owners will be able to sit down together at the table of brotherhood.

I have a dream that one day—

He had to speak louder now, to be heard over the applause that built under each line—

—even the state of Mississippi, a state sweltering with the heat of injustice, sweltering with the heat of oppression, will be transformed into an oasis of freedom and justice.

I have a dream—

The crowd's response made him pause again briefly, and then he went on:

—that my four little children will one day live in a nation where they will not be judged by the color of their skin but by the content of their character. I have a dream today!

He turned away from the lectern as the crowd screamed below him. People in the front row joined hands and swayed back and forth, shouting, "Dream some more!" He returned to the microphone, raised his right arm, and lifted his voice to a deafening wail:

I have a dream that one day, down in Alabama, with its vicious racists, with its governor having his lips dripping with the words of interposition and nullification, one day, right there in Alabama, little black boys and black girls will be able to join hands with little white boys and white girls as sisters and brothers. I have a dream today!

He paused again, and the crowd exploded. "Tell us, tell us," some members of the crowd shouted. "Dream on!" "I see it!" "Keep dreaming! Keep dreaming!"

I have a dream that one day every valley shall be exalted, and every hill and mountain shall be made low, the rough places will be made plain, and the crooked places will be made straight and the glory of the Lord shall be revealed, and all flesh shall see it together.

This is our hope. This is the faith that I go back to the South with.

He drew two sentences from near the end of his written speech, which had been lying unlooked at on the podium for several minutes:

With this faith we will be able to hew out of the mountain of despair a stone of hope. With this faith we will be able to transform the jangling discords of our nation into a beautiful symphony of brotherhood.

With the crowd calling back to him after almost every phrase in the responsive cadences of a congregation at a Sunday sermon, he left his text again:

With this faith we will able to work together, to pray together, to struggle together, to go to jail together, to stand up for freedom together, knowing that we will be free one day.

As the building applause broke over this line, he went on in lyrical improvisation:

This will be the day—this will be the day—when all of God's children will be able to sing with new meaning: "My country 'tis of thee; sweet land of liberty; of thee I sing; land where my fathers died, land of the pilgrim's pride; from every mountainside, let freedom ring!" And if America is to be a great nation, this must become true.

And so let freedom ring from the prodigious hilltops of New Hampshire.

Let freedom ring from the mighty mountains of New York.

Let freedom ring from the heightening Alleghenies of Pennsylvania.

Let freedom ring from the snow-capped Rockies of Colorado.

Let freedom ring from the curvaceous slopes of California.

But not only that.

Let freedom ring from Stone Mountain of Georgia.

Let freedom ring from Lookout Mountain of Tennessee.

Let freedom ring from every hill and molehill of Mississippi, from every mountainside—

He nearly screamed "every," and the shouts built up again under him. Many in the crowd were weeping uncontrollably.

—let freedom ring. And when this happens—

The people's calls and yells made him pause, and then he went on, drawing them with him toward the end.

—when we allow freedom ring, when we let it ring from every village and every hamlet, from every state and every city, we will be able to speed up that day when all of God's children—black men and white men, Jews and Gentiles, Protestants and Catholics—will be able to join hands and sing in the words of the old Negro spiritual,

He raised his right arm in benediction and ended in a triumphant shout:

"Free at last, free at last, thank God Almighty, we are free at last!"

He picked up his speech and stepped away from the podium to a great cry like the sound of the heavens being torn open. The cheers went on and on, as the crowd seemed to shout back to him in unison. A short distance away at the White House, President John F. Kennedy watched on television. He turned to one of his aides and said: "That guy is really good."

chapter two

Composition

Martin Luther King, Jr., began working on his speech for the March on Washington on Saturday, August 24, four days before the event was to take place. He composed the address during a period in which he also worked on a book manuscript in New York, appeared on *Meet the Press* in Washington, D.C., and visited the SCLC offices in Atlanta before traveling back to Washington the night before the march. He told one of his aides he wanted to say something short that would capture the historic resonances of the event—"sort of a Gettysburg Address," he said. But when King checked into the Willard Hotel in Washington on Tuesday night, he still did not have a final draft of his speech for the next day.

During most of the month of August 1963, King had been staying at the New York home of Clarence Jones, an attorney who had helped him since the Albany campaign, so he could work without interruption on a book about Birmingham. On the Saturday before the march, several of King's advisers joined him at Jones's house to discuss logistics for the event and to talk about ideas for King's speech. King had asked a few aides to prepare drafts of themes and language as starting points for discussion. One draft presented at the Saturday meeting contained a passage about America giving its black citizens a "bad check." Walter Fauntroy, the head of the SCLC's Washington, D.C., office, was immediately drawn to the "bad check" metaphor. "Whatever you do, keep that in there," he told King. The rest of King's advisers had other priorities. Bayard Rustin pressed King to speak about the labor movement, and a few other aides urged him to use a line of oratory they had heard in several of his speeches featuring the repeated phrase "I have a dream."

The group's principal frustration was that even though A. Philip Randolph had told King that he could take whatever time he needed, King seemed committed to staying within the five minutes that had originally been given to each speaker. Clarence Jones had earlier counseled King to ignore the time limit. "With all due respect to Roy Wilkins, James Farmer, John Lewis, Walter Reuther, Rabbi so-and-so, Reverend so-and-so, with all due respect to them, these people who came, they didn't come for them. They came for you." King tried to placate him: "Well . . . I know, Clarence," he said, "I know how you feel." But Jones went on, "I don't care if they speak for five minutes, that's fine. You are going to take as much time as you need."

At the Saturday meeting, though, King held to the idea that he would keep his speech under five minutes. The "bad check" and "I have a dream" sections would each take about four minutes, so using both of them would run over King's allotted time. After three or four hours of discussion, the conference ended. King may have seen the meeting as an opportunity to take preliminary soundings on what his advisers considered important, because nothing was written that day. Fauntroy left King with the reminder that he should not feel bound by the limits placed on the other speakers: "Look, Martin," he said, "you do what the spirit say do."

On Monday, King worked on his speech at the SCLC offices in Atlanta with Ed Clayton, the organization's public relations director. The two men went back and forth on draft passages, with Clayton writing sections and King editing them. King telephoned Clayton that night with his latest edits. He made further revisions the next day, on the plane to Washington.

Two pages of a draft speech by Clarence Jones and Stanley Levison, a longtime King adviser, still exist, as do two versions of a draft speech entitled "Normalcy—Never Again." Although the relationships among the three drafts are not clear, the shorter version of the "Normalcy" speech was probably prepared by someone who was working from both the longer "Normalcy" speech and the Jones-Levison draft, because a few sections in it appear to be revised versions of both texts. At some point, King handwrote a few sentences on the back of the last page of the shorter "Normalcy" draft:

We must live with the very people from whom we are demanding our rights

So today the whirlwinds of revolt are shaking our nation

Then America will be the home of uncompromising loyalty to social justice

Never again must our nation cast the mantle of its sanctity over the system of segregation

Through our actions we will subpoena the conscience of men to appear before the judgment seat of morality

When King arrived in Washington, D.C., on the night before the march, he did not yet have a speech that he considered satisfactory. After a meeting with the other march leaders, he gathered several aides together in the lobby of the Willard Hotel and convened another roundtable discussion about what he should say. King's advisers began to bombard him with suggestions on topics they thought he should highlight in the speech. At one point, Clarence Jones excused himself to sit at a nearby table and jot down some possible language about the federal government's failure to protect civil rights workers and the ability of the president to issue an executive order prohibiting discrimination in housing. Other aides urged King to emphasize the need for jobs and to propose a guaranteed income program. King eventually put an end to the barrage. "My brothers, I understand," he said. "I appreciate all the suggestions. Now let me go and counsel with the Lord."

King adjourned to his suite at the Willard Hotel, where his secretary, Dora McDonald, was on standby to take notes and type his drafts. He was thinking about using the "I have a dream" refrain, but he decided he did not have enough time.

Instead, he chose to begin the speech with the "bad check" metaphor, reflecting on what that meant in 1963, the centennial year of the Emancipation Proclamation. Coretta Scott King later remembered that her husband wanted to "echo some of the Lincolnian language."

Wyatt Tee Walker, the executive director of the SCLC, was installed in a Willard Hotel suite a few floors beneath King, where he spent the evening on call to provide assistance with the speech. King would tell Walker what he wanted to say, and Walker would try to produce something fitting. Walker would then sprint up several flights of stairs to King's suite and present him with a draft. King edited the drafts verbally, either accepting the suggestions or saying, "Well, no. I don't want to say it like that," and telling Walker more of the sense of what he wanted.

King finished outlining the speech at around midnight. He then began to write a draft in longhand, revising it as he went along. King occasionally called out to those who were with him for suggestions on word choice, often as not supplying the missing word himself. When Andrew Young stopped by King's suite that night, he noticed that King had crossed out words three and four times, looking for not only the right meaning, but also the right rhythm. Young thought that King was composing the Washington speech as if he were writing poetry. King finished writing the speech at about four in the morning and gave the prepared text to his aides for typing, duplication, and distribution to the press.

This meticulous process of composition, beginning with the solicitation of drafts from several advisers and culminating in a complete manuscript of a speech, was highly unusual for

King at this stage of his career. He did not have time to go through this process for every one of his speaking engagements. In the year of the March on Washington, King traveled about 275,000 miles and gave more than 350 speeches. He composed most of his speeches by stringing together a series of the "set pieces" he had developed during his career as a public speaker. Like most preachers, King had collected a repertoire of oratorical fragments—successful passages from his own sermons, sections from other preachers' works, anecdotes, Bible verses, lines from favorite poets—that he could combine to create a sermon. King's set pieces ranged from short, vivid phrases ("meet physical force with soul force") to entire paragraphs (the "I have a dream" peroration that ended his speech at the march). Most of his set pieces were memorized, and most had some natural affinities of language or theme that caused them to fit well with one another. King did not so much write his speeches as assemble them, by rearranging and adapting material he had used many times before.

As it turned out, the speech King actually delivered at the March on Washington was more indebted to set pieces from his own storehouse of oratory than it was to the prepared text he had brought with him to the podium. King added so much new material to his prepared speech that the length of his address nearly doubled. For about the first ten minutes of the speech, King read his text nearly verbatim, making only slight alterations of word choice or phrasing. But as he neared the end of his prepared text, he decided to omit its penultimate peroration:

And so today, let us go back to our communities as members of the international association for the advancement of creative dissatisfaction. Let us go back and work with all the strength we can muster to get strong civil rights legislation in this session of Congress. Let us go down from this place to ascend other peaks of purpose. Let us descend from this mountaintop to climb other hills of hope.

Instead he inserted several set pieces from his own repertoire that he hadn't originally intended to deliver. Just before King spoke, both Andrew Young and Clarence Jones noticed that he had already marked up his copy of his prepared text, crossing out lines and scribbling new ones as he awaited his turn to speak. Andrew Young thought that it looked like King was still editing the speech until he walked to the podium to deliver it. A side-by-side comparison of the speech he prepared with the speech he actually gave illustrates how King improvised minor alterations throughout his prepared text before finally deciding to abandon it completely:

Prepared Speech	*Delivered Speech*
(omissions in italics)	(additions in bold)
	I am happy to join with you today in what will go down in history as the greatest demonstration for freedom in the history of our nation.

(continued)

Prepared Speech

(*omissions in italics*)

Five score years ago, a great American, in whose symbolic shadow we stand today, signed the Emancipation Proclamation. This momentous decree came as a great beacon light of hope to millions of Negro slaves who had been seared in the flames of withering injustice. It came as a joyous daybreak to end the long night of captivity.

But one hundred years later, *we must face the tragic fact that* the Negro still is not free. One hundred years later, the life of the Negro is still sadly crippled by the manacle of segregation and the chains of discrimination. One hundred years later, the Negro lives on a lonely island of poverty in the midst of a vast ocean of material prosperity. One hundred years later, the Negro is still languished in the corners of American society

Delivered Speech

(additions in bold)

Fivescore years ago, a great American, in whose symbolic shadow we stand today, signed the Emancipation Proclamation. This momentous decree came as a great beacon light of hope to millions of Negro slaves who had been seared in the flames of withering injustice. It came as a joyous daybreak to end the long night of **their** captivity.

But one hundred years later, the Negro still is not free. One hundred years later, the life of the Negro is still sadly crippled by the manacles of segregation and the chains of discrimination. One hundred years later, the Negro lives on a lonely island of poverty in the midst of a vast ocean of material prosperity. One hundred years later, the Negro is still languished in the corners of American society and finds and finds himself an exile in his own land.

So we have come here today to dramatize an *appalling* condition. In a sense we have come to our nation's Capitol to cash a check. When the architects of our republic wrote the magnificent words of the Constitution and the Declaration of Independence, they were signing a promissory note to which every American was to fall heir. This note was a promise that all men would be granted the unalienable rights of life, liberty, and the pursuit of happiness.

It is obvious today that America has defaulted on this promissory note insofar as her citizens of color are concerned. Instead of honoring this sacred obligation, America has given the Negro people a bad check; a check which has come back marked "insufficient funds."

himself an exile in his own land.

And so we've come here today to dramatize a **shameful** condition. In a sense we've come to our nation's capital to cash a check. When the architects of our republic wrote the magnificent words of the Constitution and the Declaration of Independence, they were signing a promissory note to which every American was to fall heir. This note was a promise that all men—**yes, black men as well as white men**—would be guaranteed the unalienable rights of life, liberty, and the pursuit of happiness.

It is obvious today that America has defaulted on this promissory note insofar as her citizens of color are concerned. Instead of honoring this sacred obligation, America has given the Negro people a bad check;

(continued)

Prepared Speech

(omissions in italics)

Delivered Speech

(additions in bold)

a check which has come back
marked "insufficient funds."

But we refuse to believe that the
bank of justice is bankrupt. We
refuse to believe that there are
insufficient funds in the great
vaults of opportunity of this nation. So we have come to cash
this check—a check that will
give us upon demand the riches
of freedom and the security of
justice.

We have also come to this
hallowed spot to remind
America of the fierce urgency of
now. This is no time to engage
in the luxury of cooling off or
to take the tranquilizing drug
of gradualism. Now is the time
to make real the promises of
Democracy. Now is the time to
rise from the dark and desolate
valley of segregation to the sunlit path of racial justice. *Now
is the time to open the doors of*

But we refuse to believe that the
bank of justice is bankrupt. We
refuse to believe that there are
insufficient funds in the great
vaults of opportunity of this nation. And so we've come to
cash this check—a check that
will give us upon demand the
riches of freedom and the security of justice.

We have also come to this hallowed spot to remind America
of the fierce urgency of now.
This is no time to engage in the
luxury of cooling off or to take
the tranquilizing drug of gradualism. Now is the time to make
real the promises of democracy.
Now is the time to rise from the
dark and desolate valley of segregation to the sunlit path of
racial justice. Now is the time
to lift our nation from the

opportunity to all of God's children. Now is the time to lift our nation from the quicksands of racial injustice to the solid rock of brotherhood.

It would be fatal for the nation to overlook the urgency of the moment *and to underestimate the determination of the Negro.* This sweltering summer of the Negro's legitimate discontent will not pass until there is an invigorating autumn of freedom and equality.

Nineteen sixty-three is not an end, but a beginning. Those who hope that the Negro needed to blow off steam and will now be content will have a rude awakening if the nation returns to business as usual.

There will be neither rest nor tranquility in America until the Negro is granted his citizenship rights. The whirlwinds of revolt will continue to shake the foun-

quicksands of racial injustice to the solid rock of brotherhood. **Now is the time to make justice a reality for all of God's children.**

It would be fatal for the nation to overlook the urgency of the moment. This sweltering summer of the Negro's legitimate discontent will not pass until there is an invigorating autumn of freedom and equality.

Nineteen sixty-three is not an end, but a beginning. And those who hope that the Negro needed to blow off steam and will now be content will have a rude awakening if the nation returns to business as usual.

There will be neither rest nor tranquility in America until the Negro is granted his citizenship rights. The whirlwinds of revolt

(continued)

Prepared Speech	*Delivered Speech*
(*omissions in italics*)	(additions in bold)

dations of our nation until the bright day of justice emerges.	**will continue to shake the foun**dations of our nation until the bright day of justice emerges.
But there is something that I must say to my people who stand on the warm threshold which leads into the palace of justice. In the process of gaining our rightful place we must not be guilty of wrongful deeds.	But there is something that I must say to my people who stand on the warm threshold which leads into the palace of justice. In the process of gaining our rightful place we must not be guilty of wrongful deeds.
Let us not seek to satisfy our thirst for freedom by drinking from the cup of bitterness and hatred.	Let us not seek to satisfy our thirst for freedom by drinking from the cup of bitterness and hatred.
We must forever conduct of [*sic*] struggle on the high plane of dignity and discipline. We must not allow our creative protest to degenerate into physical violence. Again and again we must rise to the majestic heights of meeting physical force with soul force. The marvelous new militancy which has	We must forever conduct **our** struggle on the high plane of dignity and discipline. We must not allow our creative protest to degenerate into physical violence. Again and again we must rise to the majestic heights of meeting physical force with soul force. The marvelous new militancy which has **engulfed**

engulfed the Negro community must not lead us to a distrust of all white people, for many of our white brothers [*sic*] evidenced by their presence here today, have come to realize that their destiny is tied up with our destiny and their freedom is inextricably bound to our freedom. *This offense we share mounted to storm the battlements of injustice must be carried forth by a biracial army.* We cannot walk alone.

And as we walk, we must make the pledge that we shall always march ahead. We cannot turn back. There are those who are asking the devotees of civil rights, "When will you be satisfied?" We can never be satisfied as long as the Negro is the victim of the unspeakable horrors of police brutality. We can never be satisfied as long as our bodies, heavy with the fatigue of travel, cannot gain lodging in the motels of the highways and the hotels of the cities.

the Negro community must not lead us to a distrust of all white people, for many of our white brothers, as evidenced by their presence here today, have come to realize that their destiny is tied up with our destiny **and they have come to realize that** their freedom is inextricably bound to our freedom. We cannot walk alone.

And as we walk, we must make the pledge that we shall always march ahead. We cannot turn back. There are those who are asking the devotees of civil rights, "When will you be satisfied?" We can never be satisfied as long as the Negro is the victim of the unspeakable horrors of police brutality. We can never be satisfied as long as our bodies, heavy with the fatigue of travel, cannot gain lodging in

(continued)

Prepared Speech	*Delivered Speech*
(*omissions in italics*)	(additions in bold)

	the motels of the highways and the hotels of the cities.
We cannot be satisfied as long as the Negro's basic mobility is from a smaller ghetto to a larger one.	We cannot be satisfied as long as the Negro's basic mobility is from a smaller ghetto to a larger one.
We can never be satisfied as long as our children are stripped of their selfhood and robbed of their dignity by signs stating "for whites only."	We can never be satisfied as long as our children are stripped of their selfhood and robbed of their dignity by signs stating "for whites only."
We cannot be satisfied as long as a Negro in Mississippi cannot vote and a Negro in New York believes he has nothing for which to vote.	We cannot be satisfied as long as a Negro in Mississippi cannot vote and a Negro in New York believes he has nothing for which to vote.
We will not be satisfied until justice rolls down like waters and righteousness like a mighty stream.	**No, no, we are not satisfied, and** we will not be satisfied, until justice rolls down like waters and righteousness like a mighty stream.
And so today, let us go back to our communities as members of	

*the international association for
the advancement of creative dissatisfaction.*

*Let us go back and work with all
the strength we can muster to get
strong civil rights legislation in
this session of Congress.*

*Let us go down from this place
to ascend other peaks of purpose.
Let us descend from this mountaintop to climb other hills of
hope.*

I am not unmindful that some
of you have come here out of
excessive trials and tribulation.
Some of you have come fresh
from narrow jail cells. Some of
you have come from areas
where your quest for freedom
left you battered by the storms
of persecution and staggered
by the winds of police brutality.
You have been the veterans
of creative suffering. Continue
to work with the faith that
unearned suffering is redemptive.

I am not unmindful that some
of you have come here out of
great trials and tribulations.
Some of you have come fresh
from narrow jail cells. Some of
you have come from areas
where your quest for freedom
left you battered by the storms
of persecution and staggered by
the winds of police brutality.
You have been the veterans of
creative suffering. Continue to
work with the faith that unearned suffering is redemptive.

(continued)

Prepared Speech	*Delivered Speech*
(*omissions in italics*)	(additions in bold)

Go back to Mississippi; go back to Alabama; go back to South Carolina; go back to Georgia; go back to Louisiana; go back to the slums and ghettos of our Northern cities, knowing that somehow this situation can, and will be changed. Let us not wallow in the valley of despair.

I say to you today, my friends, so even though we face the difficulties of today and to-morrow, I still have a dream.

It is a dream deeply rooted in the American dream.

I have a dream that one day this nation will rise up and live out the true meaning of its creed: We hold these truths to be self-evident, that all men are created equal.

I have a dream that one day
on the red hills of Georgia,
the sons of former slaves and
the sons of former slave-
owners will be able to sit
down together at the table of
brotherhood.

I have a dream that one day
even the state of Mississippi, a
state sweltering with the heat
of injustice, sweltering with
the heat of oppression, will be
transformed into an oasis of
freedom and justice.

I have a dream that my four
little children will one day live
in a nation where they will
not be judged by the color of
their skin but by the content
of their character. I have a
dream today!

I have a dream that one day,
down in Alabama, with its
vicious racists, with its governor having his lips dripping
with the words of interposi-

(continued)

Prepared Speech	Delivered Speech
(*omissions in italics*)	(additions in bold)

tion and nullification, one day, right there in Alabama, little black boys and black girls will be able to join hands with little white boys and white girls as sisters and brothers. I have a dream today!

I have a dream that one day every valley shall be exalted, and every hill and mountain shall be made low, the rough places will be made plain, and the crooked places will be made straight and the glory of the Lord shall be revealed and all flesh shall see it together. This is our hope. This is the faith that I go back to the South with.

Prepared Speech	Delivered Speech
With this faith we will be able to hew out of the mountain of despair a stone of hope. With this faith we will be able to transform the jangling discords	With this faith we will be able to hew out of the mountain of despair a stone of hope. With this faith we will be able to transform the jangling discords

of our nation into a beautiful symphony of brotherhood.

of our nation into a beautiful symphony of brotherhood.

With this faith we will able to work together, to pray together, to struggle together, to go to jail together, to stand up for freedom together, knowing that we will be free one day.

This will be the day—this will be the day—when all of God's children will be able to sing with new meaning: "My country 'tis of thee; sweet land of liberty; of thee I sing; land where my fathers died, land of the pilgrim's pride; from every mountain side, let freedom ring!" And if America is to be a great nation, this must become true.

And so let freedom ring from the prodigious hilltops of New Hampshire.

Let freedom ring from the mighty mountains of New York.   *(continued)*

Prepared Speech	*Delivered Speech*
(*omissions in italics*)	(additions in bold)

Let freedom ring from the heightening Alleghenies of Pennsylvania.

Let freedom ring from the **snow-capped Rockies of Colorado.**

Let freedom ring from the **curvaceous slopes of California.**

But not only that.

Let freedom ring from Stone Mountain of Georgia.

Let freedom ring from Lookout Mountain of Tennessee.

Let freedom ring from **every hill and molehill of** Mississippi, **from every mountainside, let freedom ring. And when this happens, when we allow freedom ring,**

*Let us work and march and love
and stand tall together until
that day has come when we can
join hands and sing,* "Free at
last, free at last, thank God
Almighty, we are free at last!"

when we let it ring from every
village and every hamlet, from
every state and every city, we
will be able to speed up that
day when all of God's children—black men and white
men, Jews and Gentiles,
Protestants and Catholics—
will be able to join hands and
sing in the words of the old
Negro spiritual,

"Free at last, free at last, thank
God Almighty, we are free at
last!"

As his performance at the March on Washington demon-
strates, even when King had solicited his aides for ideas on a
speech, he never ceded final control over a speech's language
to anyone but himself. King had first spoken from the Lincoln
Memorial six years before the March on Washington, at a
"Prayer Pilgrimage for Freedom," called to commemorate the
third anniversary of *Brown v. Board of Education.* He asked
Bayard Rustin and Stanley Levison to help him think through
ideas for his address. Even though King was still a relatively
young civil rights leader—the Pilgrimage occurred a few
months after the conclusion of the Montgomery bus boycott,
when King was just twenty-eight years old—he made clear to
his older and more experienced aides that he would be the
sole authority on his speech's content and language. King

turned down Rustin's suggestion that he issue a call to the labor movement to increase its presence in the South and decided instead to focus on the disenfranchisement of black Americans. Shortly before the event, Rustin gave King an edited copy of King's prepared speech, on which he had crossed out King's refrain "Give us the ballot" and substituted his own "When we have achieved the ballot." King changed the phrase back to its original wording. When Rustin complained, King just smiled, and said: "Well Bayard, I don't mind your criticizing my ideas. But I don't like your criticizing my words, because I'm better at words than you are."

The last-minute alterations King made in his prepared text at the march were only the final stage in an editing and revising process that had consumed nearly all the previous night. When King began to write his speech out in longhand the night before the march, he probably had the Jones-Levison draft and the two "Normalcy" speeches in front of him, because a few phrases and sentences from each of these three drafts appear nearly verbatim in King's prepared text.* King used these drafts as starting points for his own composition, collecting what he felt were the best turns of phrase and rewriting passages where he approved of the idea but not the wording. King's compositional hand can be seen at work in

---

* The presence of language in the Jones-Levison draft or the two "Normalcy" drafts does not necessarily mean that the material was not originally King's own. King's aides rarely worked in isolation from his input; it was common for King either to give them specific verbal instructions for what he wanted to say (as he did with Wyatt Tee Walker the night before the march) or for the aides to attempt to rework material that they had heard King use in his speeches. In effect, King's aides' drafts often enabled him to see his own material reflected back at him from different perspectives.

these revisions, as he retained the drafts' best language, made earlier versions of passages more concise, omitted confusing or unnecessary metaphors, and, in some cases, improvised at the podium final improvements to his prepared speech.

The section of the speech in which King calls for racial integration within the civil rights movement, for example, was rewritten by the author of the shorter "Normalcy" text and then rewritten a second time by King. King condensed two lengthy sentences from the Jones-Levison draft into a single clause—"The marvelous new militancy which has engulfed the Negro community must not lead us to a distrust of all white people"—and decided not to use either of the metaphors that had concluded the section in the earlier versions. King made another revision at the podium, omitting a passage about a "biracial army" that had been in his prepared text, perhaps realizing that the martial metaphor was not appropriate in a speech urging nonviolence.

Jones/Levison	"Normalcy" (Short)	Prepared Speech	Delivered Speech
		(omissions in italics)	
This new militancy which has brought us to Washington and brought much of Washington to our cause, this new militancy is a marvellous thing for we cannot and will not be free until we have ex-	This new militancy which has brought us to Washington and brought many in Washington's official and legislative family to our cause—this new militancy means that we have a great movement, vibrant	The marvelous new militancy which has engulfed the Negro community must not lead us to a distrust of all white people, for many of our white brothers [sic] evidenced by their presence here today, have	The marvelous new militancy which has engulfed the Negro community must not lead us to a distrust of all white people, for many of our white brothers, as evidenced by their pres- *(continued)*

Jones/Levison	"Normalcy" (Short)	Prepared Speech (omissions in italics)	Delivered Speech
pressed the determination to be free. But this new and necessary militancy must not lead us to the conclusion that we should distrust all white people. There is a clear and present danger that some will overlook the fact that we cannot bring about the beloved community by leaving our brother outside. A poet has said: "He drew a circle which left me out. But love and I had the wit to win. We drew a circle that took him in." The circle we draw cannot be fully rounded nor perfect in its symmetry if we seek to draw it alone. The attack upon racial injustice, the offensive to be mounted against segregation—must be bi-racial. I would hope that the great majority of us will always remember that.	with idealism; a movement which has given hundreds of thousands of Americans a sense of purpose. Many of these people of conscience are not people of color. This new militancy must not lead us to the conclusion that we should distrust all white people. We cannot bring about the beloved community by seeking to lock our brothers outside of its doors. This offense we have mounted to storm the battlements of injustice must be carried forth by a bi-racial army. We cannot walk alone.	come to realize that their destiny is tied up with our destiny and their freedom is inextricably bound to our freedom. *This offense we share mounted to storm the battlements of injustice must be carried forth by a biracial army.* We cannot walk alone.	ence here today, have come to realize that their destiny is tied up with our destiny and they have come to realize that their freedom is inextricably bound to our freedom. We cannot walk alone.

In the section of his speech that deals with nonviolence, King used the first two sentences of the Jones-Levison text nearly verbatim. He relocated the "sweltering summer" sentence elsewhere in his address. King then ignored his aides' ideas for the rest of this passage. He deleted the drafts' mixed images (the drafts combined "summer" and "winter" with the "thirst for the poisoning potion of revenge," or, in the shorter "Normalcy" draft, the "broiling waters of revenge") and substituted four new sentences of his own.

Jones/Levison	*"Normalcy" (Short)*	*Prepared Speech*
		(additions in bold)
But there is something I must say to my people who stand on the warm threshold which leads into the palace of justice. In the process of gaining our rightful place, we must not be guilty of wrongful deeds. This sweltering summer of legitimate discontent can bring us into an invigorating autumn of freedom and justice. We must not envision a winter of barricading ourselves behind walls of hatred and resentment and the thirst for the poisoning potion of revenge.	So we are here to say that in the process of gaining justice for ourselves, we will never be guilty of injustice to others. This sweltering summer of legitimate discontent can bring us into an invigorating autumn of freedom and justice. We shall not mar that splendid season of our existence in America by laying up the elements to bring about a winter of hatred or resentment of the broiling waters of revenge.	But there is something that I must say to my people who stand on the warm threshold which leads into the palace of justice. In the process of gaining our rightful place we must not be guilty of wrongful deeds. **Let us not seek to satisfy our thirst for freedom by drinking from the cup of bitterness and hatred. We must forever conduct of [sic] struggle on the high plane of dignity and discipline. We must not allow our**

(continued)

Jones/Levison	"Normalcy" (Short)	Prepared Speech
		(additions in bold)
		creative protest to degenerate into physical violence. Again and again we must rise to the majestic heights of meeting physical force with soul force.

The "Bad check" set piece was extensively revised between the two "Normalcy" drafts, the advance text, and the speech King actually delivered. King streamlined the discursive descriptions of America's promises from the shorter "Normalcy" text. The "magnificent manifestos contained in the Declaration of Independence, the Preamble to the Constitution, the Constitution itself and the Bill of Rights" became simply the "magnificent words of the Constitution and the Declaration of Independence." The "check" was no longer, as in the shorter "Normalcy" draft, "the check which gives us on demand, our rights to a life of dignity, a liberty unquestioned and the pursuit of happiness in the form of equal opportunity and justice before the law," but rather, "a check that will give us upon demand the riches of freedom and the security of justice." King made only minor modifications in two sentences from the longer "Normalcy" draft: "It is obvious today that America has defaulted on that promissory note insofar as her citizens of color are concerned. It is obvious today that, instead of honoring this promissory note sacred obligation, America has given the Negro people a bad check,

a check which has come back marked 'insufficient funds.' "
Finally, in his delivered speech, he improvised a parenthetical
explanation to his quotation from the Declaration of
Independence ("yes—black men as well as white men—"),
which brought out how racially egalitarian King thought the
Declaration was.

"Normalcy" *(Long)*	*"Normalcy"* *(Short)*	*Delivered Speech*
		(additions to prepared speech in bold)
We have come to cash a check. When the Founding Fathers of this nation came to Plymouth rock, they wrote in the script of sacrifice and deprivation, a promissory note to which every American was to fall heir. It was a promissory note created by man but simply a note which was a translation of the legacy of God. This note was a promise that, under the mores of this new society of freedom, men would be permitted to worship God in whatever manner their consciences dictated; a promise that governors of men should be selected by the governed, a promise that men might have the right of peaceful assembly and, in that assembly, the right to freely express criticism, to demonstrate protest. It was a promise that men should have the privilege and duty of suffrage, that men should have equality of opportunity and recognition of the dignity of the human personality. To the Founding Fathers, this promissory note, this pledge, this toast to the	In accordance with [our Judeo-Christian tradition and our] democratic heritage, we have come here, from all over this land, to cash a check. When the architects of our Republic wrote in indelible ink those magnificent manifestos contained in the Declaration of Independence, the Preamble to the Constitution, the Constitution itself and the Bill of Rights, they were signing a promissory note to which every American was to fall	In a sense we've come to our nation's capital to cash a check. When the architects of our republic wrote the magnificent words of the Constitution and the Declaration of Independence, they were signing a promissory note to which every American was to fall heir. This note was a promise that all men—yes, **black men as well as white men**—would be guaranteed the unalienable rights of life, liberty and the *(continued)*

"Normalcy" (Long)	"Normalcy" (Short)	Delivered Speech
		(additions to prepared speech in bold)

"Normalcy" (Long)	"Normalcy" (Short)	Delivered Speech
future, was sacrosanct. It was no wilful, thoughtless whim. It was no restrictive covenant which specified brown men or black men or yellow men or white. It was a pledge to all who came after them, as Americans, inhabitants of a new and glorious land. A promissory note! Now, this promissory note granted by the Founding Fathers was endorsed and guaranteed by others who followed them. It was endorsed by the Declaration of Independence. It was endorsed by the preamble to the Constitution and by the Bill of Rights and by those amendments to the Constitution which specifically deal with the rights for which we are still contending. It is obvious today that America has defaulted on that promissory note insofar as her citizens of color are concerned. It is obvious today that, instead of honoring this promissory note, America has given the Negro people a bad check, a check which has come back marked "insufficient funds." Insufficient funds of integrity to honor the promissory note of the Founding Fathers. Insufficient funds of justice to grant the Negro his rightful place in employment and housing and education. Insufficient funds in common decency to permit the Negro to choose with his ballot those who shall guide the destiny of his country. Insufficient funds of courage to protect the	heir. The Declaration of Independence and the 1954 Supreme Court decision were endorsements of this promissory note. Yet, in this one hundredth birthday of the existence of still another endorsement, the Emancipation Proclamation, we find that, rather than being the beneficiaries of a promissory note, we are the victims of a bad check. We refuse to believe, as some believe, that the bank of justice in America is bankrupt. We refuse to believe there are "insufficient funds" in the great vaults of opportunity of this nation. So we have come to cash this check—the check which gives us on demand, our	pursuit of happiness. It is obvious today that America has defaulted on this promissory note insofar as her citizens of color are concerned. Instead of honoring this sacred obligation, America has given the Negro people a bad check; a check which has come back marked "insufficient funds." But we refuse to believe that the bank of justice is bankrupt. We refuse to believe that there are insufficient funds in the great vaults of opportunity of this nation. And so we've come to cash this check—a check that will give us upon demand the riches of freedom and the security of justice. *(continued)*

"Normalcy" (Long)	"Normalcy" (Short)	Delivered Speech
Negro from brutalities in the same manner in which any other citizen has the right to be protected. And so we are here today to say that he who says the bank of justice and decency and morality of America is bankrupt is a liar and a scoundrel. We do not believe it. We have never believed it. We know that this nation has the resources to continue to stand and grow as a great nation. We believe this nation has the basic decency to pay off its debts at home and abroad. We stand here, united in our demand upon the bank of America. We have come to cash this check. And we demand payment, all of it, here in the halls of the Congress and not tomorrow—not next year—not next summer. We have come to cash this check and we want it redeemed NOW.	rights to a life of dignity, a liberty unquestioned, and the pursuit of happiness in the form of equal opportunity and justice before the law.	

In addition to these longer passages, there are sentences and phrases in King's prepared speech that echo his aides' drafts. The description of the "symbolic shadow" of Lincoln is in the short version of "Normalcy," and the phrase "seared in the flames of withering injustice" is in the longer version of "Normalcy." The short "Normalcy" draft includes the sentences "And, as we walk, we must make the pledge that we shall always march ahead. We cannot turn back." The refrain "We can never be satisfied" is in the short version of

"Normalcy," although King changed all the refrain's completions except "We can never be satisfied so long as a Negro in
Mississippi cannot vote and a Negro in New York believes he
has nothing for which to vote." Part of the conclusion King cut
at the podium—"Let us go down from this place to ascend
other peaks of purpose. Let us descend from this mountaintop to climb other hills of hope"—was originally in the conclusion of the shorter "Normalcy" draft.

Despite these similarities, the early drafts by King's aides
are, for the most part, nothing like the speech he actually delivered. The Jones-Levison draft included sections refuting
accusations of division among the civil rights leaders and criticizing the "chiefs of labor" for insufficiently supporting civil
rights. The longer "Normalcy" draft discussed four reasons
for coming to Washington—"to honor a great people," "to
make an abject apology," "to cash a check," and "to say to the
nation and the world that our beloved America shall never return to normalcy"—only one of which would appear in King's
final speech. The shorter "Normalcy" draft opened with a
lengthy tribute to the legacy of Abraham Lincoln, and its central theme was a series of reflections on the topic of "normalcy," concluding with a call to reject "negative normalcy"
and go forward toward "positive normalcy." Even the advance
text King prepared the night before the march resembles only
about half the speech King actually delivered.

King went on record only once to explain why he decided
to leave his written text and speak to the nation about his
dream. In a November 1963 interview with Donald Smith, a
graduate student in rhetoric, King said:

I started out reading the speech, and I read it down to a point, and just all of a sudden, I decided—the audience response was wonderful that day, you know—and all of a sudden this thing came to me that I have used— I'd used many times before, that thing about "I have a dream"—and I just felt that I wanted to use it here. I don't know why. I hadn't thought about it before the speech.

The halting tone of the answer suggests that King himself was not sure what had happened: The "I have a dream" piece came to King "just all of a sudden," and he "just felt" that he had to use it. The only reason to challenge King's explanation is on a minor point. According to Coretta Scott King and Walter Fauntroy, King thought about using the "I have a dream" refrain beforehand. But that correction does not fully explain why he decided to use it "all of a sudden" at the march.

The only hint of an explanation King offered in the Smith interview was that he left his prepared text because of something about how the audience was responding to him: "The audience response was wonderful that day, you know." When King was a student at Crozer Theological Seminary, he had learned several stylized sermon structures in his homiletics courses, such as the "Ladder Sermon," in which arguments were arranged in order of increasing persuasiveness, and the "Jewel Sermon," in which a single idea was examined from several different perspectives. Outside of class, King and his friends from the South talked about their own structures, such as "Rabbit in the Bushes," in which a preacher who feels the crowd respond should keep addressing the same idea, just as a hunter might shoot repeatedly into the bushes to see if a rabbit is there. The last seven minutes of King's speech at the march are best heard in this light, as a gifted preacher testing phrases and ideas to see what will draw a response from the crowd.

One advantage of a compositional method based on rearranging and adapting previously memorized set pieces is that it gave King the flexibility to alter his addresses as he was speaking based on what he heard from the audience. Because King did not write out many of his speeches, he effectively composed them as he went along, selecting the set pieces from his repertoire that he thought would best fit with what he was saying. In his 1956 address to the NAACP annual convention, for example, he had prepared a speech with the sequence:

> We have the strange feeling down in Montgomery that in our struggle we have cosmic companionship. We feel that the universe is on the side of right and righteousness. There is something in this universe that justifies Carlyle in saying: "No lie can live forever."

But when he delivered the speech, he said:

> We have the strange feeling down in Montgomery that in our struggle we have cosmic companionship. We feel that the universe is on the side of right and righteousness. This is what keeps us going. Oh, I would admit that, yes, it comes down to us from the long tradition of our Christian faith. Good Friday may occupy

the throne for a day, but ultimately it must give way to the triumphant beat of the drums of Easter. Evil may so shape events that Caesar will occupy the palace and Christ the cross. But one day that same Christ will rise up and split history into A.D. and B.C. so that even the life of Caesar must be dated by his name. There is something [applause], there is something in this universe that justifies Carlyle in saying "No lie can live forever."

King was probably slightly nervous when he began his speech at the march. When he had spoken from the Lincoln Memorial at the Prayer Pilgrimage for Freedom, there had been only about 30,000 people in the crowd. The 250,000 people at the March on Washington constituted the largest audience King had ever addressed. Naturally, he kept close to his prepared text for the first ten minutes, preferring not to jeopardize the success of the speech by inserting new material. But as he spoke, it became clear to him that this throng of hundreds of thousands wanted him to go on.

King had long thought the end of an address was its most important part. When Wyatt Tee Walker asked King to tell him his first priority in preparing a sermon—"Your three points?"—King replied: "Oh, no. First I find my landing strip. It's terrible to be circling around up there without a place to land." As King neared the end of his prepared text, he must have realized his written speech did not have a conclusion that matched the emotion of the moment. At the March on Washington, in his most important public address to date, he had found himself circling and circling, with no clear idea where to land. Behind him, Mahalia Jackson was calling, "Tell them about the dream, Martin." King probably did not hear her, because he didn't mention her when he later explained why he decided to use "I have a dream." But somehow, he chose the set pieces that gave the audience exactly what it wanted. It is a measure of King's compositional ability that even though he had spent four days thinking about his speech for the march, and nearly all night writing it by hand, he was able to compose a far better address at the podium, taking the best passages from his prepared text and combining them with a conclusion that he improvised as he spoke.

chapter three

Sermon

By the time of the March on Washington, King had been known as a talented preacher for over a decade. When he was in seminary at Crozer, his fellow students would crowd into the chapel to hear him practice his sermons. He had preached at churches around the country by the age of twenty-five, when he took up the pastorate at Dexter. His fame among the black clergy was already so established that his father, the minister of the Ebenezer Baptist Church in Atlanta, received a letter that began: "They told me you have a son that can preach rings around you any day you ascend the pulpit. How about that? If it is so, it is a compliment to you."

But in 1963, King's oratorical ability was, for the most part, unknown outside of the black church and the civil rights movement. Before the March on Washington, most Americans had never heard King preach a complete sermon. King's speech at the march was so powerful in part because it exposed a national audience, for the first time, to his genius as a preacher: his facility with language, his ability to transform material from different sources into set pieces that were uniquely his own, and his mastery of the art of black homiletics. The "I Have a Dream" speech was so remarkable not because it was the pinnacle of King's oratorical skill, as if he were merely an average public speaker who happened to be in particularly good form on August 28, 1963. The March on Washington simply provided a national audience with its first opportunity to witness a pulpit performance that those active in the civil rights movement could see many times a year. King transformed a political rally of the nation's citizens at the Lincoln Memorial into a vast congregation. He may have prepared a formal address for the March on Washington, but he ended up preaching a sermon, and his homiletic abilities were responsible for much of the speech's success.

1. Language

King had been fascinated with language since childhood. He once said to his mother, "You just wait and see. I'm going to get me some big words." On the inside cover of one of his seminary notebooks, King conducted experiments with wordcraft, writing "We are experiencing cold and whistling winds of despair in a world packed with turbulence" and "While Russia is poisoning the physical atmosphere with megaton bombs, America is still poisoning the moral atmosphere with racial discrimination." In his best essays in college and graduate school, he cast off his usual expository prose and wrote like a preacher. He wrote in his seminary essay on Jeremiah that the prophet "had seized on a great and revolutionary truth, and with that truth, like a pillar of cloud by day and of fire by night, went ahead of his times."

Throughout King's life, the most important source of his language was the King James translation of the Bible. He had attended his father's church nearly every Sunday since childhood, and as he recalled in a seminary essay, "The church has always been a second home for me." When King was five years old, he could recite passages of Scripture from memory. He was so immersed in the language and imagery of the Bible that he would later use it almost unconsciously. Even when he was delivering material that had been inspired by the works of other preachers, he would add turns of phrase that would make his source material sound more Biblical. For example, in a 1956 sermon, King adapted a description of the Exodus from a sermon by the famous nineteenth-century minister Phillips Brooks. But where Brooks ended, King went on to add a metaphor drawn from the Bible that he would reuse seven years later at the March on Washington: "It was a joyous daybreak that had come to end the long night of their captivity."

King's speech at the march was laden with the language of the King James Bible. Nearly every metaphor King used can be traced to a Biblical source:

King's Metaphor	*Biblical Sources*
"joyous daybreak to end the long night of their captivity"	MATTHEW 1:16: "The people which sat in darkness saw great light; and to them which sat in the region and shadow of death light has sprung up."

(continued)

King's Metaphor	Biblical Sources
	LUKE 1:79: "To give light to them that sit in darkness and in the shadow of death, to guide their feet into the way of peace."
"dark and desolate valley of segregation"	PSALM 23:4: "Yea, though I walk through the valley of the shadow of death."
"cup of bitterness and hatred"	ISAIAH 51:17: "You which hast drunk at the hand of the Lord, The cup of his fury; thou hast drunken the dregs of the cup of trembling, and wrung them out."
"from the quicksands of racial injustice to the solid rock of brotherhood"	MATTHEW 7:24–27: Parable of the houses built on the sand and on the rock.
"hew out of the mountain of despair a stone of hope"	DANIEL 2: Nebuchadnezzar's vision of a stone hewn out of a mountain.

Twice in his speech, King quoted verses from the Bible:

No, no, we are not satisfied, and we will not be satisfied until "justice [rolls] down like waters and righteousness like a mighty stream." (Amos 5:24)

I have a dream that one day "every valley shall be exalted, and every hill and mountain shall be made low, the rough places will be made plain, and the crooked places will be made straight and the glory of the Lord will be revealed and all flesh shall see it together." (Isaiah 40:4)

King's Biblical language was one reason for the speech's success. Many in the crowd at the march were as familiar with the Bible as King was. By using a few carefully chosen words, he could call up in their minds an entire story or lesson from the Bible. The "joyous daybreak"/"long night of captivity" metaphor would have evoked several Biblical narratives in the minds of his audience. The first would have been the reference to the Egyptian captivity and the Exodus flight. Another was the allusion to the birth of Christ and the beginning of a new era in God's plan, implying that the Emancipation Proclamation was one of God's acts of deliverance. "Behold, I will do a new thing" (Isaiah 43:19). A reference to segregation as a "dark and desolate valley" recalled the psalmist's promise of God's presence in times of trouble: "Yea, though I walk through the valley of the shadow of death, I will fear no evil: for thou art with me; thy rod and thy staff they comfort me" (Psalm 23:4).

King was so steeped in the King James Bible that even his sentence structure was marked by a Biblical idiom. The poets of the Hebrew Bible often wrote in parallel, pairing two ideas in consecutive lines. In the most common form of Biblical parallelism, two similar thoughts are placed next to each other. This parallel poetic structure allowed the author to intensify the import of the first thought by echoing it in slightly different language. Examples can be found throughout the Bible, particularly in the Psalms:

> Enter into his gates with thanksgiving
> 　and into his courts with praise.

> Be thankful unto him
> 　and bless his name. (Psalm 100:4)

The prophets also used this idiom, as demonstrated by the passage from Amos that King quoted in his speech:

> Let justice run down like waters,
> 　and righteousness like a mighty stream.
> 　(Amos 5:24)

King frequently used synonymous parallels at the march, both with entire sentences—

> But we refuse to believe that the bank of justice is
> 　bankrupt.
> We refuse to believe that there are insufficient funds in
> 　the great vaults of opportunity of this nation.

. . . many of our white brothers, as evidenced by
their presence here today, have come to realize that
their destiny is tied up with our destiny,
and they have come to realize that their freedom is inextricably bound to our freedom.

And as we walk, we must make the pledge that we
shall always march ahead.
We cannot turn back.

—and with brief metaphorical descriptions:

the manacles of segregation and the chains of discrimination

the riches of freedom and the security of justice

the motels of the highways and the hotels of the cities

sweltering with the heat of injustice, sweltering with
the heat of oppression

from every village and every hamlet, from every state
and every city

King's favorite rhetorical device in his speech at the
march—the anaphora, a repeated word or phrase—was a form
of parallelism. About half of his speech is made up of set
pieces constructed around anaphora: "One hundred years
later," "Now is the time," "With this faith." King would repeat

a phrase several times and complete each thought with a different reflection on the topic he was addressing. By using anaphora, King could create a series of parallel images, which allowed him to suggest connections between seemingly unrelated topics:

> But one hundred years later, the Negro still is not free.

> One hundred years later, the life of the Negro is still sadly crippled by the manacles of segregation and the chains of discrimination.

> One hundred years later, the Negro lives on a lonely island of poverty in the midst of a vast ocean of material prosperity.

> One hundred years later, the Negro is still languished in the corners of American society and finds himself an exile in his own land.

In this example, King equated the institution of slavery with contemporary segregation and poverty. In the "we can never be satisfied" section, King described the goals of the civil rights movement as an end to police brutality, open access to places of public accommodation, an end to residential segregation, the dismantling of Jim Crow, and the promotion of candidates who would represent the needs of black Americans ("We will never be satisfied so long as . . . a Negro in New York believes he has nothing for which to vote").

Another form of Biblical parallelism paired contrasting images or ideas:

> The grass withereth, the flower fadeth:
> but the word of our God shall stand forever.

> (Isaiah 40:8)

This form of parallelism appears in the passage from Isaiah that King quoted near the end of his speech: "[E]very valley shall be exalted, and every hill and mountain shall be made low, the rough places will be made plain, and the crooked places will be made straight." At several other places in his address, King contrasted opposing images:

joyous daybreak / long night of their captivity
island of poverty / vast ocean of material prosperity
dark and desolate valley of segregation / sunlit path of
    racial justice
quicksands of racial injustice / solid rock of brotherhood
sweltering summer of the Negro's legitimate discontent / invig-
    orating autumn of freedom and equality
mountain of despair / stone of hope
jangling discords of our nation / beautiful symphony of
    brotherhood
sweltering with the heat of injustice / oasis of freedom and
    justice

King often combined both synonymous and contrasting forms of parallelism. He fit pairs of contrasting images within a larger structure of synonymous thoughts:

This momentous decree came as a **great beacon light
of hope** to millions of Negro slaves who had been
seared in the flames of withering injustice.
It came as a **joyous daybreak** to end the **long night** of
their captivity.

In the process of gaining our **rightful place** we must
not be guilty of **wrongful deeds.**
Let us not seek to satisfy our **thirst for freedom** by
drinking from the **cup of bitterness and hatred.**

2. Sources

Part of King's skill as a preacher was his ability to collect
material from many sources—his own sermons, the Bible, the
sermons of other preachers—and transform it into new set
pieces. King constructed and reworked his set pieces before a
variety of audiences, testing out different versions until he had
achieved the sense he wanted. The set pieces that made up the
last seven minutes of King's speech had been in his repertoire
for several years before the March on Washington. King first
used a version of the "Let freedom ring" set piece in a 1956
speech during the Montgomery bus boycott. In a later address, he acknowledged a "great orator" as his source. That
orator was probably Archibald Carey, a Chicago preacher and
political activist who ended his 1952 address to the
Republican National Convention by reciting the lyrics of
"America," and then continuing with:

That's exactly what we mean—from every mountainside, let freedom ring. Not only from the Green

Mountains and the White Mountains of Vermont and New Hampshire; not only from the Catskills of New York; but from the Ozarks in Arkansas, from the Stone Mountain in Georgia, from the Great Smokies of Tennessee and from the Blue Ridge Mountains of Virginia—Not only for the minorities of the United States, but for the persecuted of Europe, for the rejected of Asia, for the disfranchised of South Africa and for the disinherited of all the earth—may the Republican Party, under God, from every mountain side, LET FREEDOM RING!

By the time of the March on Washington, King had made substantial alterations to Carey's set piece. He kept the recitation of "America" and the central image of freedom pealing like the tolls of a great bell from every state in the nation. But King restructured the material, inserting the anaphora "Let freedom ring" to give the piece a more rhythmic feel. The execution of the imagery was also King's own: for example, the "Green Mountains and the White Mountains of Vermont and New Hampshire" became the "prodigious hilltops of New Hampshire." King used his own version of the "Let freedom ring" set piece to conclude dozens of speeches in the late 1950s and early 1960s.

It seems that the "I have a dream" set piece first appeared in King's speeches in 1962. In an interview near the end of his life, King remembered that he had used the "I have a dream" refrain one night during the Albany campaign when the audience seemed tired and discouraged, and he couldn't get through to them. King did not give a date for this event, but

Faith Holsaert, a SNCC worker, remembers hearing King say "I have a dream" during an Albany mass meeting on November 16, 1962. The earliest known transcription of "I have a dream" comes from King's November 27, 1962, speech in Rocky Mount, North Carolina.

And so, my friends of Rocky Mount, I have a dream tonight.

It is a dream rooted deeply in the American dream.

I have a dream that one day down in Sumter County, Georgia, where they burned two churches down a few days ago because Negroes wanted to register and vote, one day right down there little black boys and little black girls will be able to join hands with little white boys and little white girls and walk the streets as brothers and sisters.

I have a dream that one day right here in Rocky Mount, North Carolina, the sons of former slaves and the sons of former slave-owners will meet at the table of brotherhood, knowing that out of one blood God made all men to dwell upon the face of this earth.

I have a dream that one day all over this nation that men will recognize that all men were created equal and endowed by their creator with certain unalienable rights.

I have a dream tonight. One day the words of Amos will become real. Let justice roll down like waters and righteousness like a mighty stream.

I have a dream tonight. One day every valley shall be exalted and every mountain and hill shall be made low. Crooked places will be made straight, the rough places will be made plain, the glory of the Lord will be revealed and all flesh shall see it together.

I have a dream tonight. One day men will do unto others as they would have others do unto them.

I have a dream tonight. One day my little daughter and my two sons will grow up in a world not conscious of the color of their skin but only conscious of the fact that they are members of the human race.

I have a dream tonight. Some day we will be free.

In the spring and summer of 1963, "I have a dream" became one of King's most frequently delivered set pieces. He used it in a Birmingham mass meeting attended by Bull Connor's deputies, who paraphrased King in their written report:

He said that he had a dream of seeing little Negro boys and girls walking to school with little white boys and girls, playing in the parks together and going swimming together. "I had a dream tonight."

King concluded a June 1963 speech at a rally in Detroit with a version of "I have a dream" that included not just the visions of the end of Jim Crow that he would make famous at the march but also visions of an end to economic inequality in the North and violence against the civil rights movement:

And so this afternoon, I have a dream.

It is a dream deeply rooted in the American dream.

I have a dream that one day, right down in Georgia and Mississippi, and Alabama, the sons of former slaves and the sons of former slave-owners will be able to live together as brothers.

I have a dream this afternoon that one day, one day little white children and little Negro children will be able to join hands as brothers and sisters.

I have a dream this afternoon, that one day, one day men will no longer burn down houses and the church of God simply because people want to be free.

I have a dream this afternoon that there will be a day when we will no longer face the atrocities that Emmett Till had to face or Medgar Evers had to face, but that all men can live with dignity.

I have a dream this afternoon that my four little children, that my four little children will not come up in the same young days that I came up within, but they will be judged on the basis of the content of their character, and not the color of their skin.

I have a dream this afternoon that one day, right here in Detroit, Negroes will be able to buy a house or rent a house anywhere that their money will carry them and they will be able to get a job.

Yes, I have a dream this afternoon that one day in this land the words of Amos will become real and justice will roll down like waters and righteousness like a mighty stream.

I have a dream this evening that one day we will recognize the words of Jefferson that all men are created equal, that they are endowed by their Creator with certain unalienable rights, that among these are life, liberty, and the pursuit of happiness.

I have a dream this afternoon.

I have a dream that one day every valley shall be exalted and every hill and mountain shall be made low. The rough places will be made plain and the crooked places will be made straight, and the glory of the Lord shall be revealed, and all flesh shall see it together.

I have a dream this afternoon that the brotherhood of man will become a reality in this day.

Although it is probable that Archibald Carey was King's source for "Let freedom ring," the origins of the "I have a dream" set piece are much more difficult to ascertain. One possibility is that King heard "I have a dream" from someone in Albany, Georgia, in 1961–62. There are two stories that explain how this might have happened. King may have heard Prathia Hall, a young SNCC worker, say "I have a dream" several times during a prayer service on September 14, 1962, at the remains of the Mount Olive Baptist Church in Sasser, Georgia, after it had been burned to the ground by segregationists. King then incorporated the evocative phrase into his own oratory.

Another story comes from Dorothy Cotton, an eminent SCLC staff member. Cotton remembers hearing a college-age white woman pray with the phrase "I have a dream" during a mass meeting in a small, crowded church in Albany. The woman went on to talk about her hope that one day her little boy could reach out and hold the hands of little black boys and girls and no one would see that as strange. Cotton was so impressed by the young woman's vision that she told King about it when she picked him up at the Albany airport the next day. King instantly recognized the beauty of the imagery and began to use it in his speeches.

The two accounts of the Albany origins of "I have a dream" find indirect support in a recollection of Ralph Allen, another Albany movement veteran. Allen remembers hearing Kathleen Conwell, a black Skidmore student who worked with SNCC in Albany, say "I have a dream" at a prayer service at Mount Olive Baptist Church several months before its arson. Conwell shared with the congregation an image of a little black girl and boy walking across the red hills of Georgia. King did not attend this meeting, so her prayers could not have inspired his later use of "I have a dream," unless someone in the movement told him what she had said. Nonetheless, Allen's recollection is additional evidence that SNCC workers in Albany were repeating the phrase "I have a dream" in their speeches and prayers.

It is possible that one of the accounts of the Albany origins of "I have a dream" is correct. King was always quick to pick up an apt turn of phrase or line of oratory and adapt it for use in his own speeches. As one of his theology professors once remarked, "All is grist that comes to his mill." The Albany explanations also make chronological sense. King's first known speeches with "I have a dream" are from November 1962— after the Mount Olive service (September 14, 1962) and probably also after Dorothy Cotton's recollection (sometime in 1961–62).

On the other hand, it is possible that King used "I have a dream" before 1961–62, which would mean he developed the set piece before he could have heard it in Albany. Many of King's speeches were never transcribed, so his earlier uses of "I have a dream" may have been lost. Wyatt Tee Walker, for example, remembers hearing King use "I have a dream" at least two years before the March on Washington. Another reason to be cautious about accepting the Albany accounts is that many veterans of the Albany campaign do not remember thinking that King had appropriated "I have a dream" from one of their members. SNCC was full of gossip, and a story as big as King's most famous refrain originating with an Albany activist would certainly have been put out along the SNCC "whisper line." The absence of this discussion is a substantial reason to be skeptical of the contention that King heard "I have a dream" in Albany.

At most, hearing the "I have a dream" refrain in Albany would have inspired King to assemble in new combinations set pieces and phrases that had been in his oratory for many years. The phrase "I have a dream" might have originated when King explained a religious experience during the Montgomery bus boycott with the words, "I had a vision." One night in January 1956, King had a spiritual experience that he would turn to as a source of strength for the rest of his life. Many years later, he would recount what had happened:

> I never will forget one night very late. It was around midnight. And you can have some strange experiences at midnight. I had been out [at a meeting] all that night. And I came home, and my wife was in the bed and I immediately crawled into bed to get some rest to get up early the next morning to try to keep things going. And immediately the telephone started ringing and I picked it up. On the other line was an ugly voice. That voice said to me in substance, "Nigger, we are tired of you and your mess now. And if you aren't out of this town in three days, we are going to blow your brains out, and blow up your house."
>
> I had heard those things before, but for some reason that night it got to me. I turned over and I tried to go to sleep, but I couldn't sleep. I was frustrated, be-wildered, and then I got up and went back to the

kitchen, and I started warming some coffee, thinking that coffee would give me a little relief. And then I started thinking about many things. I pulled back on the theology and philosophy that I had just studied in the Universities, trying to give philosophical and theological reasons for the existence and the reality of sin and evil, but the answer didn't quite come there. I sat there and thought about a beautiful little daughter who had just been born about a month earlier. . . . And she was the darling of my life; I'd come in night after night and see that little gentle smile. And I sat at that table thinking about that little girl and thinking about the fact that she could be taken away from me any minute. . . . And I started thinking about a dedicated, devoted, and loyal wife, who was over there asleep. And she could be taken from me, or I could be taken from her, and I got to the point that I couldn't take it any longer, I was weak. . . .

And I discovered then that religion had to become real to me and I had to know God for myself. And I bowed down over that cup of coffee. I never will forget it. And . . . I prayed a prayer, and I prayed out loud that night. I said, "Lord, I'm down here trying to do what's right. I think I'm right. I think the cause that we represent is right. But Lord, I must confess that I'm weak now. I'm faltering. I'm losing my courage. And I can't let the people see me like this because if they see me weak and losing my courage, they will begin to get weak." . . .

And it seemed that moment that I could hear an inner voice saying to me, "Martin Luther, stand up for righteousness. Stand up for justice. Stand up for truth. And lo I will be with you, even until the end of the world."

King described this experience to reporters the next day by saying: "Last night, in the kitchen of my home, I had a vision." "I had a vision" could easily have become "I had a dream" (as he apparently used the phrase in Birmingham) or "I have a dream."

Much of the substance of the "I have a dream" set piece appeared in a series of 1956 speeches in which King looked forward to the coming of a "new age" or a "new world." In a December 1956 speech in Montgomery, he said:

If we join together in doing all of these things we will be able to speed up the coming of the new world—a new world in which men will live together as brothers; a world in which men will beat their swords into ploughshares and their spears into pruning-hooks; a world in which men will no longer take necessities from the masses to give luxuries to the classes; a world in which all men will respect the dignity and worth of all human personality.

In the early 1960s, King gave several speeches in which he described the "American dream" in terms similar to the "new age" of the 1956 speeches. King began a 1961 address entitled "The American Dream" with:

I should like to discuss with you some aspects of the American dream. For in a real sense, America is essentially a dream, a dream as yet unfulfilled. It is a dream of a land where men of all races, of all nationalities and of all creeds can live together as brothers. The substance of the dream is expressed in these sublime words, words lifted to cosmic proportions: "We hold these truths to be self-evident, that all men are created equal, that they are endowed by their Creator with certain unalienable rights, that among these are life, liberty, and the pursuit of happiness." This is the dream.

There are several possible paths by which King could have developed the "I have a dream" set piece out of his own oratory. He could have taken "I had a vision" from his Montgomery kitchen and combined the refrain with the "new age" and "American dream" set pieces, so that his vision was not only of God's presence and promise of faithfulness but of America's redemption. Or, he could have added a two-word repetition to the "American dream" set piece and changed the sentence structure slightly, so that the anaphora was no longer "a dream" or "It is a dream" but "I have a dream," so a sentence would read, for example, "I have a dream of a land where men of all races, of all nationalities and of all creeds can live together as brothers."

It is also possible that King and the Albany students independently developed versions of "I have a dream," inspired by the dreams and visions in the Bible. The phrases "I have a dream" or "I had a dream" do not appear in the King James

Bible, but close cognates are common. "Behold, I have dreamed a dream," says Joseph in Genesis 37:9. In the book of Daniel, Nebuchadnezzar prefaces an account of a vision with "I saw a dream" (Daniel 4:5). King's vision in the kitchen fit into a Biblical tradition of God communicating through visions: "Hear now my words: If there be a prophet among you, I the LORD will make myself known unto him in a vision, and will speak unto him in a dream" (Numbers 12:6). The prophet Joel wrote, "I will pour out my spirit upon all flesh, and your sons and your daughters shall prophesy, your old men shall dream dreams, your young men shall see visions." King's "new age" set piece owes an apparent debt to Biblical visions of a new creation—"I saw a new heaven and a new earth" (Rev. 21:1)—and of the return of the Lord to Israel: "Every valley shall be exalted, and every mountain and hill shall be made low: and the crooked shall be made straight, and the rough places plain: And the glory of the LORD shall be revealed, and all flesh shall see it together: for the mouth of the LORD hath spoken it" (Isaiah 40:4–5).

The Biblical resonances in King's "I have a dream" set piece are so dense that the Bible must have influenced King's construction. The antecedents to "I have a dream" in King's own oratory are also clearly dependent on Biblical sources. It may never be possible to identify with certainty the sources of the "I have a dream" refrain, but given the theme's prominence in Scripture and its precedents in King's own oratory, it is probable that King drew the phrase, as he had drawn so much of his language, from the King James translation of the Bible.

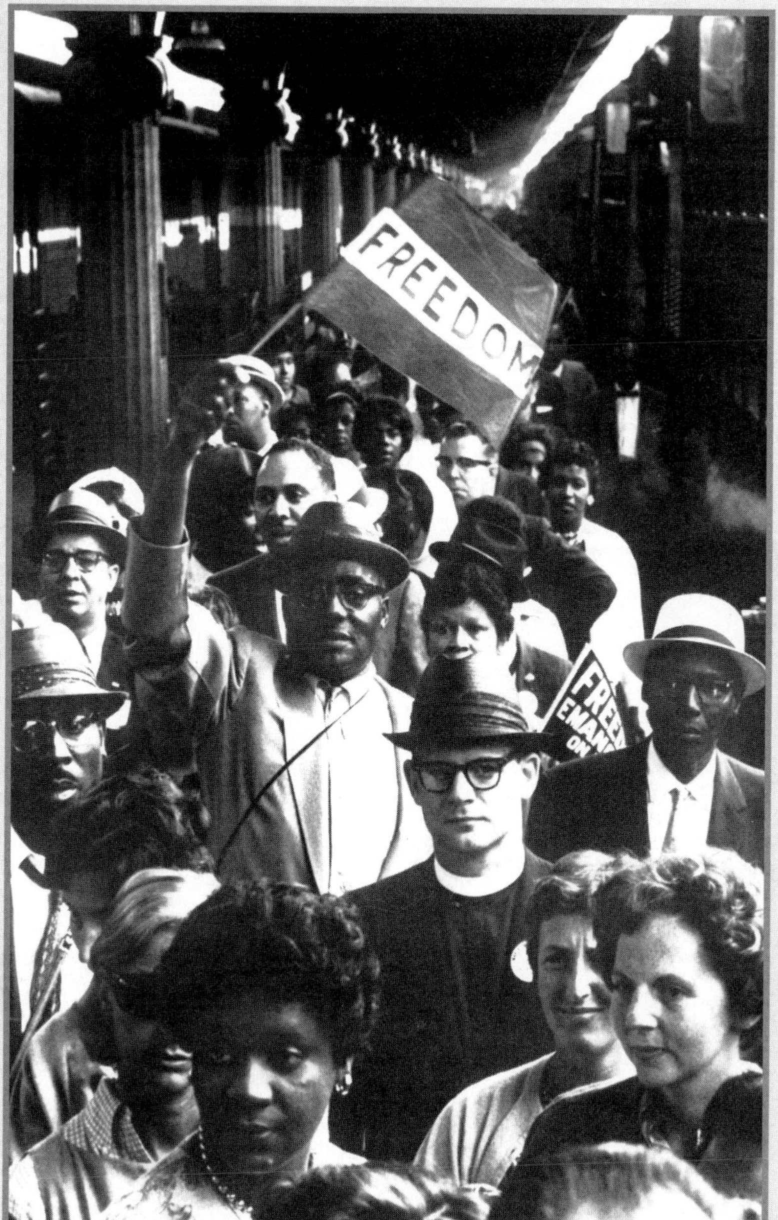

Photo © Flip Schulke

Photo © Bob Adelman/Magnum Photos

Photo © Bob Adelman/Magnum Photos

3. Delivery

King's use of a Biblical idiom in his speech at the march was made all the more powerful by his delivery of the speech in the distinctive cadences of a black Baptist preacher. James Weldon Johnson could have been describing King in his introduction to *God's Trombones,* his 1927 volume of poetry written in the voices of black ministers:

> The old-time Negro preacher of parts was above all an orator, and in good measure an actor. He knew the secret of oratory, that at bottom it is a progression of rhythmic words more than it is anything else. . . . He was a master of all the modes of eloquence. He often possessed a voice that was a marvelous instrument, a voice he could modulate from a sepulchral whisper to a crashing thunder clap. His discourse was generally kept at a high pitch of fervency, but occasionally he dropped into colloquialisms and, less often, into humor. . . . His imagination was bold and unfettered. He had the power to sweep his hearers before him; and so himself was often swept away. At such times his language was not prose but poetry.

The first feature of King's speaking style that would have been noticed by those members of the audience who had never before heard a black preacher was the way he used his voice. The *Newsweek* reporter who heard King speak at the march compared the sound of his voice to a church organ. The comparison was probably due, in part, to the timbre of King's voice: He had a magnificent, full baritone that had commanded attention even when he was young. King began his speech at the march with an almost exaggerated slowness. He drew out the vowel at the end of nearly every word in his opening (the "e" sound in "happy," the "o" in "you") until it almost filled the space before the next word in the sentence. He added a long pause after many of his phrases. Enjambed in accordance with King's delivery, the beginning of his speech would read as follows:

> I am happy to join with you today
>> in what will go down in history
>> as the greatest demonstration for freedom in the
>> history of our nation.
> Fivescore years ago,
>> a great American, in whose symbolic shadow we
>> stand today,
>> signed the Emancipation Proclamation.
> This momentous decree came
>> as a great beacon light of hope to millions of Negro
>> slaves
>> who had been seared in the flames of withering in-
>> justice.
> It came as a joyous daybreak
>> to end the long night of their captivity.

Throughout the speech, King returned to the deliberate tone of his opening. He drew out many of his long vowels (the "a" in "chains," the "i" in "island"). He paused before and after phrases of particular importance:

But one hundred years later
   the Negro
      still
  is not free.

This note was a promise that all men—
   yes,
      black men as well as white men—
  would be guaranteed the unalienable rights of life,
  liberty,
      and the pursuit of happiness.

I am not unmindful
   that some of you have come here
      out of great trials and tribulations.

Continue to work with the faith
   that unearned suffering
      is redemptive.

These pauses allowed King to emphasize themes in his speech that would otherwise be understated. His slight hesitation before and after "still" conveyed to the audience a sense of how long it had been since the Emancipation Proclamation had promised freedom to black Americans. His verbal bracketing of "black men as well as white men" was a reprimand, reminding his audience of how America had failed to live up to the promises in the Declaration of Independence.

King also used pauses to emphasize words that tied two sections of his speech together. He repeated the word "walk," setting it off with a pause, to transition from his section on the multiracial nature of the civil rights protests to his set piece with the refrain, "We can never be satisfied":

We cannot walk alone.
And as we walk,
we must make the pledge that we shall always march ahead.

King used this device to brilliant effect in his delivery of "America," where he unexpectedly paused before and after "mountainside":

. . . from every—
mountainside—
let freedom ring

King had just delivered the line about how the audience will "hew out of the mountain of despair a stone of hope." Immediately before that section he had recounted how "every hill and mountain shall be made low." He knew he was about to go into a series of images in which freedom rings from every mountain in America. The verbal bracketing of "mountainside" tied together several of the set pieces King had been stringing one after another as he neared the end of his speech.

Early in the speech—at "one hundred years later"—King almost imperceptibly quickened his delivery. Throughout the speech, King would speed up slightly as he entered one of his set pieces based on anaphora. King's quickening of pace gave these set pieces a sense of momentum that was heightened by his unusual cadence in delivering them. For example, a set piece like the "Now is the time" anaphora might conventionally be delivered with a break after each sentence:

> Now is the time to make real the promises of democracy.
>
> Now is the time to rise from the dark and desolate valley of segregation to the sunlit path of racial justice.
>
> Now is the time to lift our nation from the quicksands of racial injustice to the solid rock of brotherhood.
>
> Now is the time to make justice a reality for all of God's children.

But in King's delivery, the pause came after the refrain, not after the sentence. The unexpected placing of the pauses gave these lines a sense of propulsion, which added to the momentum of the set piece:

> Now is the time—
>
> to make real the promises of democracy. Now is the time—

to rise from the dark and desolate valley of segregation to the sunlit path of racial justice. Now is the time—

to lift our nation from the quicksands of racial injustice to the solid rock of brotherhood. Now is the time—

to make justice a reality for all of God's children.

The pauses also gave the audience a chance to respond. After a few repetitions, the marchers knew what was coming and could shout or applaud in the breaks. The crowd's reactions to King's lines often generated a call-and-response rhythm:

Now is the time
Yeah!
to make real the promises of democracy.
All right.

I am not unmindful
that some of you have come here
out of great trials and tribulations.
My Lord?
Some of you have come fresh from narrow jail cells.
My Lord.

. . . I still have a dream.
Yeah!

I have a dream
   that one day
      Yeah!

   this nation will rise up
   and live out the true meaning of its creed:
      We hold these truths to be self-evident,
     that all men are created equal.
      Yeah! [applause]

With this faith
     Yeah!
we will be able to hew out of the mountain of despair
   a stone of hope.
     All right.

King's sensitivity to meter was evident not only in the pacing of his speech but in his rhythmic delivery of selected words and phrases. Throughout the speech, King used pauses and vocal inflections to emphasize the internal rhythms of his sentences. He balanced "poverty" with "prosperity," allowing the stress on the first syllable of "poverty" to guide his pronunciation of "prosperity," in which he inserted a slight pause between "pros-" and "perity." When he improvised at the end of the speech, he balanced "Protestants" against "Catholics," giving the latter word its full three-syllable value. King used a rhythmic delivery not only with individual words ("Cath-o-lics," not "Cath-lics"), but with entire sentences, so they would seem to have an inner swing to them. For example, the phrase "symbolic shadow we stand today" has alliterative repeated sibilants, and an inner off-rhyme on "shadow," "stand," and "today." But it also has a distinctive interior beat. Even though the syllables do not precisely match, King inserted pauses in the phrase so that he delivered it in a slightly iambic tetrameter—four sets of an unstressed syllable followed by a stressed syllable:

sym-BOL-ic SHA-dow we STAND to-DAY

King did not deliver his speech in a formal meter. But part of his skill as a speaker was in accentuating the rhythmic patterns latent in his lines:

SEARED in the FLAMES of WITH-ering in-JUST-ice

in-VIG-orating AUT-umn of FREE-dom and e-QUAL-ity

NAT-ion re-TURNS to BUS-iness as U-sual

NEG-ro is GRANT-ed his CIT-izenship RIGHTS

For most of the speech, King's variations in vocal pitch or rhythm were relatively minor. The grave tone of his opening remained his default after a slight alteration of tempo or a modulation of voice. But when King left his prepared text and began to improvise, he used his full range of vocal techniques. The first real hint that he was nearing an emotional peak in his speech came near the end of his prepared text, in his recitation of the verse from the prophet Amos:

No, no, we are not satisfied, and we will not be satisfied, until justice rolls down like waters
and righteousness like a mighty stream.

King delivered the first half of the verse in the high end of his range, adding a vibrato to bring out the vowels of "rolls" and "waters." Then he rushed through the second half until the word "mighty," where he dropped down to a rough bass. He returned to his slower and more formal tone right after the verse ("I am not unmindful that some of you have come here out of great trials and tribulations"), but as he left his text ("Go back to Mississippi . . ."), he went back to a higher, louder register. As he began the "I have a dream" section, he made dramatic use of the slight vibrato he had used in "rolls" and "waters" to add a tremor to "red hills of Georgia" and "Mississippi." Then he pulled out all the stops to deliver the harshest judgment of his speech:

. . . down
   in Alabama,
          with its vicious racists,
          with its governor
having his lips dripping with the words of interposition and nullification,

He raised his voice in both pitch and volume for "down," which he hit high and cascaded off. He bent the tone of

"Alabama" and "racists" in the same way, attacking on a treble note and then sliding down several pitches.

King's theatrical delivery of these lines prepared the audience for the vocal tour de force that followed. By this point in the speech, the deliberate tone of the opening was gone entirely. King had left the more formal quality of his written text, and he was preaching an impromptu sermon. He applied a variety of vocal techniques to the last seven minutes of his speech. He deployed the vibrato that he used for "down" and "Alabama" at several points, stretching out the vowels in "valley," "ring," and the "Stone" of "Stone Mountain." He lowered the " 'tis" of "my country 'tis of thee," while retaining the vibrato, so that he delivered the word in a baritone shudder. He traveled in pitch from a baritone to a midrange tenor, returning to his natural range at the end of a phrase:

to go to JAIL together

land where my fathers died, land of the PIL-grim's pride

He also alternated his use of pauses in the anaphora. In the "I have a dream" section, King's typical delivery pattern would be to pause after the "I have a dream" refrain, so that "I have a dream" does not begin a new thought but ends the preceding one, and the stress is on the "I" of the phrase. The expectation established by this pattern made it all the more powerful when in the fourth repetition of "I have a dream," King added another repetition unexpectedly and put the accent on the word "dream," which he drew out and then punctuated with "today!", so that "I have a dream today!" was its own self-contained thought:

I have a dream—

that one day on the red hills of Georgia, the sons of former slaves and the sons of former slave-owners will be able to sit down together at the table of brotherhood. I have a dream—

that one day even the state of Mississippi, a state sweltering with the heat of injustice, sweltering with the heat of oppression, will be transformed into an oasis of freedom and justice. I have a dream—

that my four little children will one day live in a nation where they will not be judged by the color of their skin but by the content of their character. I have a dream today!

King used a similarly unexpected rhythmic pattern in his delivery of the words of "America" near the end of his speech. The song is usually sung in a straight meter:

My country 'tis of thee,
Sweet land of liberty,
Of thee I sing.

Land where my fathers died
Land of the pilgrim's pride

From every mountainside
Let freedom ring.

But in King's reading, he altered the accents and rushed some lines together to make them swing. He gave the whole hymn a longer rhythmic line than the ear expects, and reset it in an irregular meter.

"My country 'TIS of thee;

    sweet LAND of LIB-erty of THEE I sing;

    land where my fathers died land of the PIL-grim's pride;

    from every—

    —mountainside,—

    let freedom ring!" And if America is to be a GREAT nation,

    this must become true.

As he finished "Let freedom ring," he had to speak louder to be heard above the shouts of the crowd. He then entered his final peroration:

And when this happens, when we allow freedom ring, when we let it ring from every village and every hamlet, from every state and every city, we will be able to speed up that day when all of God's children—black men and white men, Jews and Gentiles, Protestants and Catholics—will be able to join hands and sing in the words of the old Negro spiritual, "Free at last, free at last; thank God Almighty, we are free at last!"

He roughened up several of the key words in his concluding paragraph by nearly shouting them: the "all" in "all of God's children," the "every" in "every mountainside," and almost every word in "black men and white men, Protestants and Catholics." All through this dazzling range of timbre and register, King never seemed to speak with any strain, not even when he punched out "Thank God Almighty," at the end of the speech.

chapter four

Prophecy

King may have sounded like a preacher, but for most of his speech, he made the familiar arguments of national politics. No one who heard the first ten minutes of King's address at the March on Washington could have predicted that it would end with a prophetic vision of a redeemed America. The prepared speech King brought with him to the podium stayed close to standard themes from the political rhetoric of the 1960s and the oratory of the civil rights movement: the appeal to American ideals, the protest against gradualism, the call for nonviolence and racial integration within the freedom movement. But the address did not become known for any of the tag lines from the prepared text—we do not speak of King's "Bad Check" speech, or his "Now Is the Time" speech. It is known as the "I Have a Dream" speech and remembered for the soaring refrains of hope that King added at the end. Had King not decided to leave his written text, it is doubtful that his speech at the march would be remembered at all.

King opened the speech by calling the nation's attention to a series of broken promises. The Emancipation Proclamation had promised freedom, but freedom had not been delivered. The Founders had drafted a promissory note guaranteeing liberty and equality to all, but the nation had defaulted on that promissory note in regard to its black citizens. This argument was not original to King. Many of the most powerful anti-slavery speeches by black orators argued that slavery was offensive to the ideals that America claimed to stand for. As Frederick Douglass said in his Glasgow Address of 1860, a speech King frequently quoted:

> [The Constitution's] language is "we the people;" not we the white people, not even we the citizens, not we the privileged class, not we the high, not we the low, but we the people; not we the horses, sheep, and swine, and wheel-barrows, but we the people, we the human inhabitants; and, if Negroes are people, they are included in the benefits for which the Constitution of America was ordained and established.

King was probably exposed to this rhetorical tradition as a child in Atlanta. When he was fifteen, he delivered a prizewinning speech called "The Negro and the Constitution," at an oratory competition sponsored by the black Elks, that made the same argument he would open with in Washington almost two decades later:

> Slavery has been a strange paradox in a nation founded on the principles that all men are created equal. Finally after tumult and war, the nation in 1865 took a new stand— freedom for all people. The new order was backed by

amendments to the national constitution making it the fundamental law that thenceforth there should be no discrimination anywhere in the "land of the free" on account of race, color or previous condition of servitude.

Black America still wears chains. The finest Negro is at the mercy of the meanest white man. . . .

Today thirteen million black sons and daughters of our forefathers continue the fight for the translation of the 13th, 14th, and 15th amendments from writing on the printed page to an actuality.

This contention had become a commonplace of national political oratory by the time of the March on Washington. Hundreds of politicians in the 1960s made the same argument that King began his Washington speech with: Racial discrimination was wrong because, among other reasons, it was un-American. President Kennedy said, in a nationally televised address on civil rights on June 11, 1963:

This Nation was founded by men of many nations and backgrounds. It was founded on the principle that all men are created equal, and that the rights of every man are diminished when the rights of one man are threatened. . . .

We are confronted primarily with a moral issue. It is as old as the scriptures and is as clear as the American Constitution.

One hundred years of delay have passed since President Lincoln freed the slaves, yet their heirs, their grandsons, are not fully free. They are not yet freed from the bonds of injustice. They are not yet freed from social and economic oppression. And this Nation, for all its hopes and all its boasts, will not be fully free until all its citizens are free.

We preach freedom around the world, and we mean it, and we cherish our freedom here at home, but are we to say to the world, and much more importantly, to each other that this is a land of the free except for the Negroes; that we have no second-class citizens except Negroes; that we have no class or caste system, no ghettoes, no master race except with respect to Negroes?

Senator Warren Magnuson of Washington State made the same argument the next year, in debates over what would become the Civil Rights Act of 1964:

Our boast is that success in American life is proportionate to talent and character—yet discrimination on the ground of race falsifies that boast every day.

Our assumption is that this is a nation of equals—yet this assumption falls to the ground as soon as discrimination to the Negro is taken into account.

The hard fact is that we have failed to redeem the promises of the Emancipation Proclamation, and of the 14th and 15th Amendments that race must not thwart the American Negro in his struggle to cast away the legacy of centuries of slavery and stand proud and erect as a free American.

The hard fact is that the American system of equality has, up to now, left out men and women whose skins were of another color.

It is now time to abolish second-class citizenship as a century ago we abolished slavery. It is now time to eliminate hypocrisy in our national life and make sure at last that our acts begin to square with our ideals.

King's decision to begin his speech at the march with an appeal to American ideals was probably based partly on location. He knew he would be speaking from the Lincoln Memorial, a particularly appropriate place from which to call on America to fulfill its promises. King had opened his speech at the Prayer Pilgrimage for Freedom six years earlier with similar endorsements of American principles, praising the Supreme Court's achievement in *Brown* as a "reaffirmation of the good old American doctrine of freedom and equality for all people." Another reason for King to begin with patriotic language was to persuade a potentially skeptical white audience. By opening with praise for the nation's founding documents, King could underscore the civil rights movement's loyalty to America—a debating point against the segregationists' accusation that the movement was controlled by communists. King would also have the rhetorical advantage of starting his speech on familiar territory, with references that his audience would have heard many times before. King crafted the argument from American ideals more eloquently than any politician of his time, with the ornate gravity of his image of the "architects of our republic" signing a "promissory note" for all Americans. Still, nothing about the substance of King's opening argument was any different from what could be found in the speeches of President Kennedy, Senator Magnuson, or any other politician of the era who supported civil rights.

King changed his tone in the next section of his speech. After the refrain, "Now is the time," he told the audience that the protests of 1963 would continue until the movement's demands were met:

> Nineteen sixty-three is not an end, but a beginning. And those who hope that the Negro needed to blow off steam and will now be content will have a rude awakening if the nation returns to business as usual. There will be neither rest nor tranquility in America until the Negro is granted his citizenship rights. The whirlwinds of revolt will continue to shake the foundations of our nation until the bright day of justice emerges.

As soon as King finished speaking, Roger Mudd on CBS singled out this passage as the main theme of his address. The *Washington Post* editorial the next day quoted only these lines from King's speech and did not mention the "I have a dream" refrains. King's guarantee of "whirlwinds of revolt" would have been challenging to many white listeners, but John Lewis had delivered a far more provocative promise of continued protest a short while earlier:

> To those who have said, be patient and wait, we must say that we cannot be patient, we do not want our freedom gradually but we want to be free now! We are tired, we are tired of being beaten by policemen. We are tired of seeing our people locked up in jail over and over again, and then you holler "Be patient." How long can we be patient? We want our freedom and we want it now. We do not want to go to jail, but we will go to jail, if this is the price we must pay for love, brotherhood and true peace.
>
> I appeal to all of you to get in this great revolution that is sweeping our nation. Get in and stay in the streets of every city, every village and hamlet of this nation, until true Freedom comes, until the revolution of 1776 is complete. We must get in this revolution and complete the revolution. For in the Delta of Mississippi, in southwest Georgia, in the black belt of Alabama, in Harlem, in Chicago, Detroit, Philadelphia, and all over this nation—the black masses are on the march for jobs and freedom.
>
> You talk about slow down and stop, we will not stop. All of the forces of Eastland, Barnett, Wallace, and Thurmond will not stop this revolution. If we do not get meaningful legislation out of this Congress, the time will come when we will not confine our marching

to Washington. We will march through the South—through the streets of Jackson, through the streets of Danville, through the streets of Cambridge, through the streets of Birmingham—but we will march with the spirit of love and with the spirit of dignity that we have shown here today. By the force of our demands, our determination, and our numbers, we shall splinter the segregated South into a thousand pieces and put them together in the image of God and democracy. We must say, "Wake up, America! Wake up!" For we cannot stop, and we will not and cannot be patient.

The original draft of Lewis's speech had been so fiery that it provoked a behind-the-scenes effort to alter it that lasted until shortly before he was scheduled to speak. His prepared speech contained such lines as, "To those who have said, 'Be patient and wait,' we must say that 'patience' is a dirty and nasty word" and "We will march through the South, through the heart of Dixie, the way Sherman did. We shall pursue our own 'scorched earth' policy and burn Jim Crow to the ground—nonviolently." On the night before the march, Courtland Cox, a SNCC representative on the march committee, distributed advance copies of Lewis's speech in an attempt to gain recognition for SNCC. Bayard Rustin was surprised when he saw copies of Lewis's address sitting out on a table, and said to Cox, "What are you doing that for? No one is seeing King's speech."

The same evening, Archbishop Patrick O'Boyle of Washington, D.C., who was scheduled to deliver the invocation at the march, was hosting a reception at the Mayflower Hotel for a few of the bishops who had come to Washington for the event. O'Boyle was as nervous about the march as most of the rest of Washington's white residents: He had forbidden the nuns in his diocese from going outside that day, because he feared they might get caught in a race riot. One of O'Boyle's aides obtained a copy of Lewis's speech and brought it to the Mayflower. The archbishop read the speech in silence. He was particularly troubled by Lewis's promise of a new Sherman's march through the South. He circulated the speech to his guests to see what they thought, and they agreed it would not be appropriate for him to give the invocation unless Lewis changed his speech.

Then, as O'Boyle would later remember, a night of hectic telephoning began. O'Boyle contacted an aide to Walter Reuther, organized labor's representative on the march committee, who got in touch with Bayard Rustin, and a bishop contacted Burke Marshall, the head of the civil rights division of the Department of Justice. The message was communicated that O'Boyle would not deliver the invocation if Lewis gave the speech he had prepared.

This presented a problem for the Kennedy administration. If the Catholic Church's most prominent representative withdrew from the march at the last minute, it would mar the image of the event as a peaceful, multiracial, and multireligious demonstration for civil rights. Burke Marshall and the Kennedys hoped the presence of priests in clerical collars and nuns wearing habits would reassure an anxious Washington public that the march would not become violent. Burke

Marshall was therefore given the task of making sure the Catholic Church didn't abandon the march because of the substance of John Lewis's speech.

Lewis returned to his hotel room Tuesday evening to find a handwritten note under his door. "John. Come downstairs. Must see you at once. Bayard." At a late-night meeting, Rustin told Lewis that O'Boyle was alarmed at Lewis's reference to "patience" as a "dirty and nasty word." Lewis didn't understand the objection. "Paaaaay-tience," said Rustin slowly. "Catholics *believe* in the word 'patience.' " So this was an eternal issue, thought Lewis. If the archbishop had a theological objection to the line, he would change it. Lewis agreed to the revision, told Rustin that he would consider any other objections to his speech the next day, and went to bed.

The next afternoon, as the marchers were arriving at the Lincoln Memorial, the march organizers received word that O'Boyle was still upset and that he had raised a specific objection to the Sherman reference in Lewis's speech. Rustin convened an emergency meeting at the Lincoln Memorial to see what could be done. Roy Wilkins was "having a fit," Lewis later remembered, saying that he just didn't understand how the SNCC people "always wanted to be different." Lewis responded, with the impatience of the student activists toward an older generation of black leaders, "I'm not just speaking for myself. I'm speaking for my colleagues in SNCC, and for the people in the Delta and the Black Belt. You haven't *been* there, Mr. Wilkins. You don't *understand.*" Rustin pulled the two men apart and suggested a smaller group assemble to consider the issue.

By this time, Eugene Carson Blake, the representative

from the National Council of Churches, had objected to Lewis's use of the words "masses" and "revolution," which he called "communist talk." This was too much for A. Philip Randolph. "There's nothing wrong with the word 'revolution,' " Randolph told Blake. "There's nothing wrong with the use of the word 'black masses.' I use it myself." But O'Boyle's objections were not so easily dismissed. Courtland Cox and James Forman, one of the SNCC leaders, were furious that someone was trying to reword Lewis's speech, and Cox told the rest of the group that anyone who didn't like the speech the way it was written could go to hell. At the ensuing stalemate, Randolph intervened again. "I have waited twenty-two years for this," he said. "Would you young men accommodate to an old man? I've waited all my life for this opportunity. Please don't ruin it." He then appealed to Lewis. "John, we've come this far together. Will you make these changes? We need to stay together." Lewis was not going to refuse a personal request from A. Philip Randolph, the acknowledged elder statesman of civil rights leaders. So, as the marchers began to fill in the area around the Reflecting Pool, James Forman hunched over a typewriter with Lewis at his side and went over the speech line by line with the rest of the group, checking each sentence to see if it raised any objections. Forman thought the changes turned out to be mostly matters of semantics. He would say afterward that he thought the speech was stronger after its redrafting, because the objections forced the SNCC group to clarify what they had meant to say.

As Lewis and Forman were rewriting the speech, it became time for the Lincoln Memorial program to start. But there was no one to give the invocation, because Archbishop O'Boyle was still some distance away at Saint Matthew's Church, threatening to boycott the march. As soon as the compromise was reached, one of Walter Reuther's aides informed John Reilly, from the Department of Justice, who was at the cutoff switch near the podium. Reilly immediately contacted General Bev Powell, the army's representative to the Department of Justice march team. "Tell O'Boyle it's settled, get him down here immediately," he said, and then ran through three blocks of blockaded streets to meet the archbishop's car. Reilly returned with O'Boyle and relayed to General Powell, "I've got the package." O'Boyle asked Matthew Ahmann, the speaker at the march from the National Catholic Conference for Interracial Justice, what he thought of Lewis's speech. "It's fine," Ahmann said, and all was settled. The archbishop never even looked at the revised speech.

Even with the revisions, Lewis delivered the address that best captured the thinking of those in the movement who had grown tired of waiting for national action on civil rights. Later in the afternoon, Malcolm X caught up with Lewis and congratulated him on what Malcolm said was an excellent speech. Many years later, Lewis would wonder whether the opening of his speech had been too harsh: "We march today for jobs and freedom, but we have nothing to be proud of." But this honest anger and impatience made his speech resonate with the feelings of a younger generation of civil rights activists. King's speech made similar arguments, but they were concealed in rhetoric (the repeated "Now is the time") and metaphor ("whirlwinds of revolt"). His speech did not have the unsparing particularity and intensity of Lewis's address.

After his promise of continued "whirlwinds of revolt," King opened the next section of his speech with the line "But there is something that I must say to my people." A typical element of King's mass meeting sermons was his encouragement of nonviolence and love for one's enemies. In his first-ever address as a civil rights leader, he told the crowd at Montgomery's Holt Street Baptist Church:

> And I want to say that we are not here advocating violence. We have never done that. I want it to be known throughout Montgomery and throughout this nation that we are Christian people. We believe in the Christian religion. We believe in the teachings of Jesus. The only weapon that we have in our hands this evening is the weapon of protest.

At the march, King reiterated this point to the civil rights movement as a whole. By August 1963, a handful of black leaders had drawn considerable media attention for their attacks on King's philosophy of nonviolence and their insistence on black Americans' right to defend themselves against white assaults. King's most well known critic at the time of the march was Malcolm X, who mocked nonviolence as "this little passive-resistance or wait-until-you-change-your-mind-and-then-let-me-up philosophy." Malcolm had first attracted national attention four years before the march, when he was featured in a documentary about the Nation of Islam. At the time, King had joined most of the other civil rights leaders in condemning the Nation for what King described as its "doctrine of black supremacy," but in private communications he was more gentle, writing to an inquirer that "as long as doors are closed in the faces of millions of Negroes and they feel dejected and dis-inherited, an organization like this will appeal to some." A few weeks before the march, Malcolm had tried to contact King, leading King to wonder to a friend whether Malcolm was trying to "unite with the main thrust" of the civil rights movement. Nonetheless, King knew that Malcolm gave voice to the feelings of many black Americans, particularly those in Northern cities. At a rally in Harlem earlier in 1963, King had been shouted down by an audience who chanted, "We Want Malcolm!" Malcolm had shown up unexpectedly at the march, where he held an impromptu press conference denouncing the event as a "Farce on Washington" and a "Chump's March," to be compared with "the Rose Bowl game, the Kentucky Derby, and the World Series."

King responded to Malcolm and other critics of nonviolence with a call to "meet physical force with soul force," a metaphor drawn from a book he had read on Gandhi. He then addressed the role of whites in the civil rights movement, another potentially divisive issue. It would be a few years before "Black Power" would become an influential slogan. But already, some members of SNCC were wondering whether their projects wouldn't be more effective if they were staffed solely with black workers, and the Nation of Islam was advocating a separate black homeland. King responded to these ideas by reaffirming his belief in racial integration within the protest movement:

The marvelous new militancy which has engulfed the Negro community must not lead us to a distrust of all white people, for many of our white brothers, as evidenced by their presence here today, have come to realize that their destiny is tied up with our destiny and they have come to realize that their freedom is inextricably bound to our freedom.

These might have sounded like minor points, but it was clear to observers familiar with the internal dynamics of the civil rights movement that King had publicly rebuked those who were becoming skeptical of nonviolence and integration. The *Atlanta Constitution* reported the next day that King "laid a hand on the extremists." In a phone conversation after the march, Stanley Levison singled out this section of King's speech for particular praise:

It was marvelous in Martin's speech, the way he handled the white and Negro question, completely repudiating this kind of nonsense of Adam Powell and the Muslims and everybody else in a way that was so positive that the crowd responded to it as they did to everything else that he said.

King would often end his mass meeting sermons by reminding the audience that demonstrations would continue until the goals of a local protest movement were met. At the march, after his call for nonviolence and integration within the civil rights movement, King told the nation that the movement would not be satisfied until all racial discrimination in America—from segregation in hotels in the South to segregation in ghettoes in the North—had ended. He closed with a

quotation from the prophet Amos: "No, no, we are not satisfied, and we will not be satisfied until justice rolls down like
waters and righteousness like a mighty stream."

At this point, King was almost finished with his prepared
text. Near the end of his written speech were the lines:

> I am not unmindful that some of you have come here
> out of great [originally "excessive"] trials and tribula-
> tions. Some of you have come fresh from narrow jail
> cells. Some of you have come from areas where your
> quest for freedom left you battered by the storms of
> persecution and staggered by the winds of police bru-
> tality. You have been the veterans of creative suffering.
> Continue to work with the faith that unearned suffer-
> ing is redemptive.

A strength of King's oratory had always been his ability to establish a rapport with his audience by communicating to them
that he knew what they had been through. James Baldwin once
wrote that the secret of King's greatness as a speaker was "in his
intimate knowledge of the people he is addressing, be they black
or white, and in the forthrightness with which he speaks of those
things which hurt or baffle them." In his speech at the beginning
of the Montgomery boycott, King had repeatedly referred to the
experience of fatigue he shared with his audience: "We are here
this evening because we're tired now," "And you know, my
friends, there comes a time when people get tired of being tram-
pled over by the iron feet of oppression." At the march, King's
audience knew that he, like many of his listeners, had recently

come "fresh from narrow jail cells." King ends this section with the core of the Christian gospel, applied to the veterans of the civil rights movement: Unearned suffering is redemptive. There was nothing particularly unusual about the substance of the first ten minutes of King's speech. He had opened with the argument from American ideals used by most progressive politicians of the era. Then he had warned of continued civil rights demonstrations until the movement's demands were met—the same message John Lewis had delivered more effectively earlier in the afternoon. The speech's most substantive message up to this point had been in the calls for nonviolence and the insistence on the importance of integration. King had composed and delivered a beautiful speech thus far, but there had not been anything extraordinary about the substance of what he was saying.

The missing element in King's prepared speech was the preacher's invocation of God. King would typically encourage congregations at mass meetings by telling them that God would lead the freedom movement to victory. He had said to the crowd at the Holt Street Baptist Church:

> And we are not wrong, we are not wrong in what we are doing. If we are wrong, the Supreme Court of this nation is wrong. If we are wrong, the Constitution of the United States is wrong. If we are wrong, God Almighty is wrong.

Nearly all of King's mass meeting addresses included some similar assurance. One of his favorite set pieces for the conclusion of a speech was a collection of triumphant lines from preachers and poets:

There is something in this universe which justifies Carlyle in saying: "No lie can live forever."

There is something in this universe which justifies William Cullen Bryant in saying: "Truth crushed to earth will rise again."

There is something in this universe which justifies James Russell Lowell in saying:

Truth forever on the scaffold,
Wrong forever on the throne.
Yet that scaffold sways the future,
And behind the dim unknown
Stands God, within the shadow,
Keeping watch above His own.

King might have felt that explicit assurances of God's deliverance would not be appropriate in a formal speech to the nation from the Lincoln Memorial. This omission might have made his speech more palatable as a political address, but it robbed it of the surging sense of hope that had powered his oratory since Montgomery. Without King's traditional promise of God's aid, his audience at the march was less likely to believe that the civil rights movement would one day succeed in remaking America. Even in 1963, it often seemed that segregation would last for decades more. The movement had won in Birmingham, but it had lost in Albany, Danville, and Americus. Medgar Evers had been murdered in front of his house. Fannie Lou Hamer had been beaten on the orders of a state trooper in a Mississippi jail. President Kennedy's civil rights bill was facing passionate opposition from segregationist senators, and no one knew if the civil rights supporters in the Senate would be able to break the filibuster.

At hundreds of mass meetings, King had told audiences, in so many words, that God would deliver the freedom movement. At the march, he did not make this direct assurance. Instead, in the last seven minutes of his speech, he seemed to be transported to see a future America where God had already led the movement to victory. With the realities of segregation in 1963, it took something close to divine inspiration for King to see beyond segregation and prophesy a day when America would be renewed. King would later tell Professor Harold DeWolf, his dissertation adviser at Boston University, that the "dream" existed first in the mind of God, and he only communicated it to the nation. One of the words for "prophet" in the Hebrew Bible is *hozeh*, a "seer"; and that day at the march, King seemed to be able to see what no one else could. When he left his prepared text, he no longer sounded like President Kennedy, John Lewis, or any other orator of the era. He sounded like Isaiah, the great visionary prophet of ancient Israel:

> The voice of him that crieth in the wilderness,
> Prepare ye the way of the LORD, make straight in
> the desert a highway for our God.

Every valley shall be exalted, and every mountain and
hill shall be made low: and the crooked shall be
made straight, and the rough places plain:

And the glory of the LORD shall be revealed, and all
flesh shall see it together: for the mouth of the
LORD hath spoken it. (Isaiah 40:3–5)

King was not the first American orator to transpose Biblical
visions of the "new creation" or the redemption of God's people to an American setting. Puritan ministers saw America as a
"city on a hill" that would be a hope for the nation. Black orators for centuries before King had been inspired by Biblical visions of national redemption to look forward to a new America
free from racism. Booker T. Washington ended his Atlanta address of 1895 by foretelling a "new heaven and a new earth" in
the South. Many of these visions featured a great choir composed of all Americans, singing anthems together. Archibald
Carey's "Let freedom ring" set piece fit into a rhetorical tradition that dates back, at least, to Ida B. Wells's 1893 address
"Lynch Law in All Its Phases":

Then no longer will our national hymn be sounding
brass and tinkling cymbal, but every member of this
great composite nation will be a living, harmonious il-
lustration of the words, and can with all honesty and
gladly join in the singing:

My country 'tis of thee, Sweet land of liberty
Of thee I sing.

Land where our fathers died, Land of the Pilgrim's pride,
From every mountainside, Freedom does ring.

The phrase "I have a dream" itself is similar to a construction that has been in American oratory since an 1876 speech by Robert G. Ingersoll:

> I see our country filled with happy homes . . .
> I see a world where thrones have crumbled . . .
> I see a world without a slave . . .
> I see a world at peace . . . a world where labor reaps its full reward . . .
> I see a world without the beggar's outstretched palm . . . the piteous wail of want . . .
> . . . and as I look, life lengthens, joy deepens, love canopies the earth; and over all, in the great dome, shines the eternal star of human hope.

Frederick Douglass once wrote, "I had a dream of freedom." Closer to the time of King's speech, James Meredith, a black Air Force veteran who was denied entrance to the University of Mississippi, composed a statement in the midst of the Ole Miss integration crisis that prefigured some of the language King would use in Washington: "I dream of the day when Negroes in Mississippi can live in decency and respect and do so without fear of intimidation and bodily harm or of receiving personal embarrassment, and with an assurance of equal justice under the law."

But by 1963, these prophetic visions of an America free

from racial discrimination had completely vanished from mainstream political discourse, even if members of the civil rights movement spoke them in private. Over and over again, politicians of the 1960s argued, on various grounds, in favor of civil rights. But they rarely set forth a vision of what America would look like if racial discrimination were no more. In the tens of thousands of pages of congressional debates and presidential speeches from the civil rights era, there is nothing resembling King's dream of a redeemed America. In the last seven minutes of King's speech at the March on Washington, he added something completely fresh to the way that Americans thought about race and civil rights. He gave the nation a vision of what it could look like if all things were made new.

Throughout his career, King told audiences that the civil rights movement was the vehicle by which God would redeem America. The freedom movement was at once a great American cause—"If we are wrong, the Constitution of the United States is wrong"—and a great religious cause—"If we are wrong, God Almighty is wrong." Appropriately, the first completion of the "I have a dream" refrain at the March on Washington was with the words of the Declaration of Independence:

> I say to you today, my friends, so even though we face the difficulties of today and tomorrow, I still have a dream.

> It is a dream deeply rooted in the American dream.

I have a dream that one day this nation will rise up
and live out the true meaning of its creed: We hold
these truths to be self-evident, that all men are created
equal.

King's subsequent completions of "I have a dream" envisioned the renewal of America, with a particular focus on the
states of the South. In each refrain, he described the coming
victory of the civil rights movement with Biblical language that
identified the movement's triumph with the arrival of the kingdom of God. King had used versions of this material many
times before, but August 28, 1963, was the first time a national
audience had heard anything like this speech. He began with
his home state of Georgia:

I have a dream that one day on the red hills of Georgia,
the sons of former slaves and the sons of former slave-
owners will be able to sit down together at the table of
brotherhood.

This vision echoed the lunch-counter protests of the early
1960s. In 1963, blacks and whites sitting together at any table
in Georgia, much less the "table of brotherhood," was un-
thinkable. King recast the image of an integrated group eating
together in the language of prophecy. A great feast is a Biblical
image of God's reign. As Isaiah wrote:

And in this mountain shall the LORD of hosts make
unto all people a feast of fat things, a feast of wines on

the lees, of fat things full of marrow, of wines on the lees well refined (Isaiah 25:6).

In the second "I have a dream" refrain, King said:

> I have a dream that one day, even the state of Mississippi, a state sweltering with the heat of injustice, sweltering with the heat of oppression, will be transformed into an oasis of freedom and justice.

Mississippi was one of the strongholds of Southern segregation. James Meredith was refused enrollment at the all-white University of Mississippi after what the Fifth Circuit Court of Appeals described as a "carefully calculated campaign of delay, harassment, and masterly inactivity." When Meredith finally enrolled in the fall of 1962, local whites started a riot that ended only after federal troops were deployed to quell it. Mississippi had been the site of some of the era's most infamous murders of blacks—Emmett Till, Medgar Evers—as well as several less well-publicized killings. After three civil rights activists were murdered in Mississippi in the summer of 1964, a search for them turned up other decomposed bodies, including one wearing a "CORE" shirt, from murders that had never been investigated. Mississippi civil rights workers lived under a regime of fear reminiscent of a totalitarian state. A Freedom Summer volunteer summarized the safety rules in a letter to his parents: "Beware of cars without tags—they are always danger; never go out alone; never go out after dark; never be the last out of a mass meeting; watch for cops without their badge; listen for an accelerating car outside; if you wake up at night thinking there is danger, wake everybody up." One SNCC worker, a former stock car driver, learned to do a U-turn at ninety miles an hour so he could outrace white harassers on Mississippi highways. As Bob Moses, the legendary organizer, explained to Freedom Summer students, "When you're not in Mississippi, it's not real, and when you're there, the rest of the world isn't real."

King recounted all the injustices in Mississippi with the image "sweltering with the heat of injustice, sweltering with the heat of oppression." But then he promised redemption: One day, even the state of Mississippi would be "transformed into an oasis of freedom and justice."

King's third completion of "I have a dream" was more personal:

> I have a dream that my four little children will one day live in a nation where they will not be judged by the color of their skin but by the content of their character. I have a dream today!

This line was modified from King's "American dream" set piece, where one aspect of the American dream was "a dream of a land where men will not argue that the color of a man's skin determines the content of his character." A fundamental assumption of segregation was that anyone who was black was automatically inferior to anyone who was white. The fifteen-year-old King was easily able to capture this racist concept in his "The Negro and the Constitution" speech: "The finest Negro is at the mercy of the meanest white man." The contrary vision imagined a society in which blacks were no longer instantly considered inferior to whites. This was a vision of an end to all racism in American life—not just an end to segregation in restaurants, housing, and schools, but an absolute end to all racial discrimination of any kind against black Americans.

King's fourth vision was the harshest:

> I have a dream that one day, down in Alabama, with its vicious racists, with its governor having his lips dripping with the words of interposition and nullification, one day, right there in Alabama, little black boys and black girls will be able to join hands with little white boys and white girls as sisters and brothers. I have a dream today!

King's attacks on the Alabama segregationists were so inflammatory that *Newsweek*'s editors omitted them from their reprint of King's speech, even though the editors left the rest of the "I have a dream" refrains intact. "Interposition" and "nullification" were references to the segregationist belief, made popular during the massive resistance to *Brown,* that the states could refuse to obey federal orders with which they disagreed, thus "interposing" the state governments in opposition to the federal government, and "nullifying" objectionable federal interference. The Supreme Court had declared that this belief could not be a permissible basis for resistance to desegregation in its 1958 decision in *Cooper v. Aaron,* a case that arose out of attempts by Arkansas state officials to resist the integration of Little Rock's Central High School. Despite the Supreme Court's rejection of interposition and nullification as doctrines of law, the ideas remained central to segregationist ideology until well into the 1960s. Two months before King's speech at the march, Governor George Wallace had stood in the schoolhouse door and physically barred federal officials from enforcing integration at the University of Alabama. A few weeks after King's speech, Governor Wallace would surround Tuskegee High School with state troopers in order to prevent the entrance of black students.

King's image of Alabama's transformation was of little black boys and girls joining hands with little white boys and girls as sisters and brothers. This sounds innocuous to the point of cliché today, but the very familiarity of this image is a measure of the influence of King's vision. In 1963, an integrated group of children holding hands would have symbolized the integration of schools and the prospect of miscegenation—two of segregationists' greatest fears. King delivered a provocative promise: Not only would children of all races live together, but this racial brotherhood was something that God demanded. In the visions of the Biblical prophets, children were often assigned the role of bringing in the new age: "A little child shall lead them." (Isaiah 11:6)

King's final, triumphant completion of the "I have a dream" refrain drew upon Isaiah's vision of the coming of the kingdom of God:

I have a dream that one day every valley shall be exalted, every hill and mountain shall be made low, the rough places will be made plain, and the crooked places will be made straight and the glory of the Lord will be revealed and all flesh shall see it together.

As soon as he finished the "I have a dream" section of his speech, King made sure that the protesters understood that his conviction that God would deliver the movement did not mean that he thought the protesters could sit back and wait for God's inexorable will to manifest itself. Instead, with the strength they took from his visions, the marchers should return to their home states and work to make the visions come true.

> With this faith we will be able to hew out of the mountain of despair a stone of hope. With this faith we will be able to transform the jangling discords of our nation into a beautiful symphony of brotherhood. With this faith we will be able to work together, to pray together, to struggle together, to go to jail together, to stand up for freedom together, knowing that we will be free one day.

King had originally planned to conclude his speech with a version of the "With this faith" refrain. He chose instead to return to the structure of "I have a dream" with the refrain, "Let freedom ring." He once more began by articulating his vision of America returning to its fundamental principles—this time, not the Declaration of Independence, but the beloved national creed expressed in the lyrics of "America."

> This will be the day—this will be the day—when all of God's children will be able to sing with new meaning:

"My country 'tis of thee; sweet land of liberty; of thee I sing; land where my fathers died, land of the pilgrim's pride; from every mountainside, let freedom ring!" And if America is to be a great nation, this must become true.

He first called out the names of the mountainsides in states outside the South, prefacing each with "Let freedom ring": New Hampshire, New York, Pennsylvania, Colorado, California. Then he prepared the audience for the dramatic climax of the piece: "But not only that." And as King called out the names of the Southern states, the audience cheered louder, anticipating the day when freedom would ring over the whole nation, South as well as North.

Let freedom ring from Stone Mountain of Georgia.

Let freedom ring from Lookout Mountain of Tennessee.

Let freedom ring from every hill and molehill of Mississippi, from every mountainside let freedom ring.

As "I have a dream" began with the Declaration of Independence and ended with Isaiah's vision of the kingdom of God, "Let freedom ring" began with "America" and ended with a promise of God's deliverance, drawn from the traditions of the black church:

And when this happens, when we allow freedom ring, when we let it ring from every village and every hamlet, from every state and every city, we will be able to speed up that day when all of God's children—black men and white men, Jews and Gentiles, Protestants and Catholics—will be able to join hands and sing in the words of the old Negro spiritual, "Free at last, free at last; thank God Almighty, we are free at last!"

For nearly every one of the 250,000 people at the march and the millions watching on television, the last seven minutes of King's speech were like nothing they had ever heard before. When King left his prepared text and began to preach about his dreams for the nation, several of his closest associates realized that something astonishing was happening. Clarence Jones was following along with an advance copy of King's speech, and when he realized King had left his text, he thought, "He's off; he's on his own now. He's inspired." As King stepped away from the podium, Ralph Abernathy embraced him and told him that the Holy Spirit had taken hold of him during the speech. King himself didn't quite know what to make of what had happened: The "I have a dream" refrain just came to him, "just all of a sudden."

In the year of Birmingham and the murder of Medgar Evers, King somehow persuaded his audience that racial discrimination would one day be no more. This was King's prophetic gift: In order for America to become a truly integrated nation, Americans first needed to be able to envision what that nation would look like. Political argument against segregation was valuable, but it was only a beginning. Imagination, as well as reason, needed to be renewed. By telling the audience about his vision of a nation healed of the sins of racial discrimination, King began the process of bringing that new nation to life—if only, at first, in the minds of his listeners.

chapter five

Reception, 1963–1968

At the time of King's death in April 1968, his speech at the March on Washington had nearly vanished from public view. There was no reason to believe that King's speech would one day come to be seen as a defining moment for his career and for the civil rights movement as a whole. Between 1963 and 1968, few people spent substantial time talking or thinking about what King had said at the march. His speech wasn't at the center of the public debate over civil rights.

This wasn't because King's audience had failed to appreciate the greatness of his speech. Many of the marchers thought that King "stole the show," as one of them told a reporter. "I was ready to march through Mississippi," a listener said to the *Amsterdam News*. Newspapers and magazines over the next week commented on how King had enraptured the crowd. The *New York Times* paid tribute to King's address with a front-page article entitled " 'I Have a Dream . . .': Peroration by Dr. King Sums Up A Day the Capital Will Remember." Several prominent black newspapers led their editions on the march with banner headlines about King's speech and front-page advertisements of their reprints of the speech's full text. Two recording companies cut records featuring the speeches from the march. Twentieth Century Fox inserted clips of King's speech into the "Fox Movietone News" newsreel. The *New York Post* published reprints of King's address, which it sold at ten cents for a single copy or one cent per copy for bulk orders.

Yet for many reporters (as well as many of the marchers), the March on Washington itself was as much of a marvel as King's speech. The nation had never before seen so many people come to the capital to petition peacefully for the redress of grievances, and the spectacle of the crowds that descended on Washington received as much media attention as King's address. The *Washington Post* headline the next day read: "MAM-MOTH RALLY OF 200,000 JAMS MALL IN SOLEMN, ORDERLY PLEA FOR EQUALITY." The television networks cut between the Lincoln Memorial program and long shots of the crowds blanketing the lawns on the Mall. Norman Mailer, writing for *Esquire*, said the best part of the day had been the walk from the Washington Monument to the Lincoln Memorial, and the speeches that followed were "anticlimactic."

Most of King's closest aides thought he had turned in a star performance. "You was smoking," Clarence Jones told King just after he finished, "The words was so hot they was just burning off the page." He compared King's address to a solo by a great jazz musician: "The rest of the band can just go home now." Stanley Levison said in a phone conversation recorded by the FBI that there was no question that King was the "man of the hour." When King returned to the Willard Hotel that night, he finally relaxed. He was plainly happy about the way the day had gone, and some of his aides teased him for how he "just got carried away" in his speech. "Watch out for Roy now," one aide said, thinking that Roy Wilkins would surely be envious of King's evident success. Over dinner, Wyatt Tee Walker told King how he felt when he heard King go into the "I have a dream" peroration, which Walker had heard many times before: "When you swung in, I said, 'Oh no, here we go again.'" King just laughed in reply, and Ralph Abernathy paid King a preacher's compliment: "Leader, you swept today."

Many prominent figures involved in civil rights agreed that King's speech had been the highlight of the march. James Farmer, the head of CORE, was scheduled to speak at the march, but he had been jailed a week earlier for leading a protest against police brutality in Plaquemine, Louisiana. He watched the march on a small television that the black citizens of Plaquemine brought to his cell.

I wept in my cell and actually regretted, momentarily, my decision not to go. When Mahalia Jackson sang and Martin Luther King, Jr., spoke, my tears disappeared and were replaced with awe.

The conscience of the nation could not be wrung any tighter. I believed then, and still do, that King's speech was an authentic American classic on a par historically with Lincoln's Gettysburg Address. There are times when divine inspiration so touches a person that he rises beyond himself. In that moment, at the march on Washington, Martin Luther King, Jr., was touched by a spirit that cannot be recaptured in our lifetime.

Mahalia Jackson thought that King's address "was the greatest speech of the day and when it was over, everybody was all used up." John Lewis and King exchanged compliments on each others' speeches, and Lewis told King, "You preached today." James Baldwin would later write in his 1972 book, *No Name in the Street*: "That day, for a moment, it almost seemed that we stood on a height, and could see our inheritance; perhaps we could make the kingdom real, perhaps the beloved community would not forever remain that dream one dreamed in agony."

But King's speech inspired a more varied reaction among others in the civil rights movement. Some in SNCC were moved by King's address: Courtland Cox thought King had "hit a home run," and the Reverend Ed King, who was active in the Mississippi movement, was impressed by King's promise that freedom would ring from every "hill and molehill in Mississippi." At least he understands the terror we're going through, Ed King thought. (King's line would become a joke among some Mississippi organizers, who identified themselves with mock pride: "We're from the molehills.") But many SNCC workers were more focused on other issues that day, such as the controversy over John Lewis's speech or the contrast between the resources that had been poured into the march—chartered buses, professionally made signs, an expensive public address system—and the spartan SNCC field offices. James Forman, who had participated in the rewriting of John Lewis's speech, thought there was nothing particularly noteworthy about

King's address. The only thing that came to his mind as he listened was that King's speech was much longer than Lewis's.

There was also some strong criticism within SNCC of the substance of King's speech. Many SNCC activists were unimpressed by the "I have a dream" refrains because they thought that King, as the most prominent figure in the movement, should have set forth some particular demands in his speech, instead of presenting a more general "dream." Some SNCC workers involved in grass-roots organizing thought King had missed an opportunity to reveal the lawlessness and horror of the segregated South to the rest of the nation. The benign image of a "dream" seemed to belittle the dangerous civil rights work that was going on across the South. Anne Moody, a student activist in Mississippi, later wrote:

> I sat on the grass and listened to the speakers, to discover we had "dreamers" instead of leaders leading us. Just about every one of them stood up there dreaming. Martin Luther King went on and on talking about his dream. I sat there thinking that in Canton we never had time to sleep, much less dream.

The general reaction to King's speech within the NAACP was, "There goes Martin again." King's speech seemed to many NAACP officials to be merely a Baptist sermon without substance, just as many within the organization saw King as a Baptist preacher who left the substantive civil rights work to others. Also, several important NAACP figures had heard King many times before, and so, to them, his speech at the march sounded like any other King address.

An even more negative response to King's speech came from Malcolm X, who had long objected to the "American dream" metaphor because he thought it encouraged blacks to be unrealistic about the extent to which whites would welcome an integrated and equal society. In a speech in New York in 1962, he had said: "What is looked upon as an American dream for white people has long been an American nightmare for black people." After Malcolm heard King speak at the march, he told Bayard Rustin, "You know, this dream of King's is going to be a nightmare before it's over."

After these initial reactions, most people in the civil rights movement didn't think or talk about King's speech between 1963 and King's death in 1968. One reason for the lack of attention to King's address was that everyone was too busy. King might have delivered a memorable speech, but there were new campaigns to plan, fundraising to worry about, legislative packages to lobby for. There was no time to sit around and speculate about what King's address might have meant for the nation. As Wyatt Tee Walker recalls, "It was just that moment, and, you know, we had work to do. We had to come down from the mountain and go into the valley and go back to Mississippi and Alabama and all of those horrible places." Another explanation for the absence of discussion was that King was constantly giving remarkable addresses between 1963 and 1968. Any number of King's speeches are now remembered by movement veterans as his "best" speech. His address at the march had been marvelous, but it was also a pastiche of familiar King set pieces. King had used the "I have a dream" refrain several times before the march, and the "Let freedom ring" set piece had been in his repertoire since 1956. To some who heard King speak on a regular basis, the setting of his speech at the march made it memorable, but most of what he said was familiar. Furthermore, the speeches at the march were less important to many in the movement than the political meaning of a pro-civil-rights demonstration of 250,000 people. The pressing question discussed within SNCC after the march was how to channel the march's energy into practical action on civil rights, not which speeches, if any, would go down in history.

King's speech did, however, have an immediate effect on his standing in relation to the leaders of the other civil rights organizations. In the months after the march, it became the common wisdom that John Lewis and SNCC were the dangerous radicals in the freedom movement, and that King was one of the moderates. As Lewis complained in a 1964 interview:

> Before the March on Washington, Martin King was considered by a lot of people, and the Southern press particularly, as an extremist. But right after the March he became the moderate of the South. Right now, SNCC is considered by the Southern press as irresponsible, extremist, radical, and militant.

Mary King, a SNCC staff member, later observed:

> As a result of Dr. King's speech, he rose on the scene and became regarded as the major personality of the

civil rights movement, and many then came to view him as Randolph had described him—the moral leader of the nation.

King's new visibility after the March on Washington did not go unnoticed by the FBI. William C. Sullivan, the assistant director in charge of the FBI's domestic intelligence division, wrote just after the March on Washington that King's "powerful demagogic speech yesterday" led him to conclude that King "stands head and shoulders over all other Negro leaders put together," and recommended: "We must mark him now, if we have not done so before, as the most dangerous Negro of the future in this Nation. . . ."

Congressional supporters of civil rights were so relieved that the march had gone off without violence that they barely discussed the speeches at all in the weeks after the event. They commended the march as a "breathtaking, moving, overpowering demonstration," a "new high in the battle of civil rights," and "a demonstration we can never forget—an intensely moving demonstration of quiet determination, of relaxed confidence, of total commitment to the ideals of democracy, of freedom and opportunity and respect for every human person." The day's speeches were almost an afterthought. Several supporters of civil rights excerpted a few of the speeches from the march, King's among them, so they could be reprinted in the *Congressional Record*. But no one in Congress singled out King's speech as the most memorable event of the day.

President Kennedy and Attorney General Robert Kennedy both thought that King had made a remarkable speech. At a White House reception for the march leaders, after the conclusion of the Lincoln Memorial program, the president greeted King with a grin and said, "I have a dream." (John Lewis, by contrast, received only an "I heard you speak" from the president.) But the Kennedy administration kept these reactions private. The president didn't mention King's speech in his official statement about the march, which praised "the deep fervor and the quiet dignity that characterizes the thousands who have gathered in the Nation's capital from across the country to demonstrate their faith and confidence in our democratic form of government."

The overwhelming grandeur and pageantry of the march wasn't the only reason that the Kennedy administration and congressional supporters of civil rights were publicly silent about King's speech. Any favorable mention of King was an invitation to the segregationists in Congress to issue furious screeds about King's supposed communist tendencies, demagoguery, and rabble-rousing. The administration's main priority was securing the passage of the president's pending civil rights bill, not publicly complimenting potential political liabilities on their speeches, no matter how great they were. To the extent that King's address would help the chances of the bill, it was welcomed. Presidential speechwriter Ted Sorensen instantly knew that King had struck exactly the right tone for the day. By delivering a message of hope, and not something that was likely to be labeled as angry or extremist, King's speech could only help the civil rights bill. But there was no reason to call attention to this and derail the debate over the bill with anti-King diatribes from the segregationists.

During the next five years, King's speech at the march received next to no attention in Congress. The paranoid hatred of the segregationists continued unabated until King's death. In 1965, Representative John Williams of Mississippi called King the "most notorious gangster of our generation" and the "most dangerous individual in America." In 1966, Representative Prentiss Walker of Mississippi compared King to Nazi and Fascist leaders. In 1968, Representative Sidney Herlong of Florida compared King to Hitler. Just three days before King's assassination, Representative John Ashbrook of Ohio inserted a lengthy statement into the record calling King a "master of deceit."

This continued anti-King sentiment explains why King's speech at the march is almost never mentioned during the monumental debates over the Civil Rights Act of 1964, which occupy around sixty-four thousand pages of the *Congressional Record*. On the few occasions when members of Congress alluded to King's speech during the debates, they concentrated on the most immediately relevant messages from the address—King's warning of continued black protest and his call for nonviolence and integration—rather than on the more visionary "I have a dream" refrain. Senator Jacob Javits quoted King's warning that "There will be neither rest nor tranquility in America until the Negro is granted his citizenship rights." Representative Seymour Halpern of New York warned Congress, in King's words, against returning to "business as usual." Senator William Proxmire of Wisconsin was the only member of Congress who spoke about the "I have a dream" section of King's speech in 1964, but even he quoted the speech not to praise its visionary refrains, but to contrast King with Malcolm X. Proxmire reminded the Senate: "The leader of the Negro movement in our country is not Malcolm X, the

leader of the Black Muslims. The leader of the Negro movement in this country is Martin Luther King. What does Martin
Luther King call for? What has he asked his people to do? He
has called for them to love the people who oppose them. He
has asked them to love, to cooperate, and to agree to work with
them." He went on:

> Last August in Washington we witnessed one of the
> most magnificent demonstrations in the history of our
> Nation. The March on Washington was a dignified
> demonstration—200,000 people, deeply moved and
> deeply indignant, marched, and yet there was not a sin-
> gle act of violence.
>
> That is a tribute to the way those people feel. Of
> course, the climax of that great march on Washington
> occurred when Martin Luther King made his great
> speech. He said, "I had a dream." What was that
> dream? The dream was not one of revenge. The dream
> was not anything of that kind. The dream was of har-
> mony—of a little white boy and a little black boy play-
> ing together, working together, and building together a
> better America.

There was also another reason why King's speech at the
March on Washington had nearly disappeared from public
memory by the time of King's death in 1968. Between 1965
and 1968, it would become more and more difficult to hold to
the assured message of hope that King had delivered at the
march. From 1963 through the summer of 1965, the civil rights

movement seemed to win victory after victory: the break-through settlement in Birmingham, the March on Washington, the dramatic success of the Selma-to-Montgomery march. The movement's legislative accomplishments during this period were even more astonishing. On July 2, 1964, President Johnson signed President Kennedy's civil rights bill into law as the Civil Rights Act of 1964, to be followed just thirteen months later by the Voting Rights Act of 1965, which provided for federal enforcement of voting rights in the South. With these two statutes, the movement achieved a goal that would have been nearly unimaginable at the time of the Montgomery bus boycott. After almost ten years of demonstrations, the civil rights movement had successfully pressured the federal government to force the end of Southern segregation.

King himself won international recognition during these years: *Time*'s "Man of the Year" for 1963, the Nobel Peace Prize in 1964. His speeches between 1963 and 1965 were jubilant in spirit, as he repeatedly returned to the themes of his address at the march. In an interview published in January 1965, he once more used the "American dream" metaphor, saying that if the problem of civil rights was solved, "America will just as surely be on the high road to the fulfillment of the Founding Fathers' dream." In December 1964, after returning from Oslo, he gave a ringing reaffirmation of his words at the march in front of a crowd in Harlem:

> For the past several days I have been on the mountaintop. I really wish I could just stay on the mountain, but

I must go back to the valley. I must go back, because my brothers and sisters down in Mississippi and Alabama can't register and vote. I've got to go back to the valley. . . . There are those who need hope. There are those who need to find a way out. . . . Oh, I say to you tonight, my friends, I'm not speaking as one who's never seen the burdens of life. I've had to stand so often amid the chilly winds of adversity, staggered by the jostling winds of persecution. I've had to stand so often amid the surging murmur of life's restless sea. But I go back with a faith. . . . And I *still* have a dream.

In the concluding speech of the Selma-to-Montgomery march, delivered from a flatbed trailer across the street from the Montgomery capitol, King moved the protesters with a triumphant address that many observers ranked as one of his best ever:

We are on the move now. The burning of our churches will not deter us. The bombing of our homes will not dissuade us. We are on the move now. The beating and killing of our clergymen and young people will not divert us. We are on the move now. The wanton release of their known murderers will not discourage us. We are on the move now.

Like an idea whose time has come, not even the marching of mighty armies can halt us. We are moving to the land of freedom.

Let us therefore continue our triumphant march to the realization of the American dream.

After several repetitions of the "Let us march" refrain, calling on the audience to march on segregated housing, segregated schools, poverty, and ballot boxes—and after a reminder to the audience that a "season of suffering" still lay ahead—King concluded with a defiant vision:

I know you are asking today, "How long will it take?" . . .
I come to say to you this afternoon, however difficult the moment, however frustrating the hour, it will not be long, because truth crushed to earth will rise again.

How long? Not long, because no lie can live forever.

How long? Not long, because you shall reap what you sow.

How long? Not long.

Truth forever on the scaffold,
Wrong forever on the throne.
Yet that scaffold sways the future.
And, behind the dim unknown,
Standeth God within the shadow
keeping watch above His own.

How long? Not long, because the arc of the moral universe is long, but it bends toward justice.

How long? Not long, because mine eyes have seen the glory of the coming of the Lord, he is trampling out the vintage where the grapes of wrath are stored. He has loosed the fateful lightning of his terrible swift sword. His truth is marching on.

He has sounded forth the trumpet that shall never call retreat. He is sifting out the hearts of man before His judgment seat. O, be swift, my soul, to answer him. Be jubilant, my feet. Our God is marching on.

The Selma-to-Montgomery speech was one of the last times that King would sound so certain that God would lead the movement to victory. Despite the astounding gains of the period from 1963 to 1965, there had been enough tragedies to cause some within the movement to begin to lose hope. Every victory that the freedom movement won in the years just after the march seemed to be accompanied by a demoralizing setback that hinted that the movement could not count on its successes to continue forever. One month after the March on Washington, the Sixteenth Street Church in Birmingham was bombed, killing four young girls. Malcolm X seized on the opportunity to tell a reporter from the *Amsterdam News* that the bombing proved the march had been a failure:

The Negroes spent a lot of money, had a good time, and enjoyed a real circus or carnival-type atmosphere. Now that the show is over, the black masses are still without land, without jobs, and without homes. . . . Their Christian churches are still being bombed, their innocent little girls murdered. So what did the march on Washington accomplish? Nothing!

This was an overstatement, but Malcolm captured a building sentiment of frustration among some in the movement. The summer of 1964 brought the enactment of the Civil Rights Act, but it also saw the assassinations of three civil rights workers in Mississippi and the refusal of the Democrats to recognize the Mississippi Freedom Democratic Party, an integrated delegation formed to protest the disenfranchisement of Mississippi blacks. The Selma campaign had shown the nation the flagrant denials of the constitutional rights of Alabama blacks, but at the cost of televised beatings of nonviolent protesters on the Pettus Bridge and the murders of civil rights activists in Selma and nearby Marion, Alabama. John Lewis still held to a commitment to nonviolence, but he sympathized with those who were growing tired. He remembered later, "I felt after Selma that it was my last demonstration. We're only flesh. I could understand people not wanting to be beaten anymore . . . Black capacity to believe [that a white person] would really open his heart, open his life to nonviolent appeal was running out."

While the veterans of the Southern civil rights movement were slowly being worn down by the cumulative effect of decades of white brutality, many activists were becoming more aware of the problems faced by the 7 million blacks living in the North, who had seen little gain from the victories of 1963–65. As early as 1959, King had delivered an entire speech devoted to employment discrimination and poverty in the North, and he regularly spoke about Northern poverty and segregation during the late 1950s and early 1960s. He told a reporter in June 1963, "I will have to face the decision soon on whether I should be limiting myself to the South . . . In the North there are brothers and sisters who are suffering discrimination that is even more agonizing, in a sense, than in the South . . . In the South, at least the Negro can see progress, whereas in the North all he sees is retrogression." The full title of the March on Washington was the "March on Washington for Jobs and Freedom," and, in the minds of the march organizers, equality in employment was as important a goal as the elimination of Jim Crow. On the Sunday before the march, in an appearance on *Meet the Press*, King reiterated his long-held belief that equality would only be achieved when both Northern and Southern segregation had ended:

> I think, in order for the Negro to approximate equality here, all of the barriers of racial segregation must be removed and all of the barriers of discrimination— whether it is in housing conditions, whether it is in employment, where the Negro confronts a great deal of discrimination, whether it is in the actual legal segregation of the South in schools or the *de facto* segregation in the Northern schools. All of these barriers must be removed before the Negro can even begin moving up the highways of freedom in all of its dimensions.

In 1964, King suggested on several occasions that he was interested in starting a campaign against Northern segregation. In an interview with *U.S. News & World Report*, King said: "We feel that it is necessary to grapple with the very difficult problem of *de facto* segregation," and promised that there would be movement activity against segregation in the schools, in employment, and in housing. On a radio program in New York, King said, "The movement will have to move in a more determined, creative, and inventive manner in the North," and "more and more I feel that the problem is so national in its scope that I will have to do more work in the North than I have in the past."

But King had no time to oversee a major civil rights campaign in the North. The Birmingham and Selma campaigns occupied most of his attention through the beginning of 1965. When the Selma protests concluded in the spring of 1965, King finally had an opportunity to plan his Northern campaign. He scheduled a trip through the North to pick a target city, visiting Chicago, Cleveland, Philadelphia, and Washington, D.C. In his initial tour of Chicago, King kept to a packed schedule of sermons, neighborhood rallies, lunches, and meetings, giving about twenty speeches in two days. The visit ended with a rally where he told the crowd:

> [W]e come away from this revealing . . . tour of Chicago convinced more than ever that segregation is morally wrong and sinful. We come away convinced that so long as the Negro is segregated in housing that is exploited and sends his children to segregated schools that are neglected and sees them graduated with an inferior education that is useless in our rapidly automating economy we shall not be free. This is the vicious cycle of poverty and despair that segregation and discrimination have woven about the Negro in our Northern cities generally and in Chicago particularly,

and it is against this evil system that we are pledged to wage an unrelenting struggle.

Not long after King's visit to Chicago, riots broke out in the Watts neighborhood of Los Angeles, giving King a forceful reminder of the urgency of shifting his focus to the North. It took 13,900 National Guard troops to quell the riots, which killed thirty-four people and injured more than a thousand, almost all of whom were black. An onlooker who witnessed the police beatings that started the riots shouted, "We've got no rights at all—it's just like Selma!" King cut short a vacation in Puerto Rico to visit Watts, where he was personally confronted with the anger of Watts residents. "The only way that we can ever get anybody to listen to us is to start a riot," one person told King. After King toured the riot sites, a resident said, "King, and all his talk about nonviolence, didn't mean much. Watts had respect for King, but the talk about nonviolence made us laugh." Another person in Watts made mocking reference to King's speech at the march: " 'I have a dream' . . . craa-ap. We don't want dreams, we want jobs." Bayard Rustin recalled that King was "absolutely undone" by the Watts riots. King said, "You know, Bayard, I worked to get these people the right to eat hamburgers, and now I've got to do something . . . to help them get the money to buy them."

After Watts, King began to tell audiences very frankly that the civil rights movement had done almost nothing for blacks in the North. In a speech in September 1965, King said the movement "has not been national in its thrust nor objectives. . . . The explosion in Watts reminded us all that the Northern ghettos are the prisons of forgotten men." He told

New York reporters in early 1966, "[A]ll too often the civil rights movement has not gotten down to the lower levels of Negro deprivation, and I feel that it is time to take the movement to the masses of Negroes."

King fulfilled these words by returning to Chicago in the fall of 1965 and preparing for a major campaign against Chicago's slums. Some of his advisers opposed this move, arguing that King could not expect the continued support of white liberals if he started a campaign against segregation in Northern cities. King's response was, "This is where our mission is. We have received a calling to come North." King himself moved into a tenement in a Chicago ghetto to dramatize the living conditions of many Northern blacks. He described the campaign's goals in a speech in March 1966:

> Our campaign in Chicago is one to end slums. By this we mean put an end to the internal colonialism which deprives the Negro of free trade and a free share in our nation's resources and put an end to the black ghetto as an island of poverty in the midst of a sea of plenty.

King hoped that Chicago would be the breakthrough demonstration that would force national action on poverty and Northern segregation, just as Birmingham and Selma had brought about federal action on Southern segregation. At the beginning of the Chicago campaign, he said, "Selma, Alabama, was our pilot city for the Voting Rights Bill of 1965, and I have faith that Chicago . . . could become the metropolis where a meaningful nonviolent movement could arouse the conscience of the nation to deal realistically with the northern ghetto." King told his staff in October 1965, in an echo of what he had thought about Birmingham, "If we can break the system in Chicago, it can be broken any place in the country."

As the Chicago campaign got under way, King had to cope with rising discontent within the Southern movement. The disillusionment that had been kept at bay by the victories of 1963 to 1965 was slowly beginning to overcome some Southern civil rights workers. Growing sentiments of separatism and an increasing impatience with nonviolence came into public view during the Meredith march in the summer of 1966. James Meredith, famous for integrating Ole Miss, had started a solo "walk against fear" across Mississippi. He was ambushed on the second day, and as he lay recovering from shotgun wounds in a Memphis hospital, the leaders of the major civil rights groups flew to Memphis to continue his walk. Floyd McKissick, the newly elected director of CORE, signaled the presence of the internal tensions that would eventually overtake the march when he declared at Meredith's bedside that nonviolence was a "dying philosophy" that had "outlived its usefulness." The Meredith march became a media spectacle when a SNCC staffer led a group of marchers in chants of "Black Power!" to which SCLC staff members responded with "Freedom Now!" Reporters pounced on this evidence of dissension, and King worried about what it forebode for the movement. At several points along the march, white mobs and hostile police assaulted the marchers. In Canton, Mississippi, police tear-gassed the protesters after the city denied them permission to pitch their tents on the grounds of an all-black school. On the final day of the

Meredith march, King returned to his "I have a dream" refrain for the state of Mississippi: "One day, right here in Mississippi, justice will become a reality for all." But King's hopeful visions were starting to sound less and less persuasive. As the Meredith march collapsed, King returned to Chicago determined to secure a victory to quiet the dissenters. Andrew Young said: "We have got to deliver results—nonviolent results in a Northern city—to protect the nonviolent movement." King warned in Chicago, "I need some help in getting this method across. A lot of people have lost faith in the establishment. . . . They've lost faith in the democratic process. They've lost faith in non-violence. . . . [T]hose who will make this peaceful revolution impossible will make a violent revolution inevitable, and we've got to get this over, I need help. I need some victories, I need concessions."

King would never get those results in Chicago. At an open housing march led by his aides, a group of white boys carrying a noose chanted:

I'd love to be an Alabama trooper
That is what I'd really like to be
For if I were an Alabama trooper
Then I could hang a nigger legally.

King embarked on a round of marches on real estate offices that had records of discrimination against black clients. During one march, he was met by a white mob carrying Confederate and Nazi flags. The crowd threw bottles and rocks at the protesters, shouting, "Nigger go home!" "Kill the niggers!" "We want Martin Luther Coon," and "Wallace for President."

Afterward King said: "I've never seen anything like it. I've been in many demonstrations all across the South, but I can say that I have never seen—even in Mississippi and Alabama—mobs as hostile and as hate-filled as I've seen in Chicago."

The pressure of King's marches forced Chicago officials to negotiate, and they agreed to a settlement that committed the city to take steps to end residential segregation. King optimistically declared, "[t]he total eradication of housing discrimination has been made possible," but many Chicago activists were dubious, and King faced harsh criticism for signing on to the settlement. It soon became clear that city officials would evade the agreement. A new note of resignation entered King's speech at the movement's concluding rally:

> Let's face the fact: Most of us are going to be living in the ghetto five, ten years from now. But we've got to get some things straightened out right away. I'm not going to wait a month to get the rats and roaches out of my house. Morally, we ought to have what we say in the slogan, Freedom Now. But it all doesn't come now. That's a sad fact of life you have to live with.

By late 1966, the dual impact of the internal divisions in the civil rights movement and the failure of the Chicago campaign had caused King to start to sound increasingly doubtful of the hopeful profession of "I have a dream" that he had made at the March on Washington. Even before the troubles of 1966, King had occasionally responded to setbacks with an inversion of his "I have a dream" set piece. In his Chicago speech in July 1965, just after his initial tour of the city's slums,

King said: "So often in these past two years I have had to watch my dream transformed into a nightmare." He continued, "I have felt my dream falter as I have traveled through the rat-infested slums of our big city ghettos and watched our jobless and hopeless poor sweltering in an air-tight cage of poverty in the midst of an affluent society."

King continued to use this "dream into a nightmare" set piece in speeches during 1966 and 1967 as a way to express his dismay with the state of civil rights in America. The source of his disappointment was not just that the movement had met with a setback in Chicago. Even in the 1950s and early 1960s, there had been many times when local protest campaigns had been stymied, as in Albany, Georgia, in 1961–62. But the collapse of the Chicago campaign exposed a fundamental obstacle that stood in the way of King's new focus on poverty and Northern segregation. The Chicago effort failed for several reasons—divisions within the black community on goals and strategy, the difficulties of organizing in the ghettos—but one important reason was a lack of support from Northern whites for the integration of Northern cities. King was beginning to realize that addressing the problems of Northern cities such as Chicago would require a much more radical transformation of America than had been demanded by the elimination of Jim Crow, and he was not sure that a majority of Americans would welcome that transformation. The end of Jim Crow had entailed dismantling the racial caste system in only one region of the nation, and it had not required substantial government funding. Eliminating the slums and segregated schools that discriminated against Northern blacks was going to be much more far-reaching, and much more expensive. King estimated the cost of his own proposal for a "Bill of Rights for the Disadvantaged"—a massive program of housing, employment, and educational assistance for all poor Americans, modeled on the G.I. Bill—at about $10 billion per year over a ten-year period, at a time when Vietnam was already eating into a meager antipoverty budget. King began to give speeches that warned that the movement had entered a "new phase" or a "new era," different from and more challenging than the Montgomery-to-Selma period. He explained on television in June 1967:

> [W]e are in a new era of the civil rights struggle. For well now onto twelve years we worked to break down the barriers of legal segregation and we had many watershed movements to deal with these issues. . . . But with the Selma movement and the Voting Rights Bill, one phase of the civil rights struggle ended and a new phase came into being, and I would say this new phase is a struggle and a demand for genuine equality, and it is a much more difficult phase. It is much easier to integrate a lunch counter, for instance, than it is to eradicate slums. It is much easier to integrate buses than it is to create jobs.
>
> Now we are dealing with basic economic, political, and social issues that will, if dealt with properly, demand a radical redistribution of political and economic power. The other thing is that we are dealing with issues now that will cost the nation something. If we are going to get rid of slums it is going to cost the nation billions of dollars. It didn't cost the nation anything to

guarantee the right to vote, or to guarantee access to public accommodations, but we are dealing with issues now that will cost the nation something. Therefore the issues are much more difficult. Many of the allies who were with us during the first phase will not be with us now, because it does mean dispersing the ghetto, it does mean living next door to [blacks], it does mean the federal government pouring billions of dollars into programs to get rid of slums and poverty and deprivation, and I think this is why the civil rights movement has to restructure itself, in a sense, to gear itself for a new phase of struggle altogether.

The failure of the Chicago campaign caused King to realize the limits of Northern white support for his goals. The nation never rose up in outrage against mob violence in the white neighborhoods of Chicago in the way that it did against Bull Connor in Birmingham and Jim Clark in Selma. King began to argue that most whites didn't want blacks to be beaten but also didn't want blacks living next door to them or going to school with their children. He told his staff in a May 1967 retreat, "I'm convinced that a lot of the people that supported us when we were in those glowing, epic-making days in Alabama and in Mississippi, when we were in Birmingham and Selma, many of the people who supported us supported us because they were against Jim Clark, because they were against Bull Connor, but they were not for genuine equality for Negroes." In a speech in New York, he said: "White America had intended that the Negro should be spared the lash of brutality and coarse degradation, but it had never seriously intended to help him out of poverty, exploitation, or all forms of discrimination." King suggested that this absence of support could be attributed to white racism—not in the sense of virulent hatred of black Americans, but in the sense of indifference to the difficulties faced by blacks and an unwillingness to see complete equality realized. In a 1967 speech in Chicago, he said, "Racism is still alive, too much alive in our country." Before a crowd in Louisville, King said, "Our beloved nation is still a racist country," and "the vast majority of whites are racist, either consciously or unconsciously."

King was also personally beginning to feel the sense of letdown experienced by other civil rights veterans as the movement appeared to be foundering. With the slowing of tangible gains, emotionally uplifting slogans such as "I have a dream" began to seem like cruel taunts of a future that would never be realized. At one point during the Chicago movement, King had been booed during one of his speeches by a group of young black men. In a later speech, he talked about how he had responded to the incident:

> I went home that night with an ugly feeling, selfishly I thought of my sufferings and sacrifices over the last twelve years. Why would they boo one so close to them? But as I lay awake thinking, I finally came to myself and I could not for the life of me have less than patience and understanding for those young men. For twelve years, I and others like me have held out radiant promises of progress. I had preached to them about my

dream. . . . I had urged them to have faith in America and in white society. Their hopes had soared. They were now booing me because they felt that we were unable to deliver on our promises. They were booing because we had urged them to have faith in people who had too often proved to be unfaithful. They were now hostile because they were watching the dream that they had so readily accepted turn into a frustrating nightmare.

The hostile reaction to King's failure to break segregation in the North was all the greater because he had been so inspiring in his speech at the March on Washington:

> When hope diminishes, the hate element is often turned toward those who originally built up the hope. . . . The bitterness is often greater toward that person who built up the hope, who could say, "I have a dream," but couldn't produce the dream because of the failure and the sickness of the nation to respond to the dream.

By late summer 1967, the civil rights movement was at a standstill. King's Chicago campaign had failed. The year 1967 saw some of the worst riots in American history: 164 riots broke out in the first nine months of the year, and several local officials called in the National Guard. In July, Newark and Detroit exploded in week-long riots that resulted in sixty-six deaths. The riots left King "terribly distressed, more so than I had ever seen him," said Coretta Scott King. He was frustrated that people were looking to him for a solution: "People expect me to have answers, and I don't have any answers."

For the first time since Birmingham, the federal government had apparently returned to a policy of indifference toward the civil rights movement. Since the middle of 1966, King had publicly opposed the Vietnam war, which he called "a blasphemy against all that America stands for," and a conflict that sought to "turn the clock of history back and perpetuate white colonialism," but his opposition seemed to be having no effect on public opinion besides dampening support for civil rights and earning him the enmity of President Johnson. The president's 1966 civil rights bill, which would have protected civil rights workers from violence and outlawed discrimination in the sale and rental of housing, died late in the year after supporters could not break a filibuster, amid polls showing that a majority of Americans believed that the administration was moving "too fast" on civil rights. One Johnson aide said, "It would have been hard to pass the Emancipation Proclamation in the atmosphere prevailing now." Even the Supreme Court, which had so long been supportive of the movement's aims, had reversed itself. In *Walker v. City of Birmingham,* the Supreme Court sustained, by a 5-4 vote, the 1963 convictions of King and other civil rights protesters for criminal contempt, based on their violation of a Birmingham court order enjoining them from demonstrating without a permit. Justice Brennan, writing in dissent, urged his colleagues not to "permit fear of 'riots' and 'civil disobedience' generated by slogans like 'Black Power' to divert our attention from what is here at stake," but his pleas were unheard. On June 12, 1967, the Court handed down its decision and ordered King back to the Birmingham jail to serve his sentence.

The SCLC had not had a major success since Selma in 1965, and Selma had been its only real success since Birmingham. A separatist faction had taken over SNCC, ousting John Lewis from his leadership position, and several SNCC leaders had publicly encouraged rioters in the North with their fiery rejections of nonviolence. SNCC staffer Willie Ricks, who had started the "Black Power" chants during the Meredith march, said during the Atlanta riots in the summer of 1967 that SNCC militants in Atlanta would "make Vietnam look like a holiday." In a speech in Maryland, in July 1967, Rap Brown declared: "If America don't come around, we going burn it down, brother. We are going to burn it down if we don't get our share of it." A seventeen-year-old black girl in Harlem, speaking at a meeting with Stokely Carmichael, said "We intend to be the generation that says, Friends, we do not have a dream, we do *not* have a dream, we have a plan. So, TV men, do not be prepared to record our actions indoors, but be prepared to record our actions *on the streets*." King himself was beginning to doubt whether his dreams for the nation would ever be realized, and he knew that his message of hope had ceased to be persuasive to many blacks. As he became more and more preoccupied with the issues that had troubled him since Watts and the beginning of the Chicago campaign— residential segregation, discrimination in employment, and the intransigence and desperation of poverty in the North— King began planning for one last, dramatic campaign to awaken the conscience of the nation.

The plan harkened back to the movement's triumph in

Washington four years earlier. King would lead a massive, nonviolent army in a "Poor People's Campaign" to the nation's capital in order to petition the federal government to address the grievances of poor Americans. King told reporters that the movement would be multiracial, recruiting "not only Negroes, but Puerto Ricans, Mexican Americans, Appalachian whites, and American Indians." This time, the protesters would not come to Washington in a spirit of reconciliation and leave once the sun went down. In an SCLC retreat in November 1967, King said: "This will be no mere one-day march in Washington, but a trek to the nation's capital by suffering and outraged citizens, who will go to stay until some definite and positive action is taken [on] jobs and income for the poor." The Washington campaign would resemble the dramatic protests in Birmingham and Selma. "We feel that it is time now to bring a Selma-type or a Birmingham-type movement to bear on the economic problems confronting the poor people of our nation," he said in February 1968. Just as the movement had in the South, it would shut down its target city until corrective action was taken:

> I think that the time has come if we can't get anything done otherwise to camp right here in Washington . . . just camp here and stay here by the thousands and thousands until the Congress of our nation and the federal government will do something to deal with the problem . . . making it clear that the city will not function as we did in Birmingham and other cities across the South. I think we have to do it right here in the nation's capital and in other cities in our country until the problem is dealt with.

King saw the Poor People's Campaign as one last chance to show the rest of the nation that nonviolence could accomplish results in the urban North. The failure of Chicago had given many in the movement another reason to doubt nonviolence, but King held fast: "When people tell you that nonviolence won't work, tell them it has worked. We know it has worked all across the South. And if it hasn't worked in the North, it just hasn't been tried enough." King also thought that organized civil disobedience could be an alternate outlet for the anger expressed in the riots. "What we are faced with as we look toward Washington is the question of how we can transmute the inchoate rage of the ghetto into a creative and constructive force," he told his staff in January 1968. He continued: "We must bring to bear all of the power of nonviolence on the economic problem. And it must be militant enough, aggressive enough to be as attention-getting and dramatic as a riot, without destroying life or property in the process."

King knew that the Poor People's Campaign was a risky strategic move. "In a sense, we're going for broke," he said in a press conference at his home church, Ebenezer Baptist in Atlanta, in January 1968. The March on Washington had been a risk, but it had been backed by the movement's proven record in awakening America's conscience to the injustices of segregation in cities like Birmingham. King could rest on no similar evidence of success in the North. There was no reason to think that King could mobilize public opinion against poverty with protests in Washington, D.C., if he hadn't been able to do so with protests against segregation in Chicago.

For King, however, the Poor People's Campaign was grounded in the same hope he had expressed on August 28,

1963. In a reminder of what he had envisioned for the nation at the March on Washington, King called the Poor People's Campaign his "last, greatest dream." King was convinced that God hated poverty, and would deliver the nation from poverty, just as God hated segregation in the South, and was in the process of delivering the nation from Jim Crow. He said in 1966, "God never intended for some of his children to live in inordinate, superfluous wealth while others live in abject, deadening poverty, and He has left enough and to spare for all of His children to have the basic necessities of life." In a recruiting tour for the Poor People's Campaign, he said: "[W]e are going to Washington to say that all of God's children are significant. We are going to Washington to say that we demand jobs and income because we are God's children and God loves all of us and he wants us to have the basic necessities of life." During a mass meeting in Selma, he implored the crowd, "Believe in your heart that you are somebody. Believe in your heart that you are God's children. And if you are a child of God, you aren't supposed to live in any shack. If you are a child of God, you aren't supposed to live in a slum where you don't have wall-to-wall carpet but wall-to-wall rats and roaches. If you are a child of God, if you are a child of God, you aren't supposed to be at the bottom of the economic ladder." King said in a sermon:

I'm not only concerned about streets flowing with milk and honey. I'm also concerned about the fact that about two-thirds of the peoples of this world go to bed hungry at night. And I will never be content until all of God's children have the basic necessities of life. It's wonderful to talk about the "New Jerusalem." But one day we will have to start talking about the New Atlanta, the New Chicago, the New New York, the New America. And I submit to you this morning, that any preacher who isn't concerned about this, isn't preaching the true gospel. It's a nice thing to talk about long white robes over yonder, but I want some clothes to wear right down here. It's all right to talk about silver slippers in another world, but I want some shoes to wear through the snow of Chicago.

Events after 1965 had shaken King's conviction that the nation would awaken to address poverty and Northern segregation as it had addressed segregation in the South. But he kept telling people that America simply had to come to its senses and repent. In a speech in 1966, he said, "I still have faith in the future. My brothers and sisters, I can still sing 'We shall overcome.' " In a speech in 1967, he recounted his experience of God's presence at his kitchen table during the Montgomery bus boycott, and then said, "I'm not worried about tomorrow. I get weary every now and then, the future looks difficult and dim, but I'm not worried about it ultimately because I have faith in God." He insisted that detailed demands for the Poor People's Campaign were not necessary: "I don't know what Jesus had as his demands other than 'Repent, for the Kingdom of God is at hand.' My demand in Washington is 'Repent, America!' "

In the months before his death, King kept trying to hold to this hope, but he was starting to sound less sure of himself. In a speech in November 1967, he defined true faith as an attitude that says "I know that the God that I worship is able to deliver me, but if not, I'm going on anyhow, I'm going to stand up for it anyway." He continued to use the "I have a dream" refrain, but he would preface it by recalling all the ways that he had seen his dream turn into a nightmare. On Christmas Eve in 1967, King concluded a sermon at Ebenezer by reminding his congregation what had happened to his dreams since the March on Washington:

> In 1963, on a sweltering August afternoon, we stood in Washington, D.C. and talked to the nation about many things. Toward the end of that afternoon, I tried to talk to the nation about a dream that I had had, and I must confess to you today that not long after talking about that dream I started seeing it turn into a nightmare.
>
> I remember the first time I saw that dream turn into a nightmare, just a few weeks after I had talked about it. It was when four beautiful, unoffending, innocent Negro girls were murdered in a church in Birmingham, Alabama.
>
> I watched that dream turn into a nightmare as I moved through the ghettos of the nation and saw my black brothers and sisters perishing on a lonely island of poverty in the midst of a vast ocean of material prosperity, and saw the nation doing nothing to grapple with the Negroes' problem of poverty.
>
> I saw that dream turn into a nightmare as I watched my black brothers and sisters in the midst of anger and understandable outrage, in the midst of their hurt, in the midst of their disappointment, turn to misguided riots to try to solve that problem.

I saw that dream turn into a nightmare as I watched the war in Vietnam escalating, and as I saw so-called military advisors, sixteen thousand strong, turn into fighting soldiers, until today over five hundred thousand American boys are fighting on Asian soil.

But he couldn't bear to end the sermon there. King's belief that God would deliver the movement had always been based less on experience than on theological conviction. His faith had surely been easier to sustain when the movement was winning. It didn't disappear when the movement seemed no longer able to produce victories, but his hope had become a heavy burden. He told a group of psychologists in September 1967, "These have been very difficult days for me, personally, days of frustration." He told reporters, "I'm tired now. I've been in this thing thirteen years now and I'm really tired." Roger Wilkins noticed at a meeting with King in February 1968 that King had become "a profoundly weary and wounded spirit," and that a "profound sadness" had descended upon him. King closed his 1967 Christmas Eve sermon at Ebenezer with a weary attempt to once more describe his vision for America:

Yes, I am personally the victim of deferred dreams, of blasted hopes, but in spite of that I close today by saying I still have a dream, because, you know, you can't give up in life. If you lose hope, somehow you lose that vitality that keeps life moving, you lose that courage to be, that quality that helps you go on in spite of all. And so today I still have a dream.

I have a dream that one day men will rise up and come to see that they are made to live together as brothers.

I still have a dream this morning that one day every Negro in this country, every colored person in the world, will be judged on the basis of the content of his character rather than the color of his skin, and every man will respect the dignity and worth of human personality.

I still have a dream that one day the idle industries of Appalachia will be revitalized, and the empty stomachs of Mississippi will be filled, and brotherhood will be more than a few words at the end of a prayer, but rather the first order of business on every legislative agenda.

I still have a dream today that one day justice will roll down like water, and righteousness like a mighty stream.

I still have a dream today that in all of our state houses and city halls men will be elected to go there who will do justly and love mercy and walk humbly with their God.

I still have a dream today that one day war will come to an end, that men will beat their swords into plowshares and their spears into pruning hooks, that nations will no longer rise up against nations, neither will they study war any more.

I still have a dream today that one day the lamb and the lion will lie down together and every man will sit under his own vine and fig tree and none shall be afraid.

I still have a dream today that one day every valley shall be exalted and every mountain and hill will be made low, the rough places will be made smooth and the crooked places straight, and the glory of the Lord shall be revealed, and all flesh shall see it together.

The ringing phrases and vivid metaphors were at the same emotional pitch as they had been four years earlier, but they now sounded far removed. His speech in 1963 had been soaring and hopeful, full of the faith that God would lead the movement to victory. "Free at last, free at last, thank God Almighty, we are free at last!" But in 1967, his professions of hope sounded strained: "I still have a dream, because, you know, you can't give up in life." In 1963, King had moved a national audience with visions of the movement's triumph: the "vicious racists" of Alabama would be no more; Mississippi would be "transformed into an oasis of freedom and justice." Four years later, he no longer held out these promises of the movement's success. The most particular vision in his Christmas Eve sermon—that the "idle industries of Appalachia will be revitalized, and the empty stomachs of Mississippi will be filled"—reflected his crusade against poverty, and King probably knew from his experiences in Chicago that this vision would not be realized in his lifetime. The "I have a dream" refrains are now completed with general, Biblical images of the reign of God's kingdom: the prophet Micah's instruction to "do justly and love mercy and walk humbly with their God"; the prophet Isaiah's promises of a time when people will "beat their swords into plow-shares," when the "lamb and the lion will lie down together," and when God's kingdom would come on earth. The only deliverance for America would be in God's eschatological age.

A few months after his Christmas Eve sermon, King traveled to Memphis to lend support to a sanitation workers' strike as part of a recruiting mission for the Poor People's Campaign. King knew that his field organizers had been unable to locate many people who were willing to go to Washington, and he was becoming pessimistic about whether the campaign would succeed. His growing desperation escaped during a recruiting tour of Mississippi, when he told the crowd, "Let us see that God has called us at this particular moment in history to save America. And if we don't save it, it's going straight to Hell." A second visit to Memphis gave him further reason to despair. On a protest march that King led through the city's downtown, a few of the younger protesters started to break store windows and loot goods along the march route. King tried to call off the march, but the riots spread through the city as angry youths threw rocks at police, who tear-gassed the rioters and shot and killed a young black man they thought was looting. King was despondent. "This is terrible," he told Ralph Abernathy, as he watched live television coverage of the riot, "Now we'll never get anybody to believe in nonviolence." "Maybe we'll just have to let violence have its chance," he said. "Maybe we'll have to let violence run its course. Maybe the people will listen to the voice of violence. They certainly won't listen to us."

One week later, on April 3, 1968, King delivered what would be his last public address. Before a packed crowd in the

Mason Temple in Memphis, he reeled off the high points of the movement: the sit-ins, the Birmingham campaign, the moment in 1963 when he got up to "tell America about a dream that I had had." Then he confessed to the audience:

> Well, I don't know what will happen now; we've got some difficult days ahead. But it really doesn't matter with me now, because I've been to the mountaintop. And I don't mind. Like anybody, I would like to live a long life—longevity has its place. But I'm not concerned about that now. I just want to do God's will. And He's allowed me to go up to the mountain. And I've looked over, and I've seen the Promised Land. I may not get there with you. But I want you to know tonight that we, as a people, will get to the Promised Land. And so I'm happy tonight; I'm not worried about anything; I'm not fearing any man. Mine eyes have seen the glory of the coming of the Lord.

King was still sure that the movement would reach the promised land, but he couldn't say how long it would take. Nearly five years after the March on Washington, it was no longer possible to declare with assurance that the movement would triumph. King's final act of prophetic vision was to hold to the hope that the day of victory would come, even as he was slowly beginning to realize that he would not live to see the fulfillment of all the dreams he had shown the nation on August 28, 1963. "I may not get there with you."

chapter six

Recovery

On April 4, 1968, the day after he delivered his "I've Been to the Mountaintop" speech, Martin Luther King, Jr., was assassinated. His coffin was carried through the Atlanta streets on a farm wagon pulled by a brace of mules, emblematic of his last crusade against poverty. An estimated 150,000 to 200,000 people, nearly as many as were present at the March on Washington, followed King's casket in a funeral cortege that lasted nearly three hours. Approximately 120 million people watched the proceedings on television. Flags across the nation were flown at half-mast. The United Nations flag was lowered. Schools, banks, stores, and stock exchanges were closed for the day.

Within a few weeks of King's death, the "I Have a Dream" speech had regained all the public visibility it had lost since 1963. Newspapers and magazines reprinted lengthy sections from the speech in commemorative articles about King's career. Members of Congress—no longer skittish about publicly praising King—recalled how moved they had been when they heard King speak at the march.

The attention given to "I Have a Dream" in retrospectives

of King's life was appropriate. The speech had marked a high point in King's career. Writing about King's life without mentioning his speech at the march would have been as absurd as writing about King without discussing the Montgomery bus boycott, the Selma-to-Montgomery march, or the sanitation workers' strike in Memphis. But King's speech at the march wasn't merely listed in tributes to King as one among many successes of his career. President Johnson, members of Congress, book publishers, and the media used the "I Have a Dream" speech as a mystical synecdoche for King's life (King didn't just work to eliminate racial prejudice, he "dreamed of an America without racial prejudice"). Eulogy after eulogy used the image of the "dream" as a shorthand for all that King had tried to accomplish. President Johnson told the nation on the day after King's death: "No words of ours—and no words of mine—can fill the void of the eloquent voice that has been stilled. But this I do believe deeply: The dream of Dr. Martin Luther King, Jr., has not died with him." *Life* magazine began its tribute article to King with: "Martin Luther King, Jr., lived by this exalted dream of freedom for his people, and he died in Memphis for daring to have it." The *Washington Post* editorial after King's assassination concluded:

> The dream of which he spoke so eloquently at the Lincoln Memorial in 1963 must seem tonight, to many of his sorrowing countrymen and embittered fellow citizens, farther than ever from fulfillment. But that shining vision and bright hope will yet prevail. It must be our resolve to go forward with a greater sense of ur-

gency to make a reality of his dream of racial equality and social justice.

By the middle of April 1968, a short biography called *I Have a Dream* and an unauthorized book of King quotations (also called *I Have a Dream*) had appeared for sale. *Life*'s excerpts from Coretta Scott King's book about her husband were titled "He Had a Dream."

The frequent references to King's speech immediately after his death occasionally seemed to be an attempt by politicians and the media to influence the perceived direction of black protest. Riots and looting struck 130 cities in the days after King's assassination, causing over 45 million dollars in property damage and resulting in 43 deaths and more than 20,000 arrests. Many politicians feared that more-violent black leaders would take over the civil rights movement in King's absence. Representative Jack Edwards of Alabama, who had been no ally of King's, said: "[A] vacuum has been created in the civil rights movement and it looks like Stokely Carmichael is moving into that void. . . . So whatever we thought of Martin Luther King, the assassin's bullet only made matters worse." Public statements by some of these leaders ratified this fear. "When white America killed Dr. King, she declared war on us," said Stokely Carmichael. "We have to retaliate for the deaths of our leaders." Floyd McKissick said that King's assassination proved that nonviolence was a "dead philosophy." In the weeks after King's death, quotations from "I Have a Dream" would have been more likely to remind these leaders that King had never given up his faith in nonviolence than would quotations from speeches at the end of his life, when he was becoming frustrated at the inability of non-violent protest to awaken the nation's conscience on poverty and Northern segregation.

There were still enough reminders of King's post-1963 career in the first years after his death that the "I Have a Dream" speech did not immediately become the public's only memory of King's legacy. The Poor People's Campaign—King's "last, greatest dream"—went forward without him. Shortly after the assassination, Ralph Abernathy, the new head of the SCLC, announced that the Poor People's Campaign would bring hundreds of impoverished Americans to Washington, D.C., to camp on the Mall in a shantytown called "Resurrection City" until Congress agreed to their demands. (The SCLC considered naming the encampment "Dream City," but rejected the title as too ethereal.) Once more, officials in Washington reacted with hysteria at the prospect of being lobbied by the nation's disadvantaged citizens. Attorney General Ramsey Clark described the capital's mood as "Paranoia, literally." Southern members of Congress who had railed against civil rights shifted their attacks to welfare recipients, saying that the recruits for the campaign were "being told to go to Washington one night and get on welfare the next day."

The Poor People's Campaign began well, as it had bene-fitted from an outpouring of support at King's death. Ralph Abernathy drove two mules named "Eastland" and "Stennis," after Mississippi's two segregationist senators, in the lead wagon of a mule train carrying marchers from the South. Demonstrators from across the nation arrived in Washington, D.C., during the month of May and moved into A-frame huts—some bearing stickers that read "I HAVE A DREAM"—that had been constructed on sixteen acres of the Mall. But within a few weeks, Resurrection City had become a debacle. Steady rains mired parts of the settlement in mud, and an odor of raw sewage pervaded the camp. There was mistrust and tension among different racial groups in the settlement, and several muggings and assaults occurred within the camp's borders.

The SCLC tried to salvage the Poor People's Campaign with a climactic Washington rally entitled "Solidarity Day." Comparisons to the March on Washington abounded: Ralph Abernathy asked for a massive turnout at Solidarity Day to show that America still believed in the spirit of the 1963 march and had the will to "redeem the national dream." He said: "It is sad for us to say today that the dream has not been fulfilled. On that day we felt that America had great promise for her poor people. Today we can see that that promise was empty." Police and press estimated that only 50,000 to 100,000 people showed up for Solidarity Day, as compared with the 250,000 that had marched on Washington in 1963. Coretta Scott King recited portions of the "I Have a Dream" speech for the crowd, but King's words no longer seemed appropriate. Observers noticed that the mood of the assembly was far different than it had been five years earlier. One journalist later wrote: "Few seemed optimistic about the rally's chances of having much impact. One got the impression they came out of a sense of duty, and once there they were a little bored." By the end of June, Resurrection City was abandoned, to be bull-dozed by the D.C. police.

Another of King's legacies had a better record. A bill pro-hibiting racial discrimination in housing, which had broken a filibuster shortly before King's assassination, was rapidly passed by the House and signed by President Johnson one week after King's death as the Civil Rights Act of 1968. Many members of Congress saw the bill as a monument to King's last crusades against poverty and Northern segregation. The fair housing provisions of the statute were the first significant federal legislation mandating freedom from housing discrimination, the issue that had motivated King in Chicago.

Over the next decades, there were fewer reminders of King's campaigns against poverty and segregation in the North. The Civil Rights Act of 1968 was the last major civil rights legislation that Congress enacted until the early 1990s. The SCLC, after its conspicuous failure with the Poor People's Campaign, regrouped sufficiently to assist in a handful of successful union-organizing efforts but never regained the public profile it had enjoyed under King's leadership.

With few images of King's later career to compete with, the "I Have a Dream" speech gradually came to dominate public memory of King's legacy. Members of Congress regularly quoted the speech in tributes to King during the 1970s. When President Carter awarded the Presidential Medal of Freedom posthumously to King on July 11, 1977, the citation read: "From the pain and exhaustion of his fight to fulfill the promises of our founding fathers for our humblest citizens, he wrung his eloquent statement of his dream for America. He made our nation stronger because he made it better. His dream sustains us yet." In 1979, an editorial in the *Washington Post* called King's "I Have a Dream" speech "the speech by which he is best remembered."

There were good reasons for King's speech at the march to

become America's most enduring memory of King's career. The speech had been glorious, with King's musical delivery, the address's poetic, Biblical language, and its visionary refrains of "I have a dream" and "Let freedom ring." King's speech also had an irresistible metaphorical attraction. It seemed fitting that a martyred visionary like King would be remembered with the poetic image of a "dream." The "I have a dream" phrase itself was short, simple, and easy to remember. "The dream," "he dreamed," "his dream" and other variants proved to be useful hooks for authors of tributes to King, who could add rhetorical flair to their writing by referring to King's "dream."

But there was also an unappealing side to the memorialization of King in terms of the "I Have a Dream" speech. The constant quotation of King's speech at the march in the decades after his death often seemed to be shot through with an eagerness to forget King's post-1965 career. Even though King's speech at the march condemned Northern as well as Southern segregation (with, for example, his reference to the exile of black Americans on a "lonely island of poverty," and his statements, "We cannot be satisfied as long as the Negro's basic mobility is from a smaller ghetto to a larger one"; "We cannot be satisfied so long as a Negro in Mississippi cannot vote and a Negro in New York believes he has nothing for which to vote"), the speech was, for many Americans, emblematic of King's career as a crusader against Jim Crow in the South. King delivered the speech in a year when he was engaged in protest campaigns in Southern states, and the visions in the "I have a dream" and "Let freedom ring" sections of the speech were primarily about the triumph of the Southern civil rights movement. By talking about King's speech at the march, politicians and the media could underscore how the nation had responded to King's calls for the end of Jim Crow by enacting the Civil Rights Act in 1964 and the Voting Rights Act in 1965. This was a much more pleasant subject to remember than King's defeat in Chicago and the collapse of the Poor People's Campaign. Remembering King through the "I Have a Dream" speech allowed the nation to tell itself a comforting but inaccurate story about King's legacy: King had called on America from the Lincoln Memorial to abolish Jim Crow, the nation had done so, and King had died victorious. The constant repetition of refrains from King's speech at the march drowned out memories of other speeches King had given since 1963. The reproduction of photographs of King addressing the crowds below the Lincoln Memorial blotted out images of King in Chicago or at the march in Memphis. King's later career was not explicitly repudiated, but it was overwhelmed by the attention paid to his successful campaigns against Jim Crow.

At some point in the late 1970s or early 1980s, the "I Have a Dream" speech came to be known not just as the defining moment of King's career, but as an address that gave voice to America's most fundamental ideals—the oratorical equivalent of the Declaration of Independence. This was a surprising development, considering that most politicians would not even quote King's speech during his lifetime. It is difficult to mark with any certainty exactly when "I Have a Dream" came to be regarded so highly, but a useful reference point is the enactment of the Martin Luther King, Jr., national holiday legislation in 1983. In order for King's speech at the march to be appreciated as an expression of America's most cherished values, King himself had to be accepted as an American hero, which was impossible until decades after his death. In 1968, when Representative John Conyers first introduced a bill to commemorate King's birthday with a national holiday, hatred of King in Congress was still so hot that the bill had no chance of passage. Six days after King's death, Representative William Tuck from Virginia said on the House floor that King "fomented discord and strife between the races," and implied that King had gotten what was coming to him: "He who sows the seed of sin shall reap and harvest a whirlwind of evil." Variations on these themes, supplemented with charges of communism and anti-Americanism, appeared in congressional speeches through the 1970s. In the 1979 congressional hearings on the King holiday bill, several witnesses dredged up allegations that King had been controlled by communists. One speaker claimed that he "deliberately brought violence to America's streets." Another witness said: "If this measure is passed honoring Martin Luther King, we may as well take down the Stars and Stripes that fly over this building and replace it with a Red flag."

The King holiday bill finally passed in 1983, but only after overcoming a malicious anti-King crusade led by Senator Jesse Helms. Senator Helms threatened a filibuster of the bill and distributed to his Senate colleagues a sheaf of Hoover-era FBI documents detailing King's alleged communist sympathies. Senator Daniel Moynihan threw the papers to the floor during one of the Senate debates, calling them a "packet of filth." Helms began a crusade to open the remaining FBI files on King, which had been sealed by a federal judge, on the theory that those files would enable him to assess whether King was a communist—even though the sealed files would have revealed little information about King's political beliefs because they consisted mainly of transcripts of recordings from bugged hotel rooms and personal telephones. When President Reagan was asked at a press conference what he thought about Helms's allegations that King was a communist, he replied: "Well, we'll know in about thirty-five years, won't we?"—an inapposite reference to the sealed FBI files. He told reporters that he would have preferred an informal commemorative day for King rather than a federally recognized holiday, but "since they seem bent on making it a national holiday, I believe the symbolism of that day is important enough that I will sign that legislation when it reaches my desk." The bill was approved by a 78-22 Senate vote in October 1983 and signed into law by President Reagan.

The enactment of the King holiday legislation marked the completion of a gradual transformation in the national perception of King and the civil rights movement. Twenty years after King's death, nearly everyone in America recognized that King and the freedom movement's veterans had been responsible for one of the greatest peaceful revolutions in American history. King was no longer a suspected communist or a demagogue, but a national hero on a par with Abraham Lincoln and George Washington. With this acknowledgment of King as a great American leader came the acceptance of the "I Have a Dream" speech as a statement of fundamental American values. Every time America undergoes a great social revolution, some speech or document comes to be accepted as the definitive expression of the spirit of that revolution. The

Constitution and the Declaration of Independence interpret the Founding; the Gettysburg Address interprets the Civil War. King's "I Have a Dream" speech became the definitive statement of the meaning of the civil rights revolution. During the 1983 King holiday debates, Representative Wright said:

> It was 20 years ago this month that Martin Luther King stood in the shadow of the Lincoln Memorial and proclaimed his now-famous phrase, "I have a dream." Is it not the same dream to which this Nation proclaims its allegiance enshrined in the Jeffersonian words, "All men are created equal"?

Senator Bill Bradley said something similar in the Senate:

> The dream he shared that hot August afternoon in 1963 on the steps of the Lincoln Memorial—the dream he gave his life for—was a dream shared by millions of Americans black and white alike. It was a dream that challenged America to live up to its ideals, to rise above the assumed rights of prejudice and to assert the inherent rights of humanity once again, just as 100 years earlier Abraham Lincoln had urged Americans to rise above the assumed rights of property and to assert the inherent rights of humanity. . . . He preached that America was still an idea becoming—becoming what its people would have it be. And he labored for an America in which men and women were not judged by color but stood equal in the eyes and practices of the State just as they do in the eyes of God. His message

told us what we knew, that America was incomplete without addressing the injustice, festering in our national soul, of a dual society of black and white. But he believed that even in the face of blatant discrimination, America—its institutions and its people—had the capacity for righting the wrong course. His message offered redemption from our original sin. His message spawned the civil rights revolution of the 1960s—the 1964 Civil Rights Act, 1965 Voting Rights Act, the 1968 Fair Housing Act. These laws secured long-withheld civil rights for black Americans but they also changed the attitudes of white Americans, and led to a legitimate moral awakening, and made America a better place.

But by the time that "I Have a Dream" was recognized as one of the greatest addresses in American history, its prophetic message had largely been lost. King's speech had originally been so powerful partly because his visions of a redeemed America were so sharply at odds with the realities of segregation in 1963: the murder of Medgar Evers, the beating of Fannie Lou Hamer, Bull Connor's police dogs and fire hoses. In the years after King's assassination, these obvious brutalities of segregation were eliminated. Much of King's speech started to sound almost anachronistic, with its references to the "governor having his lips dripping with the words of interposition and nullification," or the "children stripped of their selfhood and robbed of their dignity by signs stating 'for whites only.' " King's visions of America's renewal never completely lost their ability to inspire awe. Many of the speech's lines remained uncomfortably relevant for decades, such as King's reference to protesters "staggered by the winds of police brutality." But after Jim Crow segregation had been dismantled, the speech started to sound more and more like a historical artefact, describing a past of racial injustice that had since been overcome, than a prophetic address about God's future deliverance of America.

This seeming anachronism of King's speech at the march was probably part of its appeal for politicians and the media in the 1980s. By constantly quoting the "I Have a Dream" speech, and de-emphasizing most of King's other speeches, King's legacy could be limited to issues that were matters of history. In 1983, there was no serious disagreement that Jim Crow segregation had been backward and immoral. There was no similar consensus on the issues that had preoccupied King toward the end of his life: residential segregation, inequalities in education, and poverty among Americans of all races. Poverty and Northern segregation still existed in the early 1980s, and it was easier to ignore King's speeches and campaigns on these issues than it was to admit that King would have been dissatisfied with the unfinished state of his crusades. Nearly any of King's speeches after 1965 would have been as explosively controversial in the 1980s as they had been during King's lifetime, such as his Gandhi Memorial Lecture at Howard University in November 1966:

People talk about the white backlash. . . . Now, my answer to this question is that there is really no white backlash, because that gives the impression that the nation had decided it was going to solve this problem and then there was a step back because of developments in the civil rights movement. Now, the fact is that America has been backlashing on the civil rights question for centuries now. . . .

[T]he backlash is merely the surfacing of prejudices, of hostilities, of hatreds and fears that already existed and they are just now starting to open. And this must be faced factually. The fact is that demands are being made now which the nation was not willing to yield to in the very beginning.

Public accommodations did not cost the nation anything; the right to vote did not cost the nation anything. Now we are grappling with basic class issues between the privileged and the underprivileged. In order to solve this problem, not only will it mean the restructuring of American society but it will cost the nation something, and the backlash is just responding to the fact that now we are saying everybody ought to have a job and everybody ought to have a guaranteed annual income and everybody ought to have the right to live in a decent house wherever he wants to live and everybody ought to have an adequate education. This is the problem—that there are those who are not willing to have this come about.

Or this speech, given in Georgia just a few weeks before his assassination:

And there is no point in our going around acting like we are free. We are still not free, we are still facing slavery. And you know why we aren't free? Because we are poor. We are poor.

But calling attention to this critical legacy would have made it impossible to celebrate King as an American hero. Figures of present political controversy do not have their birthdays commemorated with federal holidays. President Reagan's statement when he signed the King holiday bill in 1983 was silent about any aspect of King's career that could challenge modern America. His remarks mentioned the bus boycott, the Nobel Prize, and the "I Have a Dream" speech—and then cut right away to King's assassination in 1968, erasing King's entire career after 1964. In the year in which King was finally given his due recognition as an American hero, his legacy was sealed off so that it was safely in the past.

By the early 1980s, the "I Have a Dream" speech had become omnipresent in American consciousness. It was excerpted in countless American studies textbooks, reprinted on posters sold in college bookstores, and emblazoned on pins and T-shirts sold at civil rights rallies. King's address found its way into hip-hop songs. On King's birthday, radio stations and television networks broadcast clips of King speaking from the Lincoln Memorial. In political debates over civil rights, the "I Have a Dream" speech became one of the few documents that nearly all sides could agree expressed the nation's aims. It became impossible to repudiate King's speech without removing oneself from the mainstream public debate on civil rights. Freedom movements around the world quoted King's words. In Nelson Mandela's victory speech after South Africa's first multiracial elections, he declared that black Africans were "Free at last." Protesters in Tiananmen Square held up billboards with pictures of King and the words, "I have a dream."

In the 1980s and 1990s, the history of King's speech at the march took a peculiar turn. Some politicians and writers seized on King's line about his children being judged not by the color of their skin but by the content of their character—a line that referred to the end of white racist assumptions of black inferiority—as a justification for opposing affirmative action programs that had been designed to benefit blacks. This use of the "I Have a Dream" speech was picked up in the 1980s by several Reagan administration officials and by President Reagan himself, who said in 1986, "We are committed to a society in which all men and women have equal opportunities to succeed, and so we oppose the use of quotas. We want a colorblind society, a society that, in the words of Dr. King, judges people not on 'the color of their skin but by the content of their character.' " The anti-affirmative-action quotation of the "content of their character" line reached its highest point of public visibility in the mid-1990s, during the battles over state referenda banning affirmative action. In 1996, supporters of Proposition 209 ran an advertisement on California television stations featuring a clip of King delivering the "content of their character" line, followed by a voice-over saying, "Martin Luther King was right. . . . Let's get rid of all discrimination." In 1998, Washington State radio talkshow host John Carlson invoked this line from King's speech in the campaign to pass the anti-affirmative-action Initiative 200. Hundreds of newspaper editorials and law review articles used King's words to explain their opposition to affirmative action. By the mid-1990s, the most common ways in which most Americans heard the "I Have a Dream" speech were either during celebrations of King's birthday or in editorials, speeches, or political ads against affirmative action.

King's supporters immediately criticized this use of the "I Have a Dream" speech. John Lewis said the Proposition 209 advertisement was "almost obscene," Jesse Jackson called it "vulgar and blasphemous," and the Republican party pulled the ad under threat of a copyright infringement lawsuit from the King estate. The objection of King's allies wasn't just that the phrase that was most frequently quoted by opponents of affirmative action was not a reference to affirmative action programs, which did not exist in any widespread way in 1963. Their objection was that there was good evidence from King's speeches and writings that he would have supported a variety of race-based programs benefitting black Americans to compensate for centuries of racial discrimination. Even before the March on Washington, King had praised the Indian government's efforts to end the caste system, not just by enforcing antidiscrimination laws but by enacting preferential measures to give equal opportunities in employment to the lower castes. King actively supported some forms of compensatory preferential treatment for black Americans. He said in his testimony before the National Advisory Commission on Civil Disorders in 1967:

[T]he nation must not only radically readjust its attitude toward the Negro and the compelling present, but must incorporate in its planning some compensatory consideration for the handicaps he has inherited from the past. It is impossible to create a formula for the future which does not take into account that our society has been doing something special against the Negro for hundreds of years. How then can he be absorbed into the mainstream of American life if we do not do something special for him now in order to balance the equation and equip him to compete on a just and equal basis? Whenever this issue of compensatory or preferential treatment for the Negro is raised, some of our friends recoil in horror. The Negro should be granted equality, they argue, but he should ask nothing more. On the surface this appears reasonable, but it is not realistic, for it is obvious that if a man is entered at the starting line in a race 300 years after another man, the first would have to perform some impossible feat in order to catch up with his fellow runner.

Even aside from King's express support for compensatory programs for blacks, there was something incongruous about using one of King's speeches as a reason to oppose affirmative action. King's career was devoted to breaking down the racial caste system that kept blacks in subjugation. When Jim Crow segregation—the most obvious manifestation of this caste system—had been eliminated, King turned his attention to its subtler forms: segregation of cities into "white" and "black" neighborhoods, underfunding of schools in black areas, racial discrimination in employment. Many modern-day defenders of affirmative action programs see them as mechanisms for breaking down the subtle forms of racial caste that King spent the last years of his life fighting against.

The ability of the "I Have a Dream" speech to highlight King's early career at the expense of his later career accounts for the tone of impatience and betrayal that often appears when modern-day supporters of King's agenda talk about the speech. Julian Bond said in 1986 that commemorations of King seemed to "focus almost entirely on Martin Luther King the dreamer, and not on Martin King the antiwar activist, not on Martin King the challenger of the economic order, not on Martin King the opponent of apartheid, not on the complete Martin Luther King." Andrew Young said that when members of Congress voted for the King holiday, "they voted for Martin's 'I have a dream' speech. They didn't vote for his anti-Vietnam speech, or his challenge to Lyndon Johnson about ending poverty." In a 1983 sermon that Jesse Jackson preached at Ebenezer Baptist, he criticized the way in which King was being distorted into a "nonthreatening dreamer": "That so-called 'I have a dream' speech. . . . was not a speech about dreamers and dreaming. It was a speech describing nightmare conditions." Vincent Harding, another King associate, published an article in the *Union Seminary Quarterly Review* in 1986, when the first King birthday would be celebrated, about the public perception of King:

> Somehow, it seemed that the furthest most Americans could go with King was to that magnificent day in August, 1963, before the Lincoln Memorial, when he

spoke of his "dream." (Of course, he also pointed that day to "the unspeakable horrors of police brutality" inflicted on black people, and said he refused to be satisfied "as long as the Negro's basic mobility is from a smaller ghetto to a larger one." But it was easier to deal with the dream of an America where black and white children would hold hands in unity.) As a result, in most of the celebrations of King's life which prepared the way for this month's inauguration of the official national holiday, the dominant image has been that of the great orator at the Mall, the dreamer of interracial harmony, the stirring and mildly challenging preacher.

One King scholar, Michael Eric Dyson, has proposed a ten-year moratorium on reading or listening to the "I Have a Dream" speech, in the hopes that America will then discover the rest of King's legacy.

This proposal effectively concedes that King's magnificent address cannot be recovered from the misuse and overquotation it has suffered since his death. But it is not clear that this is so. Even now, upon hearing the speech, one is struck by the many forms of King's genius. Many people can still remember the first time they heard "I Have a Dream," and they tend to speak of that memory with the reverence reserved for a religious experience. At the very least, reflecting on the "I Have a Dream" speech should be an opportunity to be grateful for the astonishing transformation of America that the freedom movement wrought. In just under a decade, the civil rights movement brought down a system of segregation that had stood essentially unaltered since

Reconstruction. King's dreams of an America free from racial discrimination are still some distance away, but it is astounding how far the nation has come since that hot August day in 1963. Jim Crow segregation in the South has been dismantled; there are no longer "Whites Only" signs; segregationist governors do not try to prevent black children from entering public schools. Toward the end of his life, King preached a sermon entitled "Ingratitude," in which he called ingratitude "one of the greatest of all sins," because one "fail[s] to realize his dependence on others." The annual Martin Luther King, Jr., holiday is properly also a day of national thanksgiving, a time for the nation to recognize the immense debt it owes to King and the thousands of heroes of the civil rights movement for saving the soul of America.

The contribution of "I Have a Dream" to America's transformation was not apparent at first. King's speech did not instantly alter anything in the South. In the days just after the March on Washington, Alabama did not become integrated, and Mississippi did not become an oasis of freedom and justice. King's address at the march did less practical good than, for example, nearly any SNCC field secretary in the deep South. But on August 28, 1963, King began the long-overdue process of changing America's idea of itself. He gave the nation a vocabulary to express what was happening in the civil rights revolution. We must not be a segregated nation, but an integrated one. We must not be a nation enslaved to the sin of racial discrimination, but a nation where all people are free. This transformation in America's self-conception has happened only over many years, as King's speech at the march has slowly remade the American imagination:

For as the rain cometh down, and the snow from heaven, and returneth not thither, but watereth the earth, and maketh it bring forth and bud, that it may give seed to the sower, and bread to the eater:

So shall my word be that goeth forth out of my mouth: it shall not return unto me void, but it shall accomplish that which I please, and it shall prosper in the thing whereto I sent it. (Isaiah 55:10–11)

Forty years after it was first delivered, the "I Have a Dream" speech has helped to change our conception of America so completely that it is no longer possible to argue that America should be anything less than the redeemed nation King envisioned on August 28, 1963.

Perhaps today, when Jim Crow segregation has long been abolished, and no reasonable person argues that it was ever a just or moral system, King's speech at the march does not have the same prophetic impact that it once did. But King did not definitively articulate his vision for America on August 28, 1963. In his Christmas Eve sermon at Ebenezer in 1967, he delivered another "I Have a Dream" speech, in which he envisioned a future America that God had delivered from poverty, as well as from racial discrimination:

I still have a dream that one day the idle industries of Appalachia will be revitalized, and the empty stomachs of Mississippi will be filled, and brotherhood will be more than a few words at the end of a prayer, but rather the first order of business on every legislative agenda.

In the days just after King's assassination, his closest associates recounted among themselves a verse from Genesis: "Behold, this dreamer cometh. Come now therefore, and let us slay him . . . and we shall see what will become of his dreams." Andrew Young remembers that this verse "sort of gave us our marching orders." After King's assassination, Young thought, the burden had been placed on those who remained to see that his dreams were fulfilled.

Forty years later, that burden is still ours. At the end of his life, King started to realize that America would not be free from all its evils in his lifetime. But he never abandoned his faith that God would one day lead America to the promised land. King's legacy to our country is the gift of prophecy: a vision of what a redeemed America might look like, and a hope that this redemption will one day come to pass. The arc of the moral universe is indeed long, but it bends toward justice. This dream can sustain us yet.

Notes

Abbreviations used in source notes

1 King Papers   *The Papers of Martin Luther King, Jr.,* volume 1: "Called To Serve, January 1929–June 1951" (ed. Clayborne Carson et al.) (Berkeley: University of California Press, 1992)

2 King Papers   *The Papers of Martin Luther King, Jr.,* volume 2: "Rediscovering Precious Values, July 1951–November 1955" (ed. Clayborne Carson et al.) (Berkeley: University of California Press, 1994)

3 King Papers   *The Papers of Martin Luther King, Jr.,* volume 3: "Birth of a New Age, December 1955–December 1956" (ed. Clayborne Carson et al.) (Berkeley: University of California Press, 1997)

4 King Papers   *The Papers of Martin Luther King, Jr.,* volume 4: "Symbol of the Movement, January 1957–December 1958" (ed. Clayborne Carson et al.) (Berkeley: University of California Press, 2000)

AA   *Baltimore Afro-American*

AC   *Atlanta Constitution*

ADW   *Atlanta Daily World*

AN   *Amsterdam News*

MLK-Atlanta   Martin Luther King, Jr., Papers; Martin Luther King, Jr., Center for Nonviolent Social Change, Atlanta, Georgia

MLK-BU   Martin Luther King, Jr., Papers; Mugar Library, Boston University, Boston, Massachusetts

NAACP	NAACP Papers, Library of Congress, Washington, D.C.
NYC	*New York Courier*
NYT	*New York Times*
PC	*Pittsburgh Courier*
WP	*Washington Post*

Prologue

1–2 Fewer than one-half of one percent of black children: Southern Education Reporting Service, *A Statistical Summary, State by State, of School Segregation-Desegregation in the Southern and Border Area from 1954 to the Present* (Nashville: Southern Education Reporting Service, 1965), p. 29.

  1 Not a single black child: Southern Education Reporting Service, *A Statistical Summary*, p. 29.

1–2 Voter registration statistics: United States Commission on Civil Rights, *Civil Rights '63: Report of the United States Commission on Civil Rights* (Washington, D.C.: United States GPO, 1963), pp. 14–15.

  2 "FRDUM FOOF SPETGH": *United States v. Louisiana,* 225 F. Supp. 353, 384 (E.D. La. 1963).

  2 shut down the registration offices: *United States v. Alabama,* 192 F. Supp. 677, 679 (M.D. Ala. 1961).

  2 Madison Parish, Louisiana: *United States v. Ward,* 222 F. Supp. 617, 618 (W.D. La. 1963).

  2 Wilcox County, Alabama: *United States v. Logue,* 344 F.2d 290, 291 (5th Cir. 1965).

  2 Panola County, Mississippi: *United States v. Duke,* 332 F.2d 759, 760 (5th Cir. 1964).

  2 *Strauder v. West Virginia:* 100 U.S. 303 (1879).

  3 picked jurors based on personal acquaintance: *Whitus v. Georgia,* 385 U.S. 545 (1967).

  3 Mitchell County, Georgia: *Whitus v. Balkcom,* 333 F.2d 496, 498 (5th Cir. 1964).

3   Lynching statistics: Robert L. Zangrando, *The NAACP Crusade Against Lynching* (1980), pp. 6–7, tab. 2 (figures are for all lynchings nationwide).

3   George Lee and Lamar Smith murders: Henry Hampton and Steve Fayer, *Voices of Freedom: An Oral History of the Civil Rights Movement from the 1950s through the 1980s* (New York: Bantam, 1990), p. 2; *Jet,* May 26, 1955, pp. 8–9; *Jet,* Aug. 25, 1955, pp. 3–4.

4   *Shelley v. Kraemer:* 334 U.S. 1 (1948).

4   Residential segregation in the North: Douglas S. Massey and Nancy A. Denton, *American Apartheid: Segregation and the Making of the Underclass* (Cambridge: Harvard University Press, 1993); Arnold R. Hirsch, *Making the Second Ghetto: Race and Housing in Chicago, 1940–1960* (Cambridge, NY: Cambridge University Press, 1983).

4   Black ownership of retail outlets and banks: Andrew F. Brimmer, "The Negro in the National Economy," in *Race and Poverty: The Economics of Discrimination* (John F. Kain, ed.) (Englewood Cliffs, NJ: Prentice-Hall, 1969), pp. 89, 90.

4   Income statistics: U.S. Census Bureau, "Historical Income Tables—People (Table) P-2, Race and Hispanic Origin of People by Median Income and Sex: 1947 to 1998," published May 25, 1999; *www.census.gov/hhes/income/histinc/p02.htm.*

4   Unemployment and arrest statistics: Hugh Davis Graham, *Civil Rights and the Presidency: Race and Gender in American Politics, 1960–1972* (New York: Oxford University Press, 1992), p. 13; William H. Harris, *The Harder We Run: Black Workers Since the Civil War* (New York: Oxford University Press, 1982), pp. 123–46.

4   "other-cheek-turners": James Patterson, *Grand Expectations: The United States, 1945–1974* (New York: Oxford University Press, 1996), p. 382.

4   Integration of sports: Patterson, *Grand Expectations,* pp. 382–83.

4   President's cabinet, Federal Reserve Board, New York Stock Exchange, mayors: Gerald David Jaynes and Robin M. Williams, Jr.,

eds., *A Common Destiny: Blacks and American Society* (Washington, D.C.: National Academy Press, 1989), pp. 68–69 (chart: "Selected Black Firsts in American Society: 1945–1982").

5   Nathan Glazer and Daniel Moynihan: Patterson, *Grand Expectations*, p. 384. The authors changed this sentence in the second edition of *Beyond the Melting Pot*.

5   "vivid memories" of King's interest in the prophets: James Bennett Pritchard to Coretta Scott King, Feb. 22, 1987, in 1 King Papers, p. 162.

6   King's essay on Jeremiah: King, "The Significant Contributions of Jeremiah to Religious Thought," Sept. 14–Nov. 24, 1948, in 1 King Papers, p. 194.

6   King's essay on the concept of religion: "A Conception and Impression of Religion from Dr. W. K. Wright's Book Entitled *A Student's Philosophy of Religion,*" Dec. 19, 1950, in 1 King Papers, p. 389.

6   King's activism in Montgomery: King, *Stride Toward Freedom: The Montgomery Story* (New York: Harper & Row, 1958), pp. 30–34.

6   Refused NAACP Presidency: King, *Stride Toward Freedom*, p. 56.

7   "Well, if you think I can render some service, I will": Ralph David Abernathy, *And the Walls Came Tumbling Down* (New York: Harper & Row, 1989; New York: HarperPerennial, 1990), p. 148.

7   King's preparations for Holt Street address: King, *Stride Toward Freedom*, pp. 58–60.

7   King and Abernathy arriving at the church: Abernathy, *And the Walls*, pp. 149–50.

8   King's speech at Holt Street: King, "MIA Mass Meeting at Holt Street Baptist Church," Dec. 5, 1955, in 3 King Papers, p. 72. The program for the evening is in 3 King Papers, p. 68, and Abernathy, *And the Walls*, pp. 150–51.

8   "Open your mouth and God will speak for you": King, *Stride Toward Freedom*, p. 63.

8   Supreme Court decision ending the Montgomery bus boycott: *Gayle v. Browder,* 352 U.S. 903 (1956).

9   "The Red Sea has opened for us": King, "Address to MIA Mass

Meeting at Holt Street Baptist Church," Nov. 14, 1956, in 3 *King Papers*, p. 433.

9   Supreme Court decision prohibiting segregation in interstate bus terminals: *Boynton v. Virginia*, 364 U.S. 454 (1960).

9   Senator Javits quotation from Edward Murrow: Congressional Record, May 25, 1961, p. 8918 (statement of Sen. Jacob Javits, R-NY).

10 Southern cities desegregating buses: Adam Fairclough, *To Redeem the Soul of America: The Southern Christian Leadership Conference and Martin Luther King, Jr.* (Athens: University of Georgia Press, 1987), pp. 42–43.

10 Pritchett and "nonviolence" in Albany: David L. Lewis, *King: A Critical Biography* (New York: Praeger, 1970), p. 151; Laurie Pritchett in *Voices of Freedom*, pp. 105–6.

10–11 Beatings of Marion King and C. B. King: Howard Zinn, *Albany: A Study in National Responsibility* (Atlanta: Southern Regional Council, 1962), pp. 11–13.

12 President Kennedy's reaction to Birmingham photographs: Arthur M. Schlesinger, Jr., *A Thousand Days: John F. Kennedy in the White House* (Boston: Houghton Mifflin, 1965), p. 959.

12 "great victory" for the movement: *NYT*, May 11, 1963, p. 8.

12 *New York Times* stories about civil rights: Taylor Branch, *Pillar of Fire: America in the King Years, 1963–1965* (New York: Simon & Schuster, 1998; New York: Touchstone, 1999), p. 87.

12 Civil rights demonstrations after Birmingham: Taylor Branch, *Parting the Waters: America in the King Years, 1954–1963* (New York: Simon & Schuster, 1988), p. 825.

12 Conversation between Carl Albert and President Kennedy: Branch, *Pillar of Fire*, p. 115.

12–13 King's plans for demonstration in Washington: FBI 100-106670, Memorandum July 22, 1963, regarding King phone conversation with Stanley Levison, June 1, 1963, p. 9.

13 "Mr. President, sign it": Letter from Aubrey Williams to King (n.d.), Bayard Rustin Papers.

13   King had assented to the use of his name: Letter from Clarence Jones to A. Philip Randolph, May 6, 1963, Bayard Rustin papers.

13   Whitney Young had declined: Letter from Whitney Young to A. Philip Randolph, Apr. 30, 1963, Bayard Rustin papers.

14   Exchange between Wilkins and King: James Farmer, *Lay Bare the Heart: An Autobiography of the Civil Rights Movement* (New York: Arbor House, 1985; New York: Plume, 1985), p. 216.

14   at the risk of seeming outside the mainstream of civil rights activism: Jervis Anderson, *Bayard Rustin: Troubles I've Seen* (New York: HarperCollins, 1997; Berkeley: University of California Press, 1998), pp. 240–41; interview with James Forman, Dec. 17, 2001.

14   Announcement of March plans: *NYT,* June 12, 1963, p. 25.

15   Timing of President Kennedy's invitation: David Garrow, *Bearing the Cross: Martin Luther King, Jr., and the Southern Christian Leadership Conference* (New York: William Morrow, 1986; New York: Vintage, 1988), p. 271.

15   Meeting with President Kennedy: Schlesinger, *Thousand Days,* pp. 968–71.

16   Reasons for selecting August 28: Interview with Bayard Rustin (Herbert Allen), July 27–28, 1983, Bayard Rustin papers; interview with Walter Fauntroy, July 10, 2001.

16   King on goals of the march: King, "Statement After Negro Summit Meeting," July 2, 1963, MLK-Atlanta.

17   Compared to a congressional campaign: *Nation,* Sept. 7, 1963, pp. 104–7.

17   Marshals and FBI's reaction: *AA,* Aug. 31, 1963, p. 2; SAC New York to Director, Aug. 14, 1963, FBI 157-970-210: SAC Washington Field Office to Director, Aug. 21, 1963, FBI 157-970-541.

17   March plans: Gentile, *March on Washington,* pp. 46–56; *Nation,* Sept. 7, 1963; interview with Rachelle Horowitz, Oct. 22, 2001.

18   Department of Justice team: Interview with John Douglas, July 9, 2001; interview with John Reilly, October 25, 2001; interview with Burke Marshall, Feb. 16, 2000; interview with Nick Katzenbach, July 27, 2001; interview with John Nolan, Aug. 15, 2001.

18 Department of Justice paid for the toilets: Interview with Burke Marshall, Feb. 16, 2000.

18 "No dogs": Thomas Gentile, *March on Washington: August 28, 1963* (Washington, D.C.: New Day, 1983), pp. 63–64: Brennan to Sullivan, Aug. 26, 1963, FBI 157-970-illegible.

18–19 FBI surveillance of March: Director to SAC Albany, Aug. 8, 1963, FBI 157-970-89; interview with John Reilly, Oct. 25, 2001.

19 Willis Barber Shop: SAC New Haven to Director, Aug. 14, 1963, FBI 157-970-316.

19 FBI memos on conduct of Bureau: Morrell to DeLoach,Aug. 5, 1963, FBI 157-970-242; To Callahan, July 25, 1963, FBI 157-970-200.

19 Roy Wilkins in Jackson: Mrs. Medgar Evers with William Peters, *For Us, The Living* (New York: Doubleday, 1967), p. 281.

20 "We've baptized brother Wilkins": Stanley Levison to Clarence Jones, June 2, 1963 (recalling June 1 conversation with King), FBI 100-111180-9-186a, p. 3.

20 "It was just some kind of prank,": Evers, *For Us, The Living*, p. 276.

20 Danville violence: Mary King, *Freedom Song: A Personal Story of the 1960s Civil Rights Movement* (New York: William Morrow & Co., 1987), pp. 87–88.

20 Danville, "the most critical city in the country at the moment": Michael Dorman, *We Shall Overcome: A Reporter's Eyewitness Account of the Year of Racial Strife and Triumph* (New York: Delacorte. 1964), p. 335.

20 Americus violence: King, *Freedom Song*, pp. 159–60.

20 Fannie Lou Hamer testimony: Partial Proceedings of the Democratic National Convention Credentials Committee, Atlantic City, Aug. 22, 1964, Papers of Joseph L. Rauh, Jr., Box 29, Library of Congress.

22 Speeches by each leader and time limits: Al Duckett to Jones and King, Aug. 23, 1963, FBI 100-73250-1C-19a; interview with Rachelle Horowitz, Oct. 22, 2001.

22 "This is silly": Clarence Jones to Walter Fauntroy, Aug. 21, 1963, FBI 100-73250-1A-illegible, p. 6.

22–23 King's proposal of longer speaking times or extending program: King to Jones, Aug. 22, 1963, FBI 100-73250-1C-18a, p. 5; King to Ted Brown, Aug. 23, 1963, FBI 100-73250-1C-19, p. 2.

23 King feeling leaders trying to throttle him: King to Ted Brown, Aug. 23, 1963, FBI 100-73250-1C-19, p. 2.

23 *Newsday* reporter: Pat Patterson to King, Aug. 23, 1963, FBI 100-73250-1C-19.

23 King was asked not to attend the meeting: Interview with Bayard Rustin (Herbert Allen), July 27–28, 1983, Bayard Rustin papers.

23 Randolph's arrangement with King's aides: Ted Brown to King, Aug. 23, 1963, FBI 100-73250-1C-19a, p. 16. Wyatt Walker spoke separately with Bayard Rustin, who told Walker that King would be the last speaker and be allowed to "take the time he needs." Walker to King, Aug. 23, 1963, FBI 100-73250-1C-19a, p. 2.

23 Whether King or Roy Wilkins should speak last: Interview with Wyatt Tee Walker, Dec. 11, 2001; interview with Matthew Ahmann, July 6, 2001.

23–24 Rustin wanting to put King last, "You are wise": Interview with Bayard Rustin (Herbert Allen), July 27–28, 1983, Bayard Rustin papers; Anderson. *Troubles I've Seen*, p. 261.

24 Additional reason for other leaders allowing King to speak last: Andrew Young, *An Easy Burden: The Civil Rights Movement and the Transformation of America* (New York: HarperCollins, 1996), p. 271; interview with Andrew Young, Jan. 17, 2002; interview with Walter Fauntroy, Dec. 18, 2001.

1. The March on Washington for Jobs and Freedom

25 Marchers leaving: *Ebony*, Nov. 1963, pp. 38, 42; *Newsweek*, Sept. 2, 1963, p. 17; Buffalo SAC to Director, Aug. 28, 1963, FBI 157-970.

25 Chicago marchers: *Ebony*, Nov. 1963, p. 40.

26 Alabama marchers: *Ebony*, Nov. 1963, p. 38; *NYT*, Aug. 29, 1963, p. 19.

26 Buses and trains leaving: Lerone Bennett, "Introduction," in Doris E. Saunders, *The Day They Marched* (Chicago: Johnson Publishing Co., 1963); *Ebony*, Nov. 1963, p. 38.

26   Marchers from Boston, Memphis, and New York: Interview with Margaret "Peggy" McCarter, July 1999; *NYT*, Aug. 29, 1963, pp. 19, 20.

26   SNCC vigil: Thomas Gentile, *March on Washington: August 28, 1963* (Washington, D.C.: New Day, 1983), p. 160. The Albany indictments are described in Howard Zinn, *SNCC: The New Abolitionists* (Boston: Beacon, 1965), pp. 211–12.

27   New York marchers: Saunders, *Day*, pp. 7–8; *WP*, Aug. 29, 1963, p. D15; *AN*, Sept. 7, 1963, p. 14; Rosen to Belmont, Aug. 28, 1963, FBI 157-970-796.

27   FBI tracking demonstrators: SAC Knoxville to Director, Aug. 27, 1963, FBI 157-970-758; SAC Phoenix to Director, Aug. 26, 1963 (March on Washington file), FBI 157-970; (deleted) to (deleted), July 22, 1963, FBI 157-970-868; SAC Houston to Director, Aug. 26, 1963, FBI 157-970-603.

28   Bus journeys: Interview with Margaret ("Peggy") McCarter, July 1999; *Newsweek*, Sept. 2, 1963, p. 15; *Newsweek*, Sept. 9, 1963, p. 20.

29   "scare stories or bad news": Congressional Record, May 21, 1963, p. 9117 (statement of Senator John Stennis, D-MS).

29   throwing stones at them: Burke Marshall, in Henry Hampton and Steve Fayer, *Voices of Freedom: An Oral History of the Civil Rights Movement from the 1950s through the 1980s* (New York: Bantam, 1990), p. 161.

29   *Life* magazine: *Life*, Aug. 23, 1963, p. 63.

29   "mob spirit": *U.S. News & World Report*, Aug. 5, 1963, p. 104.

29   Representative Dorn quotation: Congressional Record, Aug. 26, 1963, p. 15818 (statement of Representative William Jennings Bryan Dorn, D-SC).

30   President Kennedy's comments: Public Papers of the Presidents: Jan. 1 to Nov. 22, 1963 (Washington, D.C.: United States Government Printing Office, 1964), p. 305 (July 17, 1963); Arthur M. Schlesinger, Jr., *A Thousand Days: John F. Kennedy in the White House* (Boston: Houghton Mifflin, 1965), p. 972.

30   Federal government precautions for the march: Interview with John Douglas, July 9, 2001; interview with John Reilly, Oct. 25, 2001;

Gentile, *March on Washington*, pp. 146–49; McGowan to Rosen, Aug. 26, 1963, FBI 157-970-985; SAC Washington Field Office to Director, Sept. 3, 1963, FBI 157-970-1015; Brennan to Sullivan, Aug. 26, 1963, 157-970-illegible; Evans to Belmont, Aug. 26, 1963, FBI 157-970-885; Evans to Belmont, Aug. 26, 1963, FBI 157-970-891.

31 Security of the public address system and plans for the cutoff switch: Interview with John Reilly, Oct. 25, 2001; Evans to Belmont, Aug. 26, 1963, FBI 157-970-885; Evans to Belmont, Aug. 26, 1963, FBI 157-970-891; interview with John Douglas, July 9, 2001; interview with Nick Katzenbach, July 27, 2001.

31 Washington on the morning of the March: *NYT*, Aug. 29, 1963, p. 17; *AC*, Aug. 29, 1963, p. 14; *WP*, Aug. 29, 1963, pp. A13, A17; *Ebony*, Nov. 1963, p. 44; *Economist*, Aug. 31, 1963, p. 744; *Newsweek*, Sept. 9, 1963, p. 31; interview with Roger Wilkins, July 6, 2001; interview with Stephen Friedman, July 1999; Belmont to Director, Aug. 23, 1963, FBI 157-970-1018; Brennan to Sullivan, Aug. 22, 1963, FBI 157-970-534; D.C. Police Traffic Control Plan, Aug. 21, 1963, NAACP Papers, Washington Bureau, Box 154; Peter Goldman, *The Death and Life of Malcolm X* (2d ed. 1979) (Urbana: University of Illinois Press, 1979), p. 104.

32 First busloads: *WP*, Aug. 29, 1963, p. A22.

33 Marchers at the Monument: *Time*, Sept. 6, 1963, p. 14; *New Yorker*, Sept. 7, 1963, p. 30.

33 Worries of march organizers: Interview with Rachelle Horowitz, Oct. 22, 2001; Jervis Anderson, *Bayard Rustin: Troubles I've Seen* (New York: HarperCollins, 1997; Berkeley: University of California Press, 1998), p. 255.

33 King on the morning of the march: Coretta Scott King, *My Life with Martin Luther King, Jr.* (New York: Holt, Rinehart, and Winston, 1969), pp. 236–37; Ralph Abernathy, *And the Walls Come Tumbling Down* (New York: Harper & Row, 1989), p. 275.

34 First trains: *AA,* Sept. 7, 1963, pp. 2–3; *WP*, Aug. 29, 1963, p. A23; *Time*, Sept. 6, 1963, p. 14; *Ebony*, Nov. 1963, p. 40; Branch, *Parting the Waters*, p. 876.

35   Washington Monument crowd: *WP*, Aug. 29, 1963, p. A14; *AA*, Sept.
     7, 1963, p. 11; *AC*, Aug. 29, 1963, p. 14; *NYT*, Aug. 29, 1963, pp. 16, 17;
     Ebony, Nov. 1963, p. 46; *New Yorker*, Sept. 7, 1963, pp. 30–31;
     Newsweek, Sept. 2, 1963, p. 20; interview with Marvin Caplan, July,
     1999.

37   White counterdemonstrators: McGowan to Rosen, Aug. 29, 1963,
     FBI 157-970-972 (attached memorandum from Washington Field
     Office regarding March on Washington); SAC Richmond to
     Director, Sept. 3, 1963, FBI 157-970-1047; SAC Richmond to
     Director, Aug. 25, 1963, FBI 157–970-744; George Lincoln Rockwell
     to National Park Service, Aug. 10, 1963, FBI 157-970, no file number;
     SAC Richmond Aug. 22, 1963, FBI 157-970-illegible; SAC Los
     Angeles to Director, Aug. 22, 1963, FBI 157-970-554; *WP*, Aug. 29,
     1963, pp. A12, A27; interview with Walter Fauntroy, July 10, 2001; let-
     ter from Corrinne M. Brooks, Fort Wayne, Ind., NAACP Papers, Box
     A226.

39   Program and crowd at the Washington Monument: *ADW*, Aug. 29,
     1963, p. 1; *NYT*, Aug. 29, 1963, p. 17; *New South*, Sept. 1963, pp. 5–7;
     WP, Aug. 29, 1963, p. A13.

39   Walk to the Lincoln Memorial: *WP*, Aug. 29, 1963, p. A1, A13; *AC*,
     Aug. 29, 1963, p. 14; *NYT*, Aug. 29, 1963, pp. 17, 20; John Lewis,
     Walking with the Wind: A Memoir of the Movement (New York:
     Simon & Schuster, 1998; New York: Harcourt Brace, 1998), p. 223;
     King, *My Life*, p. 238; *Newsweek* Sept. 9, 1963, p. 20; *Time*, Sept. 6,
     1963, p. 14; Interview with John Lewis, July 10, 2001; McGowan to
     Rosen, Aug. 29, 1963, FBI 157-970-972 (attached memorandum from
     Washington Field Office regarding March on Washington); William
     H. Oliver to Bayard Rustin, Aug. 13, 1963, Bayard Rustin papers.

41   Crowd and program at the Lincoln Memorial: *WP*, Aug. 29, 1963, p.
     A13; *AC*, Aug. 29, 1963, p. 14; *Life*, Sept. 6, 1963, pp. 22–24; interview
     with Marvin Caplan, July, 1999; *Newsweek*, Sept. 9, 1963, p. 22; *AA*,
     Sept. 7, 1963, p. 8.

43   John Lewis's speech: The speeches from the March on Washington
     are available in several sources. The march organizers made two

records: *We Shall Overcome* and *The March on Washington*. The
Museum of Television and Radio has the CBS News broadcast of the
march in its collection. A generally accurate transcription of the day's
speeches can be found in NAACP, *Speeches by the Leaders: The
March on Washington for Jobs and Freedom* (New York: NAACP,
n.d.). John Lewis's speech can also be found in Gentile, *March*, pp.
178–83. John Lewis's recollections are from an interview with John
Lewis, July 10, 2001; and Lewis, *Walking with the Wind*, pp. 227–28.
The reference to "Title Three" in Lewis's speech is to a section in a
civil rights bill that would protect civil rights workers from violence.
The reference to "FEPC" is to a Fair Employment Practices
Commission, an entity that would protect blacks against racial discrimination in employment.

48   every black speaker: Murray Kempton, "The March on
Washington," *New Republic*, Sept. 14, 1963, p. 20.

48   Roy Wilkins's speech: Speech recordings as noted above; in addition, David L. Lewis, *W. E. B. DuBois: Biography of a Race:
1868–1919* (New York: Henry Holt and Co., 1993), pp. 2–3.

49   Mahalia Jackson: Recordings of the march as noted above; in addition, *NYT,* Aug. 29, 1963, p. 17; *AC,* Aug. 29, 1963, p. 14; King, *My
Life*, p. 238. King's reaction to Mahalia Jackson is from an interview
with Courtland Cox, Nov. 20, 2001.

51   television networks had all interrupted their regular programming:
Branch, *Parting the Waters*, p. 881.

52   King's speech: The text of King's speech is available in a transcription at MLK-Atlanta. King's speech is also available in *A Call to
Conscience* (New York: Warner Books, 2001), and in audio form on
the audio version of *A Call to Conscience*. The King Center also has a
videotape entitled "The 'I Have A Dream' Speech." The crowd's reaction to King's speech is from what is audible on recordings and
also from Oates, *Let the Trumpet Sound*, p. 261; *Newsweek*, Sept. 9,
1963, p. 22.

57   "Tell them about the dream, Martin!": Branch, *Parting the Waters*,
p. 882. The *Washington Post* reported that an unidentified person on

the speakers' platform repeatedly shouted, "Tell us your dream, Martin!" *WP,* Aug. 29, 1963, p. E3. In her autobiography (Mahalia Jackson, *Movin' On Up* [New York: Hawthorn, 1966]), Mahalia Jackson does not mention saying anything to King while he was speaking at the march.

63 "That guy is really good": Garrow, *Bearing the Cross,* p. 677, n. 62.

2. Composition

65 "sort of a Gettysburg Address": King to Al Duckett, Aug. 24, 1963, FBI 100-73250-1C-20a, p. 5. In Jackie Robinson's autobiography, Duckett would try to claim credit for King's speech: "Al was also a writer for Martin Luther King, and, in fact, he did a major job on the famous 'I Have a Dream' speech." Jackie Robinson and Alfred Duckett, *I Never Had It Made: An Autobiography* (New York: Putnam, 1972; New York: Ecco, 1995), p. 213.

65 Saturday meeting at Jones's house: Interviews with Walter Fauntroy, July 10 and Dec. 18, 2001; interview with Clarence Jones, Jan. 4, 2002; King affidavit, *King v. Mister Maestro, Inc.,* 63 Civ. 2889 (S.D.N.Y. 1963), MLK-BU.

66 Draft with "bad check" passage: Walter Fauntroy does not recall the author of this draft but remembers that one of King's advisers brought it to the Saturday meeting. Interview with Walter Fauntroy, Dec. 18, 2001.

67 Worked on the speech in Atlanta: King affidavit in *King v. Mister Maestro*; David L. Lewis, *King: A Critical Biography* (New York: Praeger, 1970), p. 227; Xernona Clayton, *I've Been Marching All the Time* (Marietta, Georgia: Longstreet Press, 1991), p. 68; interview with Xernona Clayton, March 1, 2002.

67 Revisions on the plane to Washington: Lewis, *King,* p. 227. The *SCLC Newsletter,* Sept. 1963, p. 6, has a photograph by Wyatt Tee Walker of King on the plane, with the caption: "Aboard plane for Washington, Dr. King adds finishing touches to draft speech."

67 Surviving drafts by King's aides: The three extant drafts by King's aides are a two-page fragment entitled "Dr. King MOW Address,"

pages 10 and 12, a shorter (four-page) draft speech entitled "Normalcy-Never Again," and a longer (nine-page) draft speech entitled "Normalcy-Never Again." All three documents are in MLK-Atlanta. Clarence Jones has identified the two-page fragment as belonging to the speech he wrote with Stanley Levison. Interview with Clarence Jones, Jan. 4, 2002.

Although it is reasonably certain that each of the three drafts by King's aides independently influenced King's prepared text, the relationship among the three drafts is not clear. The two "Normalcy" speeches may have been written by someone with a background in journalism, based on their use of slashes for above-the-line insertions, and by someone who read newspapers and magazines, based on their references to newspaper editorials and magazine articles. Among King's aides involved in the March on Washington speech, this would narrow the possible authors to Al Duckett and Ed Clayton. Also, the typeface on the two "Normalcy" speeches, particularly the longer one, resembles that of a typewriter used by Ed Clayton in early 1964 correspondence. If the "Normalcy" speeches are indeed from Ed Clayton, then they were probably prepared by Clayton and King, working together, on the Monday before the March. (I am grateful to David Garrow for these observations.)

Another possibility, however, is that the nine-page "Normalcy" speech originated in New York. It is possible that the nine-page "Normalcy" speech was put together with the Jones-Levison speech into a long compilation document of drafts by King's New York aides. Two facts about the drafts support this conclusion: First, the nine-page "Normalcy" speech ends on page 9, with the conclusion of the "Bad check" set piece, and the two surviving pages of the Jones-Levison draft begin on page 10, with a sentence referring back to the "Bad check" set piece. Second, the longer "Normalcy" draft and the Jones-Levison draft share a similar heading.

67   Handwritten sentences on back of last page of draft: "Normalcy—Never Again" (short version), MLK-Atlanta.

68 Willard Hotel lobby on Tuesday night: Interview with Clarence Jones, Jan. 4, 2002; Clarence Jones affidavit in *Estate of Martin Luther King, Jr., Inc. v. CBS Inc.*, No. 1:96-CV-3052 (N.D. Ga. 1998).

68 King went up to his suite at the Willard Hotel and began thinking about what he would say: Coretta Scott King, *My Life with Martin Luther King, Jr.* (New York: Holt, Rinehart and Winston, 1969), p. 236; Jones affidavit in *Estate of King v. CBS.*

69 Wyatt Tee Walker at the Willard Hotel: Interview with Wyatt Tee Walker, Dec. 11, 2001. Wyatt Tee Walker remembers working on a new conclusion for King to use. He particularly remembers wanting to send the marchers away with a challenge, so the day was not just a Sunday picnic. Interview with Wyatt Tee Walker, Dec. 11, 2001.

69 King outlining and drafting the speech in his room at the Willard: King, Affidavit in *King v. Mister Maestro*; interview with Martin Luther King, Jr. (Donald H. Smith), Nov. 29, 1963, MLK-Atlanta; King, *My Life*, p. 236; interview with Andrew Young, Jan. 17, 2002.

70 King traveled about 275,000 miles and gave more than 350 speeches: *Time*, Jan. 3, 1964, p. 27.

70 Preacher's set pieces: See, for example, the sermons and explanations in William H. Pipes, *Say Amen, Brother! Old Time Negro Preaching: A Study in American Frustration* (William-Frederick Press, 1951; Michigan: Wayne State Univ. Press, 1991).

70 King's compositional method: Wyatt Tee Walker said in a 1963 interview: "I think Dr. King has basically maybe two dozen speeches, which he changes introductions and intersperses, drops in on different points . . ." Interview with Wyatt Tee Walker (Donald H. Smith), Dec. 2, 1963, MLK-Atlanta.

71 King's markings on his prepared text: Interview with Clarence Jones, Jan. 4, 2002; interview with Andrew Young, Jan. 17, 2002. The manuscript with King's markings has apparently been lost. The only surviving manuscript that King had with him at the podium is now in the private collection of George Raveling, who was a volunteer marshal

for the march. As soon as King finished speaking, Raveling asked, "Dr. King, could I have that copy of the speech?" King handed him a manuscript, and just then, his attention was distracted by a rabbi on the speakers' platform who complimented him on his address. Raveling folded the manuscript up and put it in his pocket. Interview with George Raveling, Oct. 1, 2001.

Raveling's manuscript is identical to the hundreds of copies of the "Advance Text" of King's speech that were handed out to the press on the morning of the march. There is not a single handwritten cross-out, addition, or alteration on the document. This means that King probably had at least two copies of his prepared speech with him at the podium: One to mark up, and one to keep clean, so he could see what his original text had been in case he wanted to return to it.

71   Prepared speech: King, "Advance Text of Speech to Be Delivered by Dr. Martin Luther King, Jr.," Aug. 28, 1963, MLK-Atlanta.

71   Delivered speech: As noted in chapter 1, I have transcribed the speech that King gave from several recordings of the speech, and checked it against the transcript in MLK-Atlanta and the reprint of the speech in *A Call to Conscience*. The unreliability of many older published transcriptions of King's speech at the march is noted in Haig Bosmaijan, "The Inaccuracies in the Reprintings of Martin Luther King's 'I Have A Dream' Speech," 31 *Communication Education* 107 (Apr. 1982).

86   King turned down Rustin's suggestion: Bayard Rustin to King (May 10, 1957), in 4 King Papers, pp. 199–201.

86   "I'm better at words than you are": Taylor Branch, *Parting the Waters: America in the King Years 1954–63* (New York: Simon & Schuster, 1988), p. 217.

95   King explanation for why he used "I have a dream": Interview with Martin Luther King, Jr. (Donald H. Smith), Nov. 29, 1963, MLK-Atlanta.

95   Coretta Scott King and Walter Fauntroy's recollections of King's consideration of "I have a dream": King, *My Life*, p. 236; interview with Walter Fauntroy, July 10, 2001

96 "Rabbit in the Bushes": Branch, *Parting the Waters*, pp. 76–77.

96 Change his speeches: King explained in the Donald Smith interview: "I started out in high school in oratorical contests and one of the things that I developed then was a means of speaking without being tied down to a manuscript, which means that I'm usually free when I'm speaking to communicate with my audience, communicate by actually looking at the audience . . ." Interview with Martin Luther King, Jr. (Donald H. Smith), Nov. 29, 1963, MLK-Atlanta.

96 Alterations in NAACP speech: King, "The Montgomery Story: Address Delivered at the Forty-seventh Annual NAACP Convention," in 3 King Papers, p. 306.

97 "First I find my landing strip": Lischer, *The Preacher King*, p. 139.

3. Sermon

99 King's reputation as a preacher at Crozer: Branch, *Parting the Waters*, pp. 75–76.

99 "They told me you have a son that can preach rings around you": J. Raymond Henderson to Martin Luther King, Sr. (May 12, 1955), in 2 King Papers, p. 555.

100 "You just wait and see": *New York Post*, Apr. 8, 1968, p. 37.

100 King's writings on notebooks: Richard Lischer, *The Preacher King: Martin Luther King, Jr., and the Word That Moved America* (New York: Oxford University Press, 1995), p. 69; blue notebook in Box 119, Folder 8, MLK-BU.

100 Jeremiah essay: King, "The Significant Contributions of Jeremiah to Religious Thought" (Sept. 14–Nov. 24, 1948), in 1 King Papers, p. 194.

101 "The church has always been a second home for me": King, "An Autobiography of Religious Development" (Nov. 22, 1950), in 1 King Papers, p. 361.

101 King's knowledge of the Bible as a child: Oates, *Let the Trumpet Sound*, p. 9.

101 Addition of Biblical phrase to Brooks material: The two sources are put in parallel in Keith D. Miller, *Voice of Deliverance: The Language*

of Martin Luther King, Jr., and Its Sources (New York: Free Press, 1992; Athens: University of Georgia Press, 1998), p. 15.

101   Parallelism in Hebrew Bible poetry: See generally S. E. Gillingham, *The Poems and Psalms of the Hebrew Bible* (New York: Oxford University Press, 1994).

108   King first used a version of the "Let freedom ring" piece: King's first use of this set piece appears to be in "Facing the Challenge of a New Age," Dec. 3, 1956, in 3 King Papers, pp. 451, 462.

108   Archibald Carey "Let freedom ring": Archibald Carey, "Address to the Republican National Convention," July 8, 1952, as excerpted in 3 King Papers, p. 463 n. 23. Garry Wills has observed that King also transformed Carey's set piece by inserting it into a speech that was laden with references to mountains, so that King's use of "Let freedom ring" picked up resonances that were not present in Carey's original. Garry Wills, *Certain Trumpets: The Call of Leaders* (New York: Simon & Schuster, 1994), p. 224.

109   King's use of "Let freedom ring" set piece to conclude speeches: For instance, King, "Desegregation and the Future," Dec. 15, 1956, in 3 King Papers, p. 479; King, "Facing the Challenge of a New Age," Jan. 1, 1957, in 3 King Papers, p. 88; King, "Speech Made in Savannah," Jan. 1, 1961, MLK-Atlanta.

109   King remembered using "I have a dream" in Albany: Poppy Cannon, "Martin Luther King, Jr.," in Will Yolen and Kenneth Seeman Giniger, eds., *Heroes for Our Times* (Harrisburg: Stackpole, 1968), p. 220.

110   Faith Holsaert remembers: Interview with Faith Holsaert, Oct. 31, 2001. Faith Holsaert remembers hearing King deliver "I Have a Dream" at the Albany movement's anniversary mass meeting, which took place on November 16, 1962.

110   "I have a dream" in Rocky Mount: King, "Facing the Challenge of a New Age," Nov. 27, 1962, in the collection of the city of Rocky Mount. I am grateful to Kieran Taylor for pointing me to this reference. According to the transcription, King referred to "Suffolk County," Georgia. A later annotator of the Rocky Mount text ques-

tioned whether he said "Sasser County," Georgia. I have changed the text to "Sumter County," Georgia, because there is neither a Sasser nor a Suffolk County in Georgia, and because Sumter County abuts Terrell and Lee counties, sites of some of the church burnings of the summer of 1962.

111 "I have a dream" in Birmingham: Birmingham Police Department Report, April 1963, Bull Connor Papers, Birmingham Public Library. The police officers taped the Birmingham mass meetings, but they reused their tapes, and they apparently taped over the recording of the mass meeting where King used a version of the "I have a dream" refrain. Email from Jim Baggett, Birmingham Public Library.

112 "I have a dream" in Detroit: King, "Address at March in Detroit," June 23, 1963, MLK-Atlanta; King, "Address at the Freedom Rally at Cobo Hall," in Clayborne Carson and Kris Shepard, eds. *A Call to Conscience: The Landmark Speeches of Dr. Martin Luther King Jr.* (New York: Warner Books, 2001). Just before the march, King used the "I have a dream" set piece in Chicago. Taylor Branch, *Parting the Waters: America in the King Years 1954–63* (New York: Simon & Schuster, 1988), p. 871.

114 "I have a dream" from Prathia Hall, at Mount Olive service: This account is based on an interview that Richard Lischer conducted with James Bevel. Richard Lischer, *The Preacher King: Martin Luther King, Jr., and the Word That Moved America* (New York: Oxford University Press, 1995), p. 93.

It is difficult to verify the Mount Olive account of the origins of "I Have a Dream." There were at least two prayer services at the remains of Mount Olive in Sasser. The first took place on September 10, the day after the church was burned. This service was attended by several Albany students, including Prathia Hall, and several out-of-town visitors, including Jackie Robinson and Wyatt Tee Walker, but King was not there. *NYT*, Sept. 10, 1962, p. 1; *Student Voice*, Oct. 1962, p. 1. The second service happened the next Friday, on September 14. King was there, and he announced a $10,000 pledge from Governor Nelson Rockefeller to help rebuild the church. *NYT*, Sept. 15, 1962,

p. 12; interview with Jack Chatfield, Jan. 6, 2002; interview with Ralph Allen, Jan. 9, 2002. If Prathia Hall's use of "I have a dream" inspired King, it must have occurred at the second church service, rather than the first one, which King did not attend.

One reason to be skeptical of the Mount Olive account is that Jack Chatfield, who was at the second prayer service, does not remember seeing Jim Bevel, the source of the Hall story, at the service. Bevel was such a memorable figure that Chatfield is certain he would remember if Bevel had been there. Interview with Jack Chatfield, Jan. 6, 2002. Another reason for skepticism is that Wyatt Tee Walker, who was at the first service at Mount Olive, has no recollection of hearing "I have a dream" from a student protester in King's presence and does not associate the set piece with Albany. Interview with Wyatt Tee Walker, Dec. 11, 2001.

Prathia Hall does not remember King's presence at the prayer service. She does remember using the phrase "I have a dream" at the prayer service and talking about her dream of freedom: "Being free from the bullets and the burnings, being free to worship and free to learn." Interview with Dr. Prathia Hall, Nov. 15, 2001. In any case, Dr. Hall does not want to take credit for King's subsequent use of "I have a dream." She opened our interview by making sure that I knew that if she did have a part in King's use of the phrase, she was "greatly honored," and that King "did far more with it than I could have done."

114   Dorothy Cotton account about origins of "I have a dream": Interview with Dorothy Cotton, Oct. 3, 2001. Cotton does not remember the date of this event.

114   Ralph Allen recollection of Kathleen Conwell use of "I have a dream": Interview with Ralph Allen, Jan. 9, 2002.

115   "All is grist that comes to his mill": Morton Scott Enslin, "Crozer Theological Seminary Placement Committee: Confidential Evaluation of Martin Luther King, Jr.," Nov. 21, 1950, in 1 King Papers, p. 354.

115   King's use of "I have a dream" before Albany: Wyatt Walker remem-

bers hearing King use "I have a dream" at least ten to twenty times before the March on Washington, and specifically remembers King delivering the set piece in South Bend, Indiana; Louisville; and Los Angeles. Interview with Wyatt Tee Walker, Dec. 11, 2001.

116 Not a widespread recollection of Albany students' use of "I have a dream" before King: Dr. Hall does not think that anyone at the time thought King's use of "I have a dream" was inspired by her prayers at Mount Olive. Interview with Dr. Prathia Hall, Nov. 15, 2001. Nor do any of the Albany veterans whom I have contacted remember a college-age white girl saying "I have a dream" before King did. Interview with Charles Sherrod, Feb. 11, 2002; interview with Faith Holsaert, Jan. 23, 2002; interview with Jack Chatfield, Jan. 6, 2002; interview with Penny Patch, Jan. 5, 2002; interview with Ralph Allen, Jan. 9, 2002; interview with Carolyn Daniels, Jan. 23, 2002; interview with Peggy Dammond Preacely, Feb. 10, 2002.

117 Kitchen-table experience: King, "Thou Fool," Aug. 27, 1967, MLK-Atlanta. David Garrow has argued that King's religious experience in his Montgomery kitchen was critical to his spiritual and vocational development. Garrow, *Bearing the Cross*. If this hypothesis is correct, it strengthens the case for the origins of "I have a dream" in King's vision in his Montgomery kitchen, because King would be likely to reflect back on this transforming experience with an evocative phrase such as "I had a dream."

118 "Last night, in the kitchen of my home, I had a vision": This event as a source for the "I have a dream" phrase is implied in Poppy Cannon's article about an interview that King gave near the end of his life. Poppy Cannon, "Martin Luther King, Jr.," p. 220.

118 "New world" speech: King, "Facing the Challenge of a New Age," Dec. 3, 1956, in 3 King Papers, p. 462. A version of this set piece appears in several King speeches, such as "The Birth of A New Age," Aug. 11, 1956, in 3 King Papers, p. 339.

118 "The American Dream": King, "The American Dream," in Washington, *Testament of Hope*, p. 208.

121 James Weldon Johnson: James Weldon Johnson, *God's Trombones:*

Seven Negro Sermons in Verse (New York: Viking Penguin, 1927; New York: Penguin, 1990), p. 5.

121   *Newsweek* reporter compared King's voice to the sound of a church organ: *Newsweek*, Sept. 9, 1963, p. 22.

4. Prophecy

136   King's quotation of Glasgow Address: For example, King, "The Ethical Demands for Integration," Dec. 27, 1962, in James M. Washington, ed., *A Testament of Hope: The Essential Writings and Speeches of Martin Luther King, Jr.* (New York: HarperCollins, 1986; San Francisco: HarperSanFrancisco, 1991), p. 119.

136   Glasgow Address: Frederick Douglass, "The Constitution of the United States: Is It Pro-slavery or Anti-slavery?", Glasgow, Mar. 26, 1860, in Philip S. Foner, ed., *The Life and Writings of Frederick Douglass*, vol. II, pp. 467, 477 (New York: International, 1950).

136   Black protest rhetoric: David Howard-Pitney, *The Afro-American Jeremiad: Appeals for Justice in America* (Philadelphia: Temple University Press, 1990); Wilson Jeremiah Moses, *Black Messiahs and Uncle Toms: Social and Literary Manipulations of a Religious Myth* (University Park: Pennsylvania State University Press, 1982).

136   "The Negro and the Constitution": King, "The Negro and the Consitution," May 1944, in 1 King Papers, pp. 109–111.

137   President Kennedy's June 11, 1963, speech: "Radio and Television Report to the American People on Civil Rights," Public Papers of the Presidents: Jan. 1 to Nov. 22, 1963 (Washington, D.C.: United States Government Printing Office, 1964), p. 468 (June 11, 1963).

138   Senator Magnuson speech: Congressional Record, Apr. 9, 1964, p. 7412 (Apr. 9, 1964) (statement of Sen. Warren Magnuson, D-WA).

139   King's speech at Prayer Pilgrimage for Freedom: King, "Give Us the Ballot, Address Delivered at the Prayer Pilgrimage for Freedom," May 17, 1957, in 4 King Papers, p. 208.

140   *Washington Post: WP*, Aug. 29, 1963, p. A16. A front-page *Atlanta Constitution* article the next day said that King "stressed [an] important message of the march: demonstrations will continue." *AC*, Aug.

29, 1963, p. 1. *U.S. News & World Report* quoted only these lines from King's speech. *U.S. News & World Report*, Sept. 9, 1963, p. 40.

142   Original draft of Lewis's speech: John Lewis, *Walking with the Wind: A Memoir of the Movement* (New York: Simon & Schuster, 1998; Harcourt & Brace, 1998), pp. 219–21.

142   Courtland Cox distributed advance copies: Interview with Courtland Cox, Nov. 20, 2001.

142   "What are you doing that for?": Interview with Rachelle Horowitz, Oct. 22, 2001.

143   O'Boyle's reaction: Thomas Gentile, *March on Washington: August 28, 1963* (Washington, D.C.: New Day, 1983), pp. 171–74; interview with Matthew Ahmann, July 6, 2001.

143   A night of hectic telephoning began: Gentile, *March on Washington*, p. 172.

143   Kennedy administration reaction to O'Boyle's disapproval: Interview with Burke Marshall, February 16, 2000.

144   Lewis's meeting with Rustin: Lewis, *Walking with the Wind*, pp. 221–22.

144   Lewis exchange with Roy Wilkins: Lewis, *Walking with the Wind*, p. 225.

144–45 Eugene Carson Blake objections and Randolph's response: Lewis, *Walking with the Wind*, p. 226; James Forman, *The Making of Black Revolutionaries* (New York: Macmillan, 1972), p. 334; interview with John Lewis, July 10, 2001.

145   Cox and Forman refusing to change the speech: Interview with Courtland Cox, Nov. 20, 2001; Lewis, *Walking with the Wind*, p. 226.

145   "Would you young men accommodate to an old man?" and "We've come this far together": Courtland Cox, *Voices*, p. 164; interview with John Lewis, July 10, 2001.

145   Not going to refuse A. Philip Randolph: Interview with John Lewis, July 10, 2001.

145   Forman revisions of Lewis's speech and later reactions: Interview with James Forman, Dec. 17, 2001. As one example of how the alterations improved the speech, Forman mentioned the change from "We cannot support the administration's civil rights bill" to "we sup-

port [the bill] with great reservation." SNCC did not necessarily oppose the entire bill but strongly felt that it needed a provision to protect civil rights workers from violence. In Forman's mind, the revised phrase more precisely expressed SNCC's position. Interview with James Forman, Dec. 17, 2001.

146 O'Boyle was some distance away to "I've got the package": Interview with John Reilly, Oct. 25, 2001.

146 O'Boyle never looked at the revised speech: Interview with Matthew Ahmann, July 6, 2001; interview with John Reilly, Oct. 25, 2001.

146 Malcolm X congratulations to Lewis: Taylor Branch, *Pillar of Fire: America in the King Years 1963–1965* (New York: Simon & Schuster, 1998; New York: Touchstone, 1999), p. 131.

146 Lewis later wondered whether his opening was too harsh: Interview with John Lewis, July 10, 2001.

147 King's Holt Street Address: King, "MIA Mass Meeting at Holt Street Baptist Church," Dec. 5, 1955, in 3 King Papers, p. 72.

147 Malcolm X on nonviolence: Peter Goldman, *The Death and Life of Malcolm X* (Urbana: University of Illinois Press, Second Edition, 1979), p. 73.

147 King's comments on Nation of Islam: King, "Address at the National Bar Association, Milwaukee," Aug. 20, 1959, MLK-BU; King, "Letter to Mr. Kivie Kaplan," Mar. 6, 1961, MLK-BU.

148 "unite with the main thrust": King to Dorothy Cotton, Aug. 10, 1963, FBI 100-73250-1C-6a, p. 2.

148 Malcolm at the March: James H. Cone, *Martin & Malcolm & America: A Dream or A Nightmare* (Maryknoll, New York: Orbis, 1991), p. 113; Branch, *Pillar of Fire*, pp. 130–31.

148 "meet physical force with soul force": The phrase "soul force" is probably from E. Stanley Jones, *Mahatma Gandhi: An Interpretation* (New York: Abingdon-Cokesbury Press, 1948), p. 88, as noted in 4 King Papers, p. 342 n.20.

148 SNCC projects staffed with black workers: Clayborne Carson, *In Struggle: SNCC and the Black Awakening of the 1960s* (Cambridge: Harvard University Press, 1981), pp. 74, 76–77.

149   "laid a hand on the extremists": AC, Aug. 29, 1963, p. 1.

149   Stanley Levison on King's speech: Phone call from Alice Loewi to Stanley Levison, Aug. 28, 1963, FBI 100-111180-9-273a. Bayard Rustin—a lifelong pacifist who had once been jailed as a conscientious objector—particularly welcomed King's defense of nonviolence. Interview with Rachelle Horowitz, Oct. 22, 2001.

150   Baldwin, "in his intimate knowledge": James Baldwin, "The Dangerous Road Before Martin Luther King," *Harper's*, Feb. 1961, p. 36.

151   Holt Street Address: King, "MIA Mass Meeting at Holt Street Baptist Church," Dec. 5, 1955, in 3 King Papers, p. 73.

152   "There is something in this universe": King, "Give Us the Ballot," May 17, 1957, in 4 King Papers, pp. 208, 214.

153   King to DeWolf, "dream" existed first in the mind of God: Kenneth L. Smith & Ira G. Zepp, Jr., *Search for the Beloved Community: The Thinking of Martin Luther King, Jr.* (Valley Forge: Judson Press, 1974), p. 126.

154   Puritan ministers: See the examples in Sacvan Bercovitch, *The American Jeremiad* (Madison: University of Wisconsin Press, 1978).

154   Black orators' visions of national redemption: See the examples in Howard-Pitney, *The Afro-American Jeremiad,* and Keith Miller and Elizabeth Van Der Lei, "Martin Luther King Jr.'s 'I Have a Dream' in Context: Ceremonial Protest and African American Jeremiad," 62 *College English* 1, Sept. 1999.

154   Booker T. Washington "New heaven and a new earth": Booker T. Washington, *Up From Slavery* (New York: Doubleday, Page, 1901; New York: Penguin, 1986), p. 225.

154   Image of a great choir: Miller and Van Der Lei, " 'I Have A Dream,' " pp. 89–90.

154   Wells, "My country 'tis of thee": Miller and Van Der Lei, " 'I Have A Dream,' " p. 90.

155   Ingersoll, "I see our country filled with happy homes": William Safire, *Safire's New Political Dictionary* (New York: Random House, 1978), p. 372.

155   Frederick Douglass, "I had a dream of freedom": Diane McWhorter, *Carry Me Home: Birmingham, Alabama: The Climactic Battle of the Civil Rights Revolution* (New York: Simon & Schuster, 2001), p. 490.

155   Meredith, "I dream of the day": James Meredith, *Three Years in Mississippi* (Bloomington: Indiana University Press, 1966), p. 201.

156   There is nothing resembling King's dream of a redeemed America: This conclusion is based on my review of the congressional debates and presidential addresses on civil rights between 1954 and 1964. Drew D. Hansen, "Civil Rights and the Making of the American Ideal, 1954–1964" (Sept. 1999) (unpublished manuscript). The most common arguments during this period were that civil rights legislation should be enacted to be true to America's founding ideals, to be faithful to the Bible and to Christian principles, and to deprive the communists of a propaganda weapon against the United States. There is almost no discussion in this material of what America might look like if racial discrimination were eliminated.

158   "Carefully calculated campaign": *Meredith v. Fair*, 305 F.2d 343, 344 (5th Cir. 1962).

158   Murders in Mississippi: Dave Dennis in *Voices of Freedom*, p. 194; Dave Dennis in Howell Raines, *My Soul Is Rested: The Story of the Civil Rights Movement in the Deep South* (New York: G.P. Putnam's Sons, 1977; New York: Penguin, 1983), p. 278 and note.

158   Security precautions among Mississippi civil rights workers: Elizabeth Sutherland, ed., *Letters from Mississippi* (New York: McGraw Hill, 1965; New York: Signet, 1966), p. 22; Julius Lester, "The Angry Children of Malcolm X," in August Meier et al., eds., *Black Protest Thought in the Twentieth Century* (Indianapolis: Bobbs-Merrill, 2d ed. 1971), p. 473.

159   "When you're not in Mississippi, it's not real": Sutherland, *Letters*, p. 25.

159   "A dream of a land": King, "If the Negro Wins, Labor Wins," Dec. 11, 1961, in Washington, *Testament of Hope*, p. 206.

159   "The finest Negro": King, "The Negro and the Constitution," May 1944, in 1 King Papers, p. 110. The idea can also be seen in the Rocky

Mount speech: "I have a dream tonight. One day my little daughter and my two sons will grow up in a world not conscious of the color of their skin but only conscious of the fact that they are members of the human race." King, "Facing the Challenge of a New Age," Nov. 27, 1962, in the collection of the city of Rocky Mount.

160 *Newsweek* excerpts of King's speech: *Newsweek*, Sept. 9, 1963, p. 21.

160 *Cooper v. Aaron:* 358 U.S. 1 (1958).

161 Wallace at Tuskegee High School: *Lee v. Macon County Board of Education,* 231 F. Supp. 743 (M.D. Ala. 1964).

164 "He's off; he's on his own now": Interview with Clarence Jones, Jan. 4, 2002.

164 Abernathy's reaction: Stephen B. Oates, *Let the Trumpet Sound: The Life of Martin Luther King, Jr* (New York: Harper & Row, 1982; New York: HarperPerennial, 1994), p. 262.

164 Prophetic gift: My discussion of prophecy is indebted to the works of Walter Brueggemann, particularly *The Prophetic Imagination* (Philadelphia: Fortress, 1978) and *The Hopeful Imagination: Prophetic Voices in Exile* (Philadelphia: Fortress, 1986). In *The Hopeful Imagination*, Brueggemann used the "I Have a Dream" speech as a modern example of the poetic power of Second Isaiah: "[King] was able to summon an exiled community out beyond the imperial definitions of the day which held his people in bondage. When he issued his famous poetic proposal, 'I have a dream,' that was just such a summons. He did not have a concrete notion on how to enact that dream, but it was a beginning point of energy. The dream functioned as an incredible hope, but it was also an act of heavy critique which asserted that the present social reality is not working. It was an announcement that things would not stay as they were (cf. Isa. 43:18–19)." Brueggemann, *Hopeful Imagination*, p. 9.

5. Reception, 1963–1968

167 "stole the show": *NYT*, Aug. 29, 1963, p. 17; interview with Carl Broady, July 5, 1999; interview with Margaret McCarter, July 7, 1999; interview with Stephen J. Friedman, June 29, 1999; e-mail from

George Furniss, July 1, 1999. Alice Walker wrote a decade after the march how amazed she had been at King's speech, both because of his delivery and "because no black person I knew had ever encouraged anybody to 'Go back to Mississippi.' " Alice Walker, "Choosing to Stay Home: Ten Years After the March on Washington," *New York Times Magazine*, Aug. 26, 1973, reprinted in Jon Meacham, ed., *Voices in Our Blood: America's Best on the Civil Rights Movement* (New York: Random House, 2001), p. 479. A young man standing next to a reporter for the Baltimore *Afro-American* said that King "handles words as if he invented them." *AA*, Sept. 7, 1963, p. 11.

167   "I was ready to march through Mississippi.": *AN*, Sept. 7, 1963, p. 19.

167   Newspapers and magazines: *NYT*, Aug. 29, 1963, p. 16; *WP*, Aug. 29, 1963, p. A14; *AC*, Aug. 29, 1963, p. 1; *Life*, Sept. 6, 1963, p. 22; *Newsweek*, Sept. 9, 1963, pp. 22, 31; *Ebony*, Nov. 1963, p. 31.

167   *New York Times*: *NYT*, Aug. 29, 1963, p. A1.

167   Black newspapers: *AA*, Sept. 7, 1963; *AN*, Sept. 7, 1963; *PC*, Sept. 7, 1963.

168   Two record companies, Fox Movietone News: The records were made without King's authorization and proved sufficiently popular that King eventually sued to stop their distribution. *King v. Mister Maestro, Inc.*, 224 F. Supp. 101 (S.D.N.Y. 1963), *King v. Mister Maestro, Inc.*, 63 Civ. 2889 (Dec. 13, 1963). In consultation with Clarence Jones, King himself had planned to make a record with his speech on it. Jones and King thought that any record of the march speeches would probably be bought largely because of King's speech. FBI 100-106670, Section 6, undated memorandum. The march organizers, recognizing the fundraising potential of the event, also made two records of the speeches. See orders and receipts in NAACP Box A225.

168   *New York Post* reprints: Erwin G. Krasnow, *Copyrights, Performers' Rights, and the March on Civil Rights: Reflections on* Martin Luther King, Jr. v. Mister Maestro, 53 *Georgetown Law Journal* 403, 405 (1965).

168   *Washington Post* headline: *WP*, Aug. 29, 1963, p. A1.

168   "anticlimactic": Norman Mailer, "The Big Bite," *Esquire*, Dec. 1963,

p. 22. Several other journalists thought that the speeches were boring. *U.S. News & World Report*, in a generally negative piece on the march, mentioned King only briefly, saying that the crowd "stirred momentarily" for his speech. *U.S. News & World Report*, Sept. 9, 1963, p. 40. The *Economist* didn't even mention King's speech, referring only to an "interminable afternoon of speeches delivered at the Lincoln Memorial." *Economist*, Aug. 31, 1963, p. 744.

168 Clarence Jones's reaction: Interview with Clarence Jones, Jan. 4, 2002.

168 Stanley Levison's reaction: Stanley Levison to Alice Loewi, Aug. 28, 1963, FBI 100-111180-9-273a.

169 "just got carried away": Interview with Andrew Young, Jan. 17, 2002.

169 "Watch out for Roy now": Oates, *Let the Trumpet Sound*, p. 263.

169 Wyatt Tee Walker and Ralph Abernathy's reactions: Interview with Wyatt Tee Walker, Dec. 11, 2001. Walter Fauntroy was so exhausted from the preparations for the march and so worried that a bomb would go off at the Lincoln Memorial that he couldn't pay much attention to King's speech. Interview with Walter Fauntroy, July 10, 2001.

169 James Farmer, *Lay Bare the Heart: An Autobiography of the Civil Rights Movement* (New York: Arbor House, 1985; New York: Plume, 1985), p. 245. Dick Gregory also thought King's speech was the high point of the march. Dick Gregory, *Nigger* (New York: Dutton, 1964), p. 212.

170 Mahalia Jackson's reaction: Mahalia Jackson, *Movin' On Up* (New York: Hawthorn, 1966), p. 200.

170 John Lewis's reaction: Interview with John Lewis, July 10, 2001.

170 James Baldwin's reaction: James Baldwin, *No Name in the Street* (New York: Dial, 1972), p. 140.

170 Some SNCC members were moved: Cleveland Sellers, *The River of No Return* (New York: Morrow, 1973), p. 66; interview with Dorothy Zellner, Nov. 13, 2001; interview with John Lewis, July 10, 2001.

170 Courtland Cox's reaction: Interview with Courtland Cox, Nov. 20, 2001.

170   Reverend Ed King's reaction: Interview with Ed King, Feb. 24, 2000.

170   SNCC concerns with the controversy over John Lewis's speech and waste of resources: James Forman, *The Making of Black Revolutionaries* (New York: Macmillan, 1972), pp. 333–36; Mary King, *Freedom Song: A Personal Story of the 1960s Civil Rights Movement* (New York: Morrow, 1987), p. 183; e-mail from Larry Rubin Sept. 9, 2001; interview with Dorothy Zellner, Nov. 13, 2001. Julian Bond, SNCC's communications director, only half-heard King's speech because he kept looking around to see the entertainers on the Mall and because he was irritated that John Lewis had made a copy of his speech available the night before, while King had not. Interview with Julian Bond, Aug. 15, 2001. Larry Rubin, a SNCC field secretary, thought that King was just stringing together bits and pieces of things he had heard him repeat for years. He thought the time invested in the march would have been better spent registering voters in the rural South, but at the same time, as he later remembered, he was thrilled by the sense that, for once, "no one would try to kill us SNCC workers." E-mail from Larry Rubin, Sept. 9, 2001.

170   James Forman's reaction: Interview with James Forman, Dec. 17, 2001.

171   SNCC criticisms of King's speech: E-mail from Larry Rubin, Sept. 9, 2001; Sellers, *River of No Return*, p. 66; interview with John Lewis, July 10, 2001; interview with Ed King, Feb. 24, 2000.

171   Anne Moody's reaction: Anne Moody, *Coming of Age in Mississippi*, (New York: Dell, 1968), p. 307.

171   "There goes Martin again": Reaction within the NAACP as characterized in interview with Mildred Bond Roxborough, Aug. 8, 2001.

171   Sounded like any other King address: Interview with Jack Greenberg, June 14, 1999; interview with Mildred Bond Roxborough, Aug. 8, 2001.

172   "What is looked upon as an American dream": Cone, *Martin & Malcolm*, p. 89. James Cone has observed how Malcolm increasingly used the "nightmare" image after 1963, in implicit contrast with King's hopeful vision for America. Cone, *Martin & Malcolm*, pp. 111–19.

172 "You know, this dream of King's": Goldman, *Death and Life of Malcolm X*, p. 107. In his autobiography, Malcolm wrote: "Who ever heard of angry revolutionists swinging their bare feet together with their oppressor in lily-pad park pools, with gospels and guitars and 'I Have A Dream' speeches? And the black masses in America were—and still are—having a nightmare." Malcolm X, as told to Alex Haley, *The Autobiography of Malcolm X* (New York: Ballantine, 1965), p. 281. Perhaps the most negative reaction to King's speech came from an unidentified marcher who was standing near journalist John Williams. When King was repeating "I have a dream," the man shouted "Fuck that dream, Martin! Now, now, goddamit, NOW!" John A. Williams, *This Is My Country, Too* (New York: New American Library, 1965), p. 157.

172 Didn't think much about King's speech: Interview with Wyatt Tee Walker, Dec. 11, 2001; interview with Walter Fauntroy, July 10, 2001; interview with Clarence Jones, Jan. 4, 2002; interview with John Lewis, July 10, 2001; interview with Julian Bond, Aug. 15, 2001; interview with Courtland Cox, Nov. 20, 2001; interview with James Forman, Dec. 17, 2001; interview with Robert Coles, Aug. 2001: interview with Dorothy Zellner, Nov. 13, 2001; interview with Charles Sherrod, Feb. 11, 2002.

172 Too busy: Interview with Wyatt Tee Walker, Dec. 11, 2001. James Forman remembered: "SNCC's strategy was to keep demonstrations going—whatever we could do to dramatize segregation, we'd do. The speech of Dr. King wasn't a basic issue with us." Interview with James Forman, Dec. 17, 2001.

173 More concerned with political impact of march: Interview with Courtland Cox, Nov. 20, 2001; interview with Julian Bond, Aug. 15, 2001.

173 Lewis interview: John Lewis, "A Trend Toward Aggressive Nonviolent Action" (orig. *Dialogue Magazine*, vol. 4, no. 2, Spring 1964, pp. 7–9), reprinted in August Meier et al., eds., *Black Protest Thought in the Twentieth Century* (Indianapolis: Bobbs-Merrill, 2d ed, 1971), p. 356.

173–74 Mary King quotation: King, *Freedom Song*, p. 182. Similar recollections of the speech's impact on King's stature within the movement are in Andrew Young, *An Easy Burden: The Civil Rights Movement and the Transformation of America* (New York: HarperCollins, 1996), p. 273; Sellers, *River of No Return*, p. 66. Julian Bond recalls that King's standing within the movement was already parallel to Roy Wilkins' at the time of the march, and that there was no doubt after the event that he was at least as prominent a leader as Wilkins. Interview with Julian Bond, Aug. 15, 2001.

174 Sullivan memorandum: William C. Sullivan to Alan H. Belmont, Aug. 30, 1963, in *Investigation of the Assassination of Martin Luther King, Jr.,* Hearings Before the Select Committee on Assassinations, United States House of Representatives, 95th Congress, 2d Session, November 17, 20, 21, 1978 (1979), volume 6, p. 143.

174 "breathtaking, moving, overpowering," "new high": Congressional Record, Aug. 30, 1963, p. 16182 (statement of Rep. Edward Boland, D-MA).

174 "A demonstration we can never forget": Congressional Record, Aug. 30, 1963, p. 16185 (statement of Rep. Florence Dwyer, R-NJ).

174 March speech excerpts in the *Congressional Record*: Congressional Record, Sept. 3, 1963, p. 16227 (statement of Sen. Paul Douglas, D-IL). Even though politicians were leery of quoting King's speech domestically, the United States Information Agency (USIA) instantly recognized the speech's potential propaganda value. The agency made a film featuring King's speech and distributed it abroad. Taylor Branch, *Pillar of Fire: America in the King Years 1963–1965* (New York: Simon & Schuster, 1998), p. 228.

174 President Kennedy and Attorney General Robert Kennedy's reactions: Interview with Burke Marshall, Feb. 16, 2000; interview with Nick Katzenbach, July 27, 2001; interview with Ted Sorensen, July 7, 1999.

175 President Kennedy, "I have a dream": Theodore C. Sorensen, *Kennedy* (New York: Harper & Row, 1965), p. 505. At the meeting, President Kennedy was visibly relieved that the demonstration had

occurred without violence. Interview with Matthew Ahmann. July 6, 2001; Roy Wilkins, *Standing Fast: The Autobiography of Roy Wilkins* (New York: Viking Penguin, 1982), p. 293.

175   President Kennedy to John Lewis: John Lewis, *Walking with the Wind: A Memoir of the Movement* (New York: Simon & Schuster, 1998; New York: Harcourt Brace, 1998), p. 229.

175   President Kennedy's official statement about the march: "Statement by the President on the March on Washington for Jobs and Freedom," Public Papers of the Presidents: Jan. 1 to Nov. 22, 1963 (Washington, D.C.: United States Government Printing Office, 1964), p. 645 (Aug. 28, 1963).

175   Ted Sorensen's reaction: Interview with Ted Sorensen, July 7, 1999.

176   Representative Williams: Congressional Record, Mar. 17, 1965, p. 5307 (statement of Rep. John Williams, D-MS).

176   Representative Walker: Congressional Record, July 26, 1966, p. 17138 (statement of Rep. Prentiss Walker, D-MS).

176   Representative Herlong: Congressional Record, Feb. 12, 1968, p. 2856 (statement of Rep. Albert Sidney Herlong, D-FL).

176   Representative Ashbrook: Congressional Record, Apr. 1, 1968, p. 8509 (statement of Rep. John Ashbrook, R-OH).

176   Debates over the Civil Rights Act: A few members of Congress quoted the same passage from Amos that King used at the march, but it is likely this was because of their familiarity with the Bible, rather than because of a desire to make reference to King's speech. Congressional Record, June 18, 1964, p. 14298 (statement of Sen. Hiram Fong, R-HI); Congressional Record, June 19, 1964, p. 14444 (statement of Sen. Hubert Humphrey, D-MN).

176   Senator Javits: Congressional Record, Sept. 3, 1963, p. 16240 (statement of Sen. Jacob Javits, R-NY).

176   Representative Halpern: Congressional Record, Feb. 1, 1964, p. 1628 (statement of Rep. Seymour Halpern, R-NY).

176   Senator Proxmire: Congressional Record, Apr. 18, 1964, pp. 8351–52 (statement of Sen. William Proxmire, D-WI).

178   "America will just as surely be on the high road": King, *Playboy* in-

terview, Jan. 1965, in James M. Washington, ed., *A Testament of Hope: The Essential Writings and Speeches of Martin Luther King, Jr.* (New York: HarperCollins, 1986; New York: HarperSanFrancisco, 1991), p. 377.

179 "And I *still* have a dream": Oates, *Let the Trumpet Sound*, p. 322. King's regular column in the *Chicago Defender* was entitled "My Dream."

179 Selma-to-Montgomery speech: King, "Address at the Conclusion of the Selma to Montgomery March," in Carson, *A Call to Conscience*, pp. 125–26, 130–32.

181 "The Negroes spent a lot of money": Cone, *Martin & Malcolm*, p. 113.

182 Refusal to seat the MFDP: The refusal of the Democratic party to seat the MFDP was devastating for many in the movement who were sure that the nation would realize the justice of their appeal. "Atlantic City was a powerful lesson, not only for the black people from Mississippi but for all of SNCC and many other people as well. No longer was there any hope, among those who still had it, that the federal government would change the situation in the Deep South." Forman, *Making of Black Revolutionaries*, pp. 395–96; H. Rap Brown, *Die Nigger Die!* (New York: Dial, 1969), pp. 60–61; Lewis, *Walking with the Wind*, pp. 291–92; interview with Ed King, February 24, 2000.

182 Selma and Marion murders: Jimmie Lee Jackson, a twenty-six-year-old black man, was shot by a state trooper as he tried to protect his mother from police violence after a night march. The Reverend James Reeb, a white Unitarian minister from Boston, was beaten to death by a white mob. (Many activists noted after the two murders that Reeb's family received personal messages from both Senators Kennedy and yellow roses from President Johnson, while Jackson's family received no such remembrances.) Viola Liuzzo, a white woman from Detroit, was shot as she drove two civil rights workers back through Alabama after the Selma to Montgomery march. Several months later, Jonathan Daniels, a New Hampshire seminar-

ian, was shot in the stomach by a Lowndes County deputy sheriff. Charles Fager, *Selma, 1965* (New York: Scribner, 1974).

182 "We're only flesh": *New York Times Magazine*, June 25, 1967, p. 46.

182 King speeches on poverty and Northern segregation: King, "Address at Conference of Religious Leaders Under the Sponsorship of the President's Committee on Government Contracts," May 11, 1959, MLK-Atlanta. See also King, "Address at the 11th Constitutional Convention, Transport Workers Union of America, AFL-CIO," Oct. 2–6, 1961, MLK-Atlanta; King, "Address to the National Press Club," July 19, 1962, MLK-BU; King, "Address to the 30th Anniversary of District 35, Madison Square Garden," Oct. 23, 1963, MLK-BU; King, "Address at NAACP 53rd Annual Convention. Atlanta," July 5, 1962, MLK-BU.

183 "I will have to face the decision soon": *Saturday Evening Post*, June 15, 1963, p. 18.

183 "I think, in order for the Negro to approximate equality here": *Meet the Press*, Aug. 25, 1963, MLK-Atlanta.

183 "We feel that it is necessary to grapple with": *U.S. News & World Report*, Feb. 24, 1964, p. 60.

184 "the movement will have to move": Transcript, the WINS-News Conference, May 31, 1964, MLK-Atlanta.

184 King's schedule in Chicago: Garrow, *Bearing the Cross*, p. 434.

184 "[W]e come away from this revealing tour of Chicago": King, "Address at the March on Chicago," July 26, 1965, MLK-Atlanta.

185 Watts riots: Patterson, *Grand Expectations*, p. 588.

185 "We've got no rights at all": Weisbrot, *Freedom Bound*, p. 159

185 "The only way that we can ever get anybody to listen to us": "MLK Speaking to People of Watts," Aug. 19, 1965, MLK-Atlanta.

185 "King, and all his talk about nonviolence": Cone, *Martin & Malcolm*, p. 221.

185 " 'I have a dream' . . . craa-ap": *NYT*, Apr. 5, 1968. Roy Wilkins commented in his autobiography that Watts residents "didn't need his [King's] dreams—they wanted jobs, a decent place to live." Wilkins, *Standing Fast*, p. 314.

185   "You know, Bayard": Garrow, *Bearing the Cross*, p. 439.

185   "has not been national in its thrust nor objectives": King, "Speech to Dist. 65, AFL-CIO," Sept. 17, 1965, MLK-Atlanta.

186   "All too often the civil rights movement": "Rustin, Belafonte, MLK on Vietnam," Jan. 21, 1966, MLK-Atlanta.

186   Advisers' opposition and King's response: James R. Ralph, Jr., *Northern Protest: Martin Luther King, Jr., Chicago, and the Civil Rights Movement* (Cambridge: Harvard University Press, 1993), p. 33.

186   "Our campaign in Chicago is one to end slums": King, "Speech by Dr. Martin Luther King, Jr., European Tour," Mar. 1966, MLK-Atlanta.

186   "I have faith that Chicago": Ralph, *Northern Protest*, p. 173.

187   "If we can break the system in Chicago": Garrow, *Bearing the Cross*, p. 448.

187   "dying philosophy": Lewis, *Walking with the Wind*, p. 387.

187   Meredith march and "Black Power": Carson, *In Struggle*, pp. 207-11; Renata Adler, "The Black Power March In Mississippi," in *Toward a Radical Middle: Fourteen Pieces of Reporting and Criticism* (New York: Random House, 1969), pp. 151-63; King, *My Life*, p. 277.

188   "One day, right here in Mississippi": King, *My Life*, p. 278.

188   "We have got to deliver results": Lewis, *King*, p. 331.

188   "I need some help in getting this method across": King, "MLK—'I Need Victories,' " July 12, 1966, MLK-Atlanta.

188   "I'd love to be an Alabama trooper": Ralph, *Northern Protest*, p. 120.

189   "I've never seen anything like it": Oates, *Let the Trumpet Sound*, p. 413.

189   "[the] total eradication of housing discrimination": *Nation*, Sept. 1966, p. 238.

189   "Let's face the fact": *Nation*, Sept. 1966, pp. 239-40.

190   "I have felt my dream falter": King, "Address at the March on Chicago," July 26, 1965, MLK-Atlanta.

190   King's use of "dream turn into a nightmare" in 1966 and 1967: King, n.d. (Chicago) (1966), MLK-Atlanta; King, "Remarks," Mar. 31, 1966,

MLK-Atlanta; King, "Address at the Shaw Urban Renewal Public Meeting, Washington, D.C.," Mar. 12, 1967, MLK-Atlanta; King, *Arlene Francis Show,* June 19, 1967, MLK-Atlanta.

190   Not sure that America was ready to accept that transformation: This was a theme in many of King's speeches in the last years of his life. King, "Gandhi Memorial Lecture, Howard University, Washington, D.C.," Nov. 6, 1966, MLK-Atlanta; King, "Speech at Frogmore," Nov. 14, 1966, MLK-Atlanta; King, "Civil Rights at the Crossroads," May 2, 1967, MLK-Atlanta; King, "Speech to Hungry Club," May 10, 1967, MLK-Atlanta; King, "To Charter Our Course for the Future," May 29–31, 1967, MLK-Atlanta.

191   Cost of "Bill of Rights for the Disadvantaged": *Face the Nation,* May 29, 1966, MLK-Atlanta. The "Bill of Rights for the Disadvantaged" proposal was set out in King's book *Why We Can't Wait* (New York: Penguin, 1964).

191   "[W]e are in a new era": King, ABC *Issues and Answers,*" June 18, 1967, MLK-Atlanta.

192   Nation never rose up: Ralph, *Northern Protest,* pp. 177–78.

192   "White America had intended": King, "Civil Rights at the Crossroads," May 2, 1967, MLK-Atlanta.

193   "Racism is still alive": King, "Sleeping Through A Revolution," Dec. 10, 1967, MLK-Atlanta.

193   "Our beloved nation is still a racist country": King, "Which Way Its Soul Shall Go," Aug. 2, 1967, MLK-Atlanta.

193   Cruel taunts of a future that would never be realized: "[S]logans are necessary in any revolution. And we had to have slogans. But the problem is that we couldn't produce what the slogan said. We said all here, now; I started preaching. We want all of our rights, we want them here, and we want them now. Now I guess, I knew all the time we weren't going to get all of our rights, here, and get them now. I knew that it was going to take social process and all of that. But what happens in any revolution, you've got to have these slogans to fire people up, to get them going, to give them a sense of dignity. But if

progress isn't on a continual basis, the very slogans backfire on you. Now this is what we are seeing at the present time." King, "The Crisis in Civil Rights: Address to Operation Breadbasket," July 10–12, 1967, MLK-Atlanta.

193   "I went home that night with an ugly feeling": King. "The Three Evils of Society," Aug. 31, 1967, MLK-Atlanta.

194   "When hope diminishes": Garrow, *Bearing the Cross*, p. 598.

194   1967 riots: Patterson, *Grand Expectations*, p. 663.

194   "terribly distressed, more so than I have ever seen him": King, *My Life*, p. 296.

195   King's critiques of the Vietnam War: King, "Address at the March 25 Peace and Progress Rally," Mar. 25, 1967, MLK-Atlanta. A poll in May 1967 showed that 73 percent of all Americans and 48 percent of black respondents disagreed with King's opposition to the war, and 60 percent of all Americans believed that King's stance on Vietnam would hurt the civil rights movement. Garrow, *Bearing the Cross*, p. 562.

195   "too fast": Weisbrot, *Freedom Bound*, p. 220. King's response to the bill's failure was, "I want somebody to know that when that bill died a lot of faith died in America." Ralph, *Northern Protest*, p. 194.

195   "It would have been hard to pass the Emancipation Proclamation": Ralph, *Northern Protest*, p. 194.

195   *Walker v. City of Birmingham*: 388 U.S. 307 (1967).

196   "make Vietnam look like a holiday": "If America don't come around": Carson, *In Struggle*, p. 255.

196   "We do *not* have a dream": Bernard Weinraub, "The Brilliancy of Black," *Esquire*, Jan. 1967, in Meacham, *Voices in Our Blood*, p. 353.

197   "not only Negroes": King, "Need To Go To Washington," Jan. 16, 1968, MLK-Atlanta.

197   "This will be no mere one day march in Washington": King, "Press Conference on Poor Peoples' Campaign," Dec. 4, 1967, MLK-Atlanta.

197   "We feel that it is time now": King, "A Proper Sense of Priorities," Feb. 6, 1968, MLK-Atlanta.

197   "I think that the time is come": King, "Press Conference on Poor People's Campaign," Oct. 23, 1967, MLK-Atlanta.

198 "When people tell you that nonviolence won't work" to "without destroying life or property in the process": King, "Why We Must Go to Washington II," Jan. 15, 1968, MLK-Atlanta.

198 "we're going for broke": King, "Need to Go To Washington," Jan. 16, 1968, MLK-Atlanta.

199 "last, greatest dream": Oates, *Let the Trumpet Sound*, p. 451.

199: "God never intended": King, "Gandhi Memorial Lecture," Nov. 6, 1966, MLK-Atlanta.

199 "[W]e are going to Washington to say that all of God's children are significant": King, "Rally Speech—Georgia Tour—Waycross, Georgia," Mar. 22, 1968, MLK-Atlanta.

199 "Believe in your heart that you are God's children": King, "Pre-Washington Campaign," Feb. 16, 1968, MLK-Atlanta.

199 "It's wonderful to talk about the 'New Jerusalem' ": King, "Who Are We?," Feb. 5, 1966, MLK-Atlanta.

200 "I still have faith": King, "MLK Rally with Mahalia Jackson," Aug. 4, 1966, MLK-Atlanta.

200 "I'm not worried about tomorrow": King, "Thou Fool," Aug. 27, 1967, MLK-Atlanta.

200 "I don't know what Jesus had as his demands": King, "Why A Movement," Nov. 28, 1967, MLK-Atlanta.

201 "but if not, I'm going on anyhow": King, "But, If Not . . . ," Nov. 5, 1967, MLK-Atlanta.

201 Christmas Eve sermon: King, "A Christmas Sermon on Peace," Dec. 24, 1967, in Washington, *Testament of Hope*, pp. 257–58.

202 "These have been very difficult days for me" through "profound sadness": Garrow, *Bearing the Cross*, pp. 577, 599.

205 "Let us see that God": King, "Pre-Washington Campaign," Mar. 19, 1968, MLK-Atlanta.

205 "This is terrible": Abernathy, *And the Walls*, pp. 419–20.

206 "Well, I don't know what will happen now": King, "I've Been to the Mountaintop," in Carson, *A Call to Conscience*, pp. 222–23.

6. Recovery

207 King's funeral: *AC,* Apr. 10, 1968, p. 1; *Time,* Apr. 19, 1968, p. 18; Cannon, "Martin Luther King, Jr.," p. 203.

207 Newspaper and magazine excerpts of "I Have a Dream" speech: *WP,* Apr. 5, 1968, p. A6; *AC,* Apr. 5, 1968, pp. 1, 9; *Newsweek,* Apr. 15, 1968, p. 38; *Ebony,* May 1968, pp. 132–33; *Time,* Apr. 12, 1968, p. 20.

207 Members of Congress on "I Have a Dream" speech: Congressional Record, Apr. 11, 1968, p. 9677 (statement of Rep. William Ryan, R-NY); Congressional Record, Apr. 5, 1968, p. 9139 (statement of Sen. Wayne Morse, D-OR); Congressional Record, Apr. 5, 1968. p. 9141 (statement of Sen. Warren Magnuson, D-WA); Congressional Record, Apr. 5, 1968, p. 9143 (statement of Sen. Thomas Dodd, D-CT); Congressional Record, Apr. 10, 1968, p. 9471 (statement of Sen. Ernest Gruening, D-AK); Congressional Record, Apr. 8, 1968, pp. 9164-65 (statement of Rep. William Moorhead, D-PA).

208 "dreamed of an America without racial prejudice": Congressional Record, Apr. 11, 1968, p. 9746 (statement of Rep. Henry Helstoski, D-NJ).

208 "No words of ours": "Address to the Nation Upon Proclaiming a Day of Mourning Following the Death of Dr. King," Pub. Papers of the Presidents, p. 494 (Apr. 5, 1968).

208 "Martin Luther King, Jr., lived by this exalted dream of freedom": *Life,* Apr. 12, 1968, p. 74.

208 "The dream of which he spoke so eloquently": *WP,* Apr. 5, 1968, p. A24.

209 Books entitled *I Have a Dream*: Stanley Levison to Joan Daves, Apr. 16, 1968, FBI 100-111180-9-1643; Levison to Tom Offenburger, Apr. 19, 1968, FBI 100-111180-9-1645.

209 "He had a dream": *Life,* Sept. 12, 1969.

209 Riots after King's death: *Newsweek,* Apr. 22, 1968, p. 24; *Time,* Apr. 19, 1968, p. 15.

209 "[A] vacuum has been created": Congressional Record, Apr. 8, 1968, p. 9183 (statement of Rep. Jack Edwards, R-AL).

209 "When white America killed Dr. King": *Newsweek*, Apr. 15, 1968, p. 31.

209 "dead philosophy": *Newsweek*, Apr. 15, 1968, p. 38.

210 "Dream City": Abernathy, *And the Walls*, p. 501.

210 "Paranoia, literally": Gerald D. McKnight, *The Last Crusade: Martin Luther King, Jr., the FBI, and the Poor People's Campaign* (Colorado: Westview, 1998), p. 85.

210 "being told to go to Washington one night": Senator John L. McClellan of Arkansas, May 7, 1968, in McKnight, *Last Crusade*, p. 87.

210 Poor People's Campaign began well: McKnight, *Last Crusade*, p. 84.

210 "Eastland" and "Stennis": Abernathy, *And the Walls*, p. 508.

211 Resurrection City: McKnight, *Last Crusade*, p. 111; Charlayne A. Hunter, "On the Case in Resurrection City," reprinted in *The Eyes on the Prize Civil Rights Reader* (ed. Clayborne Carson et al.) (New York: Penguin, 1991), p. 430; Walter E. Afield and Audrey B. Gibson, *Children of Resurrection City* (Washington, D.C.: Association for Childhood Education International, 1970), p. 22.

211 "redeem the national dream": Abernathy, *And the Walls*, p. 525.

211 Coretta Scott King recited portions of the "I Have a Dream" speech: Charles Fager, *Uncertain Resurrection: The Poor People's Washington Campaign* (Grand Rapids: Eerdmans, 1989), p. 80.

211 "Few seemed optimistic": Fager, *Uncertain Resurrection*, p. 76.

212 Civil Rights Act of 1968: Hugh Davis Graham, *Civil Rights and the Presidency: Race and Gender in American Politics 1960–1972* (New York: Oxford University Press, 1992), pp. 127–28.

212 Bill as a monument to King: Congressional Record, Apr. 5, 1968, pp. 9137–38 (statement of Sen. Joseph Clark, D-PA) (statement of Sen. Jacob Javits, R-NY).

212 SCLC after King's death: Adam Fairclough, *To Redeem the Soul of America: The Southern Christian Leadership Conference and Martin Luther King, Jr.* (Athens: University of Georgia Press, 1987), pp. 385–405.

212   Members of Congress quoting King's speech in the 1970s: See, e.g., Congressional Record, Feb. 17, 1971, p. 2933 (statement of Rep. Robert Nix, D-PA) ("The dream of Martin Luther King was a dream that in America and all the world our deeds would match our beliefs."); Congressional Record, Jan. 19, 1972, p. 371 (statement of Rep. William Ryan, D-NY); Congressional Record, Jan. 16, 1973, p. 1132 (statement of Sen. Hugh Scott, R-PA) ("No single man's 'dream' has had such a profound influence on modern times"); Congressional Record, Apr. 4, 1974, p. 9859 (statement of Rep. Ralph Metcalfe, D-IL) ("[H]e gave all America his dream of peace and brotherhood, a dream which is the foundation for my own efforts to right the wrongs of our society and a dream which should still be a guide by which all of us can live."); Congressional Record, Jan. 20, 1976, p. 355 (statement of Rep. Edward Boland, D-MA) ("The world will not soon forget Martin Luther King. His vision, his 'dream,' has been carried on by thousands of followers. The 'dream' of equality, peace, and brotherhood is one which we all should share and promote. We can honor Dr. King's memory in no better way than to make his dream a reality."); Congressional Record, Jan. 17, 1977, p. 1325 (statement of Rep. Peter Rodino, D-NJ) ("Martin Luther King, Jr. was great because of the imperishable dream that he nurtured throughout his life."); Congressional Record, Jan. 18, 1979, p. 496 (statement of Sen. Robert Dole, R-KN) ("Martin Luther King was a remarkable man, a man of vision whose dream of equality and brotherly love moved an entire generation.").

212   "From the pain and exhaustion": "Presidential Medal of Freedom: Remarks on Presenting the Medal to Dr. Jonas E. Salk and to Martin Luther King, Jr." (July 11, 1977) Pub. Papers of the Presidents, pp. 1228, 1230.

212   "the speech by which he is best remembered": WP, Jan. 15, 1979, p. A20.

215   "fomented discord and strife between the races": Congressional Record, Apr. 10, 1968, p. 9535 (statement of Rep. William Tuck, D-VA). See also Congressional Record, Apr. 10, 1968, p. 9574 (state-

ment of Rep. Ovie Fisher, D-TX) ("He preached nonviolence, yet in scores of instances he led marches and demonstrations which triggered violence and bloodshed.").

215 Anti-King rhetoric in Congress in the 1970s: See, e.g., Congressional Record, Apr. 2, 1970, p. 10036 (statement of Rep. John Rarick, D-LA) (calling King a "plain garden variety subversive tool" and a "Communist puppet"); Congressional Record, Jan. 20, 1976, p. 276 (statement of Rep. John Ashbrook, R-OH) (saying that King "advocated violence, advocated lawlessness, and preached an anti-American theme which was sheer radical propaganda."); Congressional Record, Sept. 26, 1977, p. 30941 (statement of Rep. John Ashbrook, R-OH); Congressional Record, Sept. 26, 1978, p. 31688 (statement of Rep. John Ashbrook, R-OH); Congressional Record, Nov. 13, 1979, p. 32139 (statement of Rep. Larry P. McDonald, D-GA) ("King practiced and preached confrontation politics. Nonviolence was the facade behind which hatred and violence were nurtured."). There was no presidential statement commemorating King's birthday in 1970, 1972, 1973, and 1974. The annual proclamation began again in 1975 and has continued since then.

215 "Deliberately brought violence to America's streets": *Martin Luther King, Jr. National Holiday*, Joint Hearings Before the Committee on the Judiciary. United States Senate, and the Committee on the Post Office and Civil Service, House of Representatives, 96th Congress, 1st Sess., S. 25, Serial 96-14, Mar. 27 and June 21, 1979 (statement of Stanley Rittenhouse), p. 34.

215 "If this measure is passed": *Martin Luther King, Jr. National Holiday*, Joint Hearings Before the Committee on the Judiciary, United States Senate, and the Committee on the Post Office and Civil Service, House of Representatives, 96th Congress, 1st Sess., S. 25, Serial 96-14, Mar. 27 and June 21, 1979 (statement of Julia Brown), p. 43.

215 "packet of filth": *Economist*, Oct. 22, 1983. p. 39.

216 "Well, we'll know in about thirty-five years, won't we?" "Since they seem bent on making it a national holiday": *WP*, Oct. 20, 1983, p. A11.

217   "It was 20 years ago this month": Congressional Record, Aug. 2, 1983, p. 22235 (statement of Rep. Jim Wright, D-TX).

217   "The dream he shared that hot August afternoon in 1963": Congressional Record, Oct. 19, 1983, p. 28359 (statement of Sen. Bill Bradley, D-NJ). See also Congressional Record, Aug. 2, 1983, p. 22209 (statement of Rep. Steny Hoyer, D-MD) (saying that King "spoke the words which have become as integral a part of American history as the Great Lincoln and Douglas debates"); Congressional Record, Aug. 2, 1983, p. 22228 (statement of Rep. Edwin Bethune, R-AR) ("His dream of a society where all men of all races could live as brothers is not a black dream, but an American dream."); Congressional Record, Aug. 2, 1983, p. 22230 (statement of Rep. Ronald Dellums, D-CA) ("In America, he was the living embodiment of the highest principles professed in the Declaration of Independence . . ."); Congressional Record, Aug. 2, 1983, p. 22235 (statement of Rep. George Gekas, R-PA) ("Martin Luther King's day must be a day for all America, because Martin Luther King's dream is the American dream."); Congressional Record, Aug. 2, 1983, p. 22236 (statement of Sen. Alan Dixon, D-IL) ("Dr. King focused this country's attention on the democratic principles and ideals upon which it was founded, and made us live up to the fundamental tenets of the Declaration of Independence and the Constitution—the equality of man and our quest for a more perfect union."); Congressional Record, Aug. 2, 1983, p. 22236 (statement of Rep. Thomas P. O'Neill, D-MA) ("He asked America to be as good as its Declaration of Independence, to be as good as its Bill of Rights. He asked all of us to take the words of our Founding Fathers and make these words come alive for all people."); Congressional Record, Aug. 2, 1983, p. 22237 (statement of Rep. Robert Borski, D-PA) ("The observance of Martin Luther King's birthday is more than the remembrance of a great man. It is a moment in which we can remember the principles on which this Nation was founded."); Congressional Record, Oct. 4, 1983, p. 26960 (statement of Sen. John Chafee, R-RI) ("The civil rights movement led by Dr. King was, in a profound sense, a second

American revolution, founded upon the dream that as a nation of law, we must judge men and women not by the color of their skin, but by their talents as individual human beings."); Congressional Record, Aug. 2, 1983, p. 22233 (statement of Rep. George Gekas, R-PA) ("The dream that [King] articulated was the same one that inspired our forefathers to give birth to the ideal we call America.").

219 Easier to ignore: Richard Lentz has observed that news magazines at King's death downplayed his later career and portrayed him solely as a moderate, nonviolent prophet from the South who brought down Jim Crow. Richard Lentz, *Symbols, the News Magazines, and Martin Luther King* (Baton Rouge: Louisiana State University Press, 1990), pp. 281-337. See also Henry Louis Gates, Jr., "Heroes, Inc.," *New Yorker*, Jan. 16, 1995, pp. 6-7.

219 "People talk about the white backlash": King, "The Seventh Annual Gandhi Memorial Lecture," Nov. 6, 1966, MLK-Atlanta.

221 "And there is no point in our going around": King, "Rally Speech—Georgia Tour—Waycross. Georgia," Mar. 22, 1968, MLK-Atlanta.

221 Reagan's remarks on King holiday: "Holiday Honoring Martin Luther King, Jr.: Remarks on Signing H.R. 3706 Into Law," Pub. Papers of the Presidents, Nov. 2, 1983.

222 Nelson Mandela, "Free at last": *Sydney Morning Herald*, May 4, 1994, p. 20.

222 Tiananmen Square. "I have a dream": *Time*, May 29, 1989, p. 36; *Portland Oregonian*, Aug. 26, 1994, p. D07.

222 Anti-affirmative action use of "I Have a Dream": It appears that the earliest use of the "I Have a Dream" speech as a way to attack affirmative action is from a 1979 book by Terry Eastland and William Bennett: "[W]hat is most pertinent to observe is the unrelenting attack the movement made against Jim Crow and the idea that Jim Crow, at root, represented: namely, that race makes a difference in the assessment of character or qualification. Here the speech made by Martin Luther King, Jr.—the 'I Have A Dream' speech—made during the March on Washington in 1963 . . . [is] instructive." Terry Eastland and William J. Bennett, *Counting by Race: Equality from the*

Founding Fathers to Bakke and Weber (New York: Basic Books, 1979), pp. 111–12.

222 Several Reagan administration officials: Clarence M. Pendleton, the Chair of the United States Commission on Civil Rights, used the phrase in a 1984 address in Ohio. Clarence M. Pendleton, Jr., "Racial Politics Has Distorted U.S. Quest for Equal Opportunity," *San Diego Union-Tribune*, Dec. 2, 1984, p. C4. William Bradford Reynolds, the assistant attorney general for civil rights, used it in a 1984 article in the *Yale Law Journal*. William Bradford Reynolds, *Individualism vs. Group Rights: The Legacy of Brown*, 93 *Yale Law Journal* 995, 1000-01 (1984).

222 "We are committed to a society": Ira R. Allen, "Washington News," *UPI*, Jan. 18, 1986.

222 Proposition 209 advertisement: *Boston Globe*, Oct. 25, 1996, p. A19.

223 John Carlson and Initiative 200: *Seattle Post-Intelligencer*, Jan. 15, 1998, p. A1.

223 Reaction of King's allies to the Proposition 209 advertisement: *Boston Globe*, Oct. 25, 1996, p. A19.

223 Anti-caste measures in India: See Clayborne Carson, "King Advocated Special Programs That Went Beyond Affirmative Action," *San Jose Mercury News*, Oct. 27, 1996.

224 "[T]he nation must not only radically readjust": King, "Statement Before the National Advisory Committee on Civil Disorders," 23 October 1967, p. 5, MLK -Atlanta.

225 Affirmative action as anti-caste: See, e.g., Orlando Patterson, *The Ordeal of Integration* (Washington, D.C.: Civitas/Counterpoint, 1997).

225 "focus almost entirely on Martin Luther King the dreamer": *NYT*, Jan. 20, 1986, p. A24.

225 "they voted for Martin's 'I have a dream' speech": *NYT*, Jan. 20, 1986, p. A24.

225 "Nonthreatening dreamer": *WP*, Jan. 16, 1983, p. A10.

225 "Somehow, it seemed that the furthest most Americans could go with King": Vincent Gordon Harding, "Recalling the Inconvenient Hero:

Reflections on the Last Years of Martin Luther King, Jr.," *Union Seminary Quarterly Review* (1986), p. 53. See also Vincent Gordon Harding, "Beyond Amnesia: Martin Luther King, Jr. and the Future of America," 74 *Journal of American History* 468 (1987).

226 Michael Eric Dyson proposal: Michael Eric Dyson, *I May Not Get There With You: The True Martin Luther King, Jr.* (New York: Free Press, 2000), pp. 15–16.

227 "Ingratitude": King, "Ingratitude." June 18, 1967, MLK-Atlanta.

229 "Behold, this dreamer cometh": The verse is Genesis 37:19–20. Andrew Young reported to Stanley Levison that the staff had been "having some religious experiences" as they talked about this verse. Young to Levison, Apr. 19, 1968, FBI 100-111180-9-1645a, p. 2. Young's recollections are from an interview with Andrew Young, Jan. 17, 2002. Ralph Abernathy's use of this verse at King's funeral is recalled in Young, *An Easy Burden*, p. 478.

Acknowledgments

I owe a substantial debt to the many people who took the time to speak or exchange e-mails with me about Dr. King, the March on Washington, and the civil rights movement: Sandra Elaine Adickes, Matthew Ahmann, Ralph Allen, Julian Bond, Carl Broady, Marvin Caplan, Jack Chatfield, Xernona Clayton, Robert Coles, Dorothy Cotton, Courtland Cox, Gloria Richardson Dandridge, Carolyn Daniels, John Douglas, Walter Fauntroy, James Forman, Stephen Friedman, George Furniss, Jack Greenberg, Prathia Hall, Charles Harris, Faith Holsaert, Rachelle Horowitz, Clarence Jones, Martha Rose Joyner, Nicholas Katzenbach, Ed King, John Lewis, Margaret McCarter, Willie Pearl Mackey, Burke Marshall, Jim Nabrit, Walter Naegle, John Nolan, Claire O'Connor, Gordon Parks, Penny Patch, Peggy Dammond Preacely, George Raveling, John Reilly, Howard MacArthur Romaine, Mildred Bond Roxborough, Lawrence Rubin, Charles Sherrod, Ted Sorensen, Wyatt Tee Walker, Lee White, Roger Wilkins, Harris Wofford, Andrew Young, and Dorothy Zellner.

I am grateful to several librarians and archivists, particularly Cynthia Lewis and Elaine Hall of the Martin Luther King, Jr., Center for Nonviolent Social Change; Jim Baggett of the Birmingham Public Library; Diana Lachatanere and Steven Sullwood of the Schomburg Center for Research in Black Culture; Charles Niles of the Mugar Library at Boston University; Brenda Lewis of the City of Rocky Mount; and Jennifer Trask of the Martin Luther King, Jr., Papers Project.

For their assistance at various stages of the project, I thank Bennett Ashley, Jack Balkin, Manie Barron, Maria Cantwell, Lincoln Caplan, Ted Cross, Drew Days, Eileen Godlis, Carolyn Hansen, Janna Hansen, Wayne

Hansen, Pierre N. Leval, Richard Lischer, David Reimer, Reva Siegel, Steve Sugarman, Olivier Sultan, Kerry Taylor, David Wenham, and John Witt. I am particularly grateful to David Garrow, who gave generously of his advice and expertise on several occasions.

For their hospitality during research trips, I am grateful to Bill Bradley in Boston; Eduardo Peñalver, Sital Kalantry, Rebecca Tushnet, and Zach Schrag in Washington, D.C.; and Elisabeth Remy and Stuart and Tina Newman in Atlanta.

Several friends kindly provided editing assistance: Kate Darnton, John Frazier, Brandon Garrett, John Kim, Troy McKenzie, Eileen Ohnell, Asha Rangappa, and Webster Younce. Matthew Polly and Amanda Schaffer read the manuscript over several drafts and gave extensive comments. I am especially indebted to Julie Cooper, who edited every page several times, from early in the writing process to the submission of the finished manuscript.

I owe a great debt to Dan Halpern and Tina Bennett for their editing and encouragement. This book would not have been possible without their assistance. I am also grateful to Patricia Fernandez, Gheña Glijansky, Robert Grover, John Jusino, and Svetlana Katz for their help. I would also like to thank Michele Rubin and Nadia Grooms of Writers' House.

Several members of the Yale Law School faculty gave considerable advice and expertise to this project. Bruce Ackerman supervised research on the congressional and presidential materials from the civil rights era, and Burke Marshall read several draft chapters and provided many invaluable insights.

Finally, I owe a particularly deep debt to Owen Fiss. Professor Fiss has given an extraordinary amount of his time to this project, which began as a series of course papers under his direction. He continued to give generously of his encouragement and advice long after I graduated. No thanks that I might give him could possibly be adequate.

Index